MORE POSTHUMAN GLOSSARY

THEORY IN THE NEW HUMANITIES

Series editor: Rosi Braidotti

Theory is back! The vitality of critical thinking in the world today is palpable, as is a spirit of insurgency that sustains it. Theoretical practice has exploded with renewed energy in media, society, the arts and the corporate world. New generations of critical 'studies' areas have grown alongside the classical radical epistemologies of the 1970s: gender, feminist, queer, race, postcolonial and subaltern studies, cultural studies, film, television and media studies. This series aims to present cartographic accounts of emerging critical theories and to reflect the vitality and inspirational force of on-going theoretical debates.

Editorial board

Stacy Alaimo (University of Oregon)

Simone Bignall (University of Technology Sydney)

Judith Butler (University of Berkeley, USA)

Christine Daigle (Brock University, Canada)

Rick Dolphijn (Utrecht University, The Netherlands)

Matthew Fuller (Goldsmiths, University of London, UK)

Engin Isin (Queen Mary University of London, UK, and University of London Institute in Paris, France)

Patricia MacCormack (Anglia Ruskin University, UK)

Achille Mbembe (University Witwatersrand, South Africa)

Henrietta Moore (University College London, UK)

Other titles in the series:

Posthuman Glossary, edited by Rosi Braidotti and Maria Hlavajova

Conflicting Humanities, edited by Rosi Braidotti and Paul Gilroy

General Ecology, edited by Erich Hörl with James Burton

Philosophical Posthumanism, Francesca Ferrando

The Philosophy of Matter, Rick Dolphijn

Vibrant Death, Nina Lykke

Visceral Prostheses, Margrit Shildrick

From Deleuze and Guattari to Posthumanism, ed. Christine Daigle and Terrance H. McDonald

Materialist Phenomenology, Manuel DeLanda

MORE POSTHUMAN GLOSSARY

Edited by Rosi Braidotti, Emily Jones and Goda Klumbytė

BLOOMSBURY ACADEMIC
LONDON • NEW YORK • OXFORD • NEW DELHI • SYDNEY

BLOOMSBURY ACADEMIC
Bloomsbury Publishing Plc
50 Bedford Square, London, WC1B 3DP, UK
1385 Broadway, New York, NY 10018, USA
29 Earlsfort Terrace, Dublin 2, Ireland

BLOOMSBURY, BLOOMSBURY ACADEMIC and the Diana logo are trademarks of
Bloomsbury Publishing Plc

First published in Great Britain 2023

Copyright © Rosi Braidotti, Emily Jones, Goda Klumbytė and Contributors, 2023

Rosi Braidotti, Emily Jones and Goda Klumbytė have asserted their right under the
Copyright, Designs and Patents Act, 1988, to be identified as Editors of this work.

For legal purposes the Acknowledgements on p. xxv constitute an extension of this
copyright page.

Cover image © Natascha Unkart, 2019 "Untitled (Salvaged)"

All rights reserved. No part of this publication may be reproduced or transmitted
in any form or by any means, electronic or mechanical, including photocopying,
recording, or any information storage or retrieval system, without prior permission
in writing from the publishers.

Bloomsbury Publishing Plc does not have any control over, or responsibility for,
any third-party websites referred to or in this book. All internet addresses given in
this book were correct at the time of going to press. The author and publisher regret
any inconvenience caused if addresses have changed or sites have ceased to exist,
but can accept no responsibility for any such changes.

A catalogue record for this book is available from the British Library.

Library of Congress Cataloging-in-Publication Data

Names: Braidotti, Rosi, editor. | Jones, Emily, 1990– editor. | Klumbytė, Goda, editor.
Title: More posthuman glossary / edited by Rosi Braidotti, Emily Jones and Goda Klumbytė.
Description: London ; New York : Bloomsbury Academic, 2023. | Series: Theory in the new
humanities | Includes bibliographical references and index.
Identifiers: LCCN 2022036575 (print) | LCCN 2022036576 (ebook) |
ISBN 9781350231429 (hardback) | ISBN 9781350231436 (paperback) |
ISBN 9781350231443 (pdf) | ISBN 9781350231450 (epub)
Subjects: LCSH: Humanism.
Classification: LCC B821 .M6225 2023 (print) | LCC B821 (ebook) |
DDC 144—dc23/eng/20220901
LC record available at https://lccn.loc.gov/2022036575
LC ebook record available at https://lccn.loc.gov/2022036576

ISBN: HB: 978-1-3502-3142-9
       PB: 978-1-3502-3143-6
       ePDF: 978-1-3502-3144-3
       eBook: 978-1-3502-3145-0

Series: Theory in the New Humanities

Typeset by RefineCatch Limited, Bungay, Suffolk

To find out more about our authors and books visit www.bloomsbury.com
and sign up for our newsletters.

Contents

List of Contributors	ix	
Preface	xx	
Donna Haraway		
Acknowledgements	xxv	
Introduction	1	
Rosi Braidotti, Emily Jones and Goda Klumbytė		

A

Acting as Country	7
Daryle Rigney	
Agrarian (Post-)Humanities	8
Sophie von Redecker	
Algorithmic Governmentality	10
Antoinette Rouvroy and Goda Klumbytė	
Art and Bioethics	12
Sarah N. Boers	

C

Collaborative Politics	15
Simone Bignall	
Collapse	17
Christopher F. Julien	

Composting	19
Astrida Neimanis and Jennifer Mae Hamilton	
Convergences	21
Rosi Braidotti, Emily Jones and Goda Klumbytė	
Cosmic Artisan	23
Kay Sidebottom	
Crip Theory	25
Kelly Fritsch	
Critical Posthuman Theory	28
Rosi Braidotti and Emily Jones	

D

Dismantling Risk	31
Helene Kazan	
Defamiliarization	33
Helen Palmer	
Disappearance	35
Rick Dolphijn and Trixie Tsang	
The Distributed University	36
Sarah Nuttall and Rosi Braidotti	

E

EcoLaw 39
Margaret Davies

Emergent Ecologies 41
Eben Kirksey

Empathy Beyond the Human 43
Danielle Sands

Endomaterialities 45
Celia Roberts

Existential Posthumanism: A Manifesto 47
Francesca Ferrando

Ex-colonialism 49
Simone Bignall

F

Feminism and Oceans 53
Gina Heathcote

Fermentation 55
Olga Goriunova

G

Geoengineering 58
Holly Jean Buck

Geontopower 59
Elizabeth Povinelli

H

Humus Economicus 62
Janna Holmstedt

Hydrofeminism 64
Astrida Neimanis

I

Internet of Trees 67
Jennifer Gabrys

Intragenerational Justice and Care 69
Christina Fredengren

L

Linguistic Incompossibility 72
Ruth Clemens

Low Trophic Theory 74
Cecilia Åsberg and Marietta Radomska

M

Manus Island and Manus Prison Theory 77
Omid Tofighian (with Behrouz Boochani)

The Meltionary 80
MELT (Ren Loren Britton and Isabel Paehr)

N

Nauru Imprisoned Exiles Collective 83
Elahe Zivardar, also known as Ellie Shakiba (with Mehran Ghadiri)

New Materialist Informatics 85
Goda Klumbytė and Claude Draude

Norms 87
Fleur Johns

O

Ontologized Plasticity 89
Zakiyyah Iman Jackson

Organoids 91
Sarah N. Boers

CONTENTS

P

Parasitology 94
Rick Dolphijn

Pattern Discrimination 95
Clemens Apprich

Petroculture 97
Josephine Taylor

Postcolonial and Decolonial Computing 99
Paula Chakravartty and Mara Mills

Postcolonial Drone Scholarship 101
Sabiha Allouche

Posthuman Agency 104
Simone Bignall

Posthuman Care 105
Rosi Braidotti and Goda Klumbytė

Posthuman Data 107
Jannice Käll

Posthuman Feminist Aesthetics 109
Nina Lykke

Posthuman International Law and Outer Space 111
Emily Jones and Rosi Braidotti

Post-humanitarian Law 113
Matilda Arvidsson

Posthuman Nursing 115
Jamie B. Smith

Posthuman Publics 117
Fiona Hillary

Posthumanism and Design 119
Laura Forlano

Proxy Reasoning 121
Olga Goriunova

Q

Queer Death Studies 124
Marietta Radomska and Nina Lykke

R

Racializing Assemblages 126
Ezekiel Dixon-Román

Relational Sovereignty 128
Simone Bignall

Rights of Nature 130
Emily Jones

S

Side Channel Attack 133
Matthew Fuller

Surface Orientations 135
Nishat Awan

Surrogacy 137
Sophie Lewis

Swarm Warfare 139
Lauren Wilcox

Syndemic 141
Joni Adamson and Steven Hartman

T

Toxic Embodiment 145
Cecilia Åsberg

Transcorporeality II: COVID-19 and Climate Change 147
Stacy Alaimo

Transjectivity 149	**Viral** 156
Christine Daigle	*Filipa Ramos*

U

Undead 152
Julieta Aranda and Eben Kirksey

V

Vibrant Death 155
Nina Lykke

W

Weird 159
Gry Ulstein

Cumulative Bibliography 162

Contributors

Stacy Alaimo is a Professor of English, and a core faculty member in Environmental Studies at the University of Oregon. Professor Stacy Alaimo researches and teaches across the environmental humanities, science studies, animal studies, American literature, cultural studies and critical theory, focusing, more specifically, on developing models of new materialism, material feminisms, environmental justice, and, most recently, the blue (oceanic) humanities.

Joni Adamson is President's Professor of Environmental Humanities in the Department of English and Distinguished Global Futures Scholar at the Julie Ann Wrigley Global Futures Laboratory (GFL), Arizona State University. She is a former President of the Association for the Study of Literature and Environment and currently serving as Founding Director of the UNESCO BRIDGES Sustainability Science Coalition Flagship Hub at GFL. Her books, special issues, articles and reviews focus on Indigenous literatures and scientific literacies, the rights of nature movement, and the food justice movement.

Clemens Apprich is Professor in Media Theory and History at the University of Applied Arts in Vienna, as well as guest researcher at the Centre for Digital Cultures at Leuphana University of Lüneburg. He is an affiliated member of the Research Centre for Media Studies and Journalism at the University of Groningen, of the Digital Democracies Institute at Simon Fraser University, and of the Global Emergent Media Lab at Concordia University. His current research deals with filter algorithms and their application in data analysis as well as machine learning methods. Apprich is the author of *Technotopia: A Media Genealogy of Net Cultures* (Rowman & Littlefield International, 2017), and, together with Wendy Chun, Hito Steyerl, and Florian Cramer, co-authored *Pattern Discrimination* (University of Minnesota Press/meson press, 2019).

Julieta Aranda is an artist and curator. She observes the altering human–earth relationship through the lens of technology, artificial intelligence, space travel and scientific hypothesis. Working with installation, video and print media, she is invested in exploring the potential of science fiction, alternative economies and the 'poetics of circulation'. As an editor of e-flux journal, and co-director of the online platform e-flux together with Anton Vidokle, Julieta Aranda has developed the projects Global Contemporary Travel, Time/Bank, Pawnshop, Supercommunity and e-flux video rental. She has held solo exhibitions in many venues worldwide, including documenta in Kassel, Istanbul, Havana, Berlin, Lyon, Moscow, Liverpool and Venice Biennales.

Matilda Arvidsson is a researcher in international law and legal philosophy at the University of Gothenburg. Her research is interdisciplinary and covers topics in international and public law, humanitarian law, posthumanism, artificial intelligence (AI), as well as the embodiment of law in its various forms and in inter-species relations.

Cecilia Åsberg is Chair of Gender, Nature, Culture at Linköping University; Professor II at Oslo Metropolitan University, and recently Guest Professor at KTH Royal Institute of Technology Stockholm, Founder and Director of The Posthumanities Hub (www.posthumanitieshub.net) and Fellow of the Rachel Carson Centre at Ludvig Maximilian University in Munich. Recent publications include 'Environmental violence and postnatural oceans: Low trophic theory in the registers of feminist posthumanities' (2021), with Marietta Radomska in *Gender, Violence and Affect*; 'A Sea Change in the Environmental Humanities' (2020) in *Ecocene: Cappadocia Journal of Environmental Humanities*; 'Checking in with Deep Time' (2020) with Christina Fredengren, in *Deterritorializing the Future* (Open Humanities Press).

Nishat Awan's research focuses on questions related to diasporas, migration and border regimes. She is interested in modes of spatial representation, particularly in relation to the digital and the limits of witnessing as a form of ethical engagement with distant places. Currently, she leads the ERC-funded project, Topological Atlas, and is Senior Research Fellow at the Borders & Territories group, Faculty of Architecture, TU Delft.

Behrouz Boochani is Adjunct Associate Professor of Social Sciences at University of New South Wales; Senior Adjunct Research Fellow at the Ngāi Tahu Research Centre, University of Canterbury; and Visiting Professor at Birkbeck Law, University of London. He is an author and journalist who was incarcerated for over six years (2013–2019) as a political prisoner by the Australian government in Manus Island and then held in Port Moresby (Papua New Guinea). His book *No Friend but the Mountains: Writing from Manus Prison* (Picador 2018) has won numerous awards including the 2019 Victorian Prize for Literature. Boochani is also co-director (with Arash Kamali Sarvestani) of the 2017 feature-length film *Chauka, Please Tell Us the Time*, and author of the anthology *Freedom, Only Freedom: The Prison Writings of Behrouz Boochani* (Bloomsbury 2023).

Simone Bignall is Senior Researcher in the Jumbunna hub for Indigenous Nations and Collaborative Futures at the University of Technology in Sydney. Primarily active as a political philosopher in the Continental European tradition, she has worked for several decades in research collaborations with Indigenous Australian communities aspiring to reclaim Aboriginal sovereignty and restore self-governance in resistance to settler-colonialism. Simone is the author of *Postcolonial Agency: Critique and Constructivism* and *Exit Colonialism: Ethics after Enjoyment* and has co-edited numerous titles on Continental Philosophy and Colonialism. With Larissa Behrendt, Daryle Rigney and Linda Tuhiwai Smith, Simone co-edits the Rowman and Littlefield International Book Series on Indigenous Nations and Collaborative Futures; and with Joanne Faulkner, Paul Patton and Diego Bubbio, she edits Continental Philosophy in Austral-Asia. She is the Associate Editor of *Interconnections: Journal of Posthumanism*.

CONTRIBUTORS

Sarah N. Boers (MD PhD) combines her postdoctoral research in bioethics with the General Practice training. Her research focuses on the ethics of emerging biotechnologies, in particular tissue engineering, biobanking and digital health. Boers combines insights from bioethics, feminist theory, science and technology studies, social sciences, (post)phenomenology and the arts. She has published in leading journals such as *Journal of Medical Ethics, Nature Cell Biology* and *Trends in Molecular Medicine.*

Rosi Braidotti is Distinguished University Professor Emerita at Utrecht University. She received honorary degrees from Helsinki, 2007 and Linköping, 2013. She is fellow of the Australian Academy of the Humanities (FAHA, 2009); a member of the Academia Europaea (MAE, 2014). Her main publications include *Nomadic Subjects* (2011a), *Nomadic Theory* (2011b), *The Posthuman* (2013), *Posthuman Knowledge* (2019) and *Posthuman Feminism* (2022). She co-edited with Paul Gilroy: *Conflicting Humanities* (2016) and with Maria Hlavajova: *The Posthuman Glossary* (2018).

Ren Loren Britton and Isabel Paehr are MELT. They are arts-design researchers who work with games, technology and radical pedagogy. Tuning to the material-discursive conditions of tech infrastructures, they trouble patterns of agency in socio-technological systems with the methods of queer play, unlearning and leaking. Their work crumbles structures, unbounds materials, melts technology and makes collectivities. MELT has been shaped by (melting) Ice, Freezers, Software, Disability Justice, Trans*feminism, Signal, moving at trans*- crip- kinship- time, Black Feminisms, Materialisms, Post/De- Colonial thinking, Gifs, Climate Protests, Anti-Racism and Dancing.

Holly Jean Buck is an Assistant Professor of Environment and Sustainability at the University at Buffalo. She's interested in how communities can be involved in the design of emerging environmental technologies. She works at the interface of environmental sociology, international development and science and technology studies. Her diverse research interests include agroecology and carbon farming, new energy technologies, artificial intelligence and the restoration of California's Salton Sea.

Paula Chakravartty is Associate Professor in the Department of Media, Culture and Communication and the Gallatin School at NYU. Her current research focuses on media infrastructures and racial capitalism, and debt and migrant supply chains. Her books include *Race, Empire and the Crisis of the Subprime* (2013); co-edited with Denise Ferreira da Silva, *Media Policy and Globalization* (2006), co-author Katharine Sarikakis and *Global Communications: Towards a Transcultural Political Economy* (2008) co-editor Yeuzhi Zhao.

Ruth Alison Clemens is a lecturer in film and literary studies at the Centre for Arts in Society, Leiden University, and an affiliated researcher with the Posthumanities Hub at Linköping University. She was awarded her PhD from Leeds Trinity University and the University of Leeds, UK, in 2020, for a nomadic and critical posthumanist exploration of multilingual paratexts in modernist literature. In 2017 Ruth was a visiting research fellow at the Utrecht University Institute for Cultural Inquiry, and she is currently a lecturer and tutor at the annual Posthuman Summer School in Utrecht. Her work is published in *Feminist Modernist Studies* and *Comparative Critical Studies*, and she has contributions in the volumes *Posthuman Pathogenesis* (2022) and *Deleuze and Guattari and Fascism* (2022).

Margaret Davies was a foundation staff member of the Law School at Flinders University in Australia. She is a Fellow of the Academy of Social Sciences in Australia and the Australian Academy of Law. Among her publications: *Asking the Law Question* (4th edition 2017), *Delimiting the Law* (1996), *Are Persons Property* (with Ngaire Naffine, 2001), *Property: Meanings, Histories, Theories* (2007), and *Law Unlimited* 2017, EcoLaw: Legality, Life, and the Normativity of Nature (2022).

Ezekiel Dixon-Román is an Associate Professor in the School of Social Policy & Practice at the University of Pennsylvania. His research seeks to make cultural and critical theoretical interventions toward rethinking and reconceptualizing the technologies and practices of quantification as mediums and agencies of systems of socio-political relations whereby race and other assemblages of difference are by-products. He is the author of *Inheriting Possibility: Social Reproduction & Quantification in Education* (2017). He co-edited 'Alternative Ontologies of Number' (2016) in *Cultural Studies-Critical Methodologies*.

Rick Dolphijn is an associate professor at Humanities, Utrecht University and Honorary Professor at the University of Hong Kong (2017–2023). His books include: *Foodscapes* (2004), *New Materialism: Interviews and Cartographies* (2012, with Iris van der Tuin). He co-edited *This Deleuzian Century: Art, Activism, Life* (2014/5); *Philosophy after Nature* (2017), and *Michel Serres and the Crises of the Contemporary* (2019/20). His latest monograph is: *The Philosophy of Matter: a Meditation* (Bloomsbury Academic, 2021).

Claude Draude is a professor in Computer Science and is head of work group Gender/Diversity in Informatics Systems (GeDIS),

and is on the directors' board of the Research Center for Information System Design (ITeG), at the University of Kassel, Germany. Her research covers intersectional Gender Studies, Feminist Science & Technology Studies and New Materialism into Computer Science to explore artistic research and critical design and enhance diversity, participation and inclusion in ICT & HCI; to explore the role of social bias in algorithmic systems and develop prototypes for critical, reflective computing.

Francesca Ferrando teaches Philosophy at NYU-Liberal Studies, New York University. They were the recipient of the Sainati Prize with the Acknowledgement of the President of Italy. They have published extensively on posthumanism; their latest book is *Philosophical Posthumanism* (2019). A very active web presence, they were the first speaker to give a talk on the topic of the posthuman in the history of TED talks.

Laura Forlano is a Fulbright award-winning writer, social scientist and design researcher. She is an Associate Professor of Design at the Institute of Design at Illinois Institute of Technology. She is an editor of three books: *Bauhaus Futures* (MIT Press 2019), *digitalSTS* (Princeton University Press 2019) and *From Social Butterfly to Engaged Citizen* (MIT Press 2011).

Kelly Fritsch is an Assistant Professor in the Department of Sociology and Anthropology and Director of the Disability Justice and Crip Collaboratory at Carleton University. As a feminist disability studies scholar and crip theorist, her work explores the generative frictions of disability and embodied difference. She is co-editor of *Disability Injustice: Confronting Criminalization in Canada* (2022), *Keywords for Radicals: The Contested Vocabulary of Late-Capitalist Struggle* (2016) and co-author of the disability justice themed children's book *We Move Together* (2021).

Matthew Fuller is Professor of Cultural Studies at Goldsmiths, University of London. His recent books include *How to Sleep, the art, biology and culture of unconsciousness*, *How to be a Geek, essays on the culture of software*, with Olga Goriunova, *Bleak Joys, aesthetics of ecology and impossibility*, and, with Eyal Weizman, *Investigative Aesthetics, conflicts and commons in the politics of truth*.

Jennifer Gabrys is Chair in Media, Culture and Environment in the Department of Sociology at the University of Cambridge. She leads the Planetary Praxis research group (planetarypraxis.org), and is Principal Investigator on the ERC-funded project, Smart Forests: Transforming Environments into Social-Political Technologies. Her recent publications include *How to Do Things with Sensors* (2019); and *Program Earth: Environmental Sensing Technology and the Making of a Computational Planet* (2016).

Mehran Ghadiri worked in Nauru in 2015 and again from 2018 to 2020 in economic development and community engagement roles within the Australian offshore border regime. He also has years of first-hand experience working in a broad range of roles supporting refugees, asylum seekers and migrants to resettle in Australia. With his background in political science and international relations, as well as his unique insights into the inner workings of Australia's refugee system both offshore and onshore, he brings a comprehensive understanding of the global interests that exacerbate and manipulate refugee flows for financial and political gain. Ghadiri is currently authoring a detailed analysis of the political, economic and societal effects of Australia's policies in Nauru, as well as producing a documentary film on this topic with Elahe Zivardar.

Olga Goriunova is Professor at Royal Holloway University of London and author of *Art Platforms* (2012) and *Bleak Joys* (2019). An editor of Fun and Software, she was a co-curator of software art platform Runme.org (2003) before the age of social platforms. She also wrote on new media idiocy, memes and lurkers. Her continuing interests are in the intersection of aesthetics, computation, ecology and subjectivation.

Jennifer Mae Hamilton is a lecturer in Literary Studies at the University of New England, on unceded Anaiwan Country. Her first book is *This Contentious Storm: An Ecocritical and Performance History of King Lear* (2017). Her current research examines the relationship between weather and housework. She is also founder of the Community Weathering Station (CoWS). Together, Astrida and Jennifer are co-convenors of the Composting Feminisms reading and research group (www.compostingfeminisms.wordpress.org) and founding members of The Weathering Collective (weatheringstation.net)

Steven Hartman is Founding Executive Director of the BRIDGES Sustainability Science Coalition in UNESCO's Management of Social Transformations Programme (MOST) and Visiting Professor in the Faculty of History and Philosophy at University of Iceland. His research engaging diverse communities of practice in integrated team-driven study of social and environmental change has been supported by the US National Science Foundation, Belmont Forum, the Swedish Foundation for Humanities and Social Sciences, the Swedish Research Council, the EEA and Norway Grants program and NordForsk. He is co-editor of the book series Global Challenges in Environmental Humanities (Bloomsbury Academic).

Gina Heathcote teaches in the School of Law, Gender and Media at SOAS University of London where she teaches across international law, the law on the use of force and gender, sexuality and law; she is interested in feminist legal methodologies and the possibilities of gender law reform. Her most recent publication: *The Law of War and Peace: a Gender Analysis Volume 1* (Zed 2021) was co-authored with Sara Bertotti, Emily Jones and Sheri Labenski. She authored: *Feminist Dialogues on International Law* (OUP 2019) and *The Law on the Use of Force: a Feminist Analysis* (Routledge 2011) and co-edited, with Dianne Otto: *Rethinking Peacekeeping, Gender Equality and Collective Security* (Palgrave 2014).

Fiona Hillary is a Melbourne-based artist working in the public realm. Working with site, neon, sound, human and non-human companion species, her work focuses on temporary, fleeting encounters in and of the everyday. Fiona has made and curated permanent, temporary, collaborative, performative works for a range of commissioning organizations. She is a member of the Algae Society – Bioart Design Lab, a global collective of interdisciplinary researchers. Fiona is a lecturer and researcher in the School of Art at RMIT University, Melbourne, Australia.

Janna Holmstedt, artist and environmental humanities researcher, investigates listening as a situated practice, the cultivation of care and environmental attention, and composition in the expanded field of genre-disobedient art practices. She is a key member of The Posthumanities Hub, co-founder of the collective (P)Art of the Biomass, and project leader (PI) for Humus economicus: Soil Blindness and the Value of 'Dirt' in Urbanized Landscapes, at National Historical Museums in Sweden, with generous support from Formas, a Swedish research council for sustainable development.

Zakiyyah Iman Jackson is Associate Professor of English at the University of Southern California. Professor Jackson is the author of *Becoming Human: Matter and Meaning in an Antiblack World* published by New York University Press, 'Sexual Cultures' series. Professor Jackson's publications can be found at: zakiyyahimanjackson.com

Fleur Johns is Professor in the Faculty of Law & Justice at UNSW Sydney and Visiting Professor in the University of Gothenburg School of Business, Economics & Law, working in the areas of public international law, legal theory and law and technology. Fleur studies emergent patterns of governance on the global plane and their social, political and economic implications. Fleur's books include *Non-Legality in International Law: Unruly Law* (Cambridge 2013) and *#Help: Digital Humanitarianism and the Remaking of International Order* (Oxford forthcoming).

Emily Jones is Senior Lecturer in the School of Law and Human Rights Centre at the University of Essex, UK. Emily is an international lawyer whose work combines theory and practice. Her current work focuses on: posthuman theory and international law; military technologies; feminist, queer and postcolonial methodologies; the rights of nature; science and technology and international law; and the regulation of deep-sea mining.

Christopher F. Julien is a researcher and strategist. His practice focuses on public innovation, art-science and climate activism, working as a Senior Research Fellow at Waag and organizer with Extinction Rebellion. He is a PhD candidate at Utrecht University, where he researches eco-philosophy and new materialisms in the context of climactic and ecological collapse. His dissertation develops the field of Ecological Governance through 'Deep Adaptation Machines'.

Jannice Käll is LL.D. in Legal Theory and Senior Lecturer in Sociology of Law at Lund University in Sweden and has published several texts on posthumanist legal theory, property and digitalization. Her current research involves developing a posthumanist framework for dealing with questions of ownership over artificial intelligence and the resources required for such technologies to come into being, including data.

Helene Kazan is a research-based practitioner, whose work engages feminist, decolonial, critical-legal and artistic methods to investigate and dismantle "risk" as a lived limit condition produced through capitalism and conflict. Kazan is a Senior Lecturer in Critical Theory at the School of the Arts, Oxford Brookes University; 2022 Graham Foundation Grant Award recipient; 2018–2020 Fellow at the Vera List Center for Art and Politics, The New School, New York and received her doctorate from the Centre for Research Architecture, Goldsmiths, University of London (2019). Kazan has exhibited and published work in exhibitions and with museums and institutions internationally.

Eben Kirksey is Associate Professor at the University of Oxford. He is author of three books: *Freedom in Entangled Worlds* (2012), *Emergent Ecologies* (2015), and *The Mutant Project* (2020). As the editor of two essay collections – *The Multispecies Salon* (2014) and 'The Emergence of Multispecies Ethnography' (2010, with Stephan Helmreich). As a curator Kirksey has staged a series of art exhibits exploring life in the age of biotechnology, edible organisms and hope in blasted landscapes.

Goda Klumbytė is a research associate and PhD candidate at the research group Gender/Diversity in Informatics Systems, University of Kassel, Germany. Her research focuses on knowledge production in and through machine learning systems and application of critical epistemologies to machine learning systems design. She has published in *Posthuman Glossary* (2018), *Everyday Feminist Research Praxis* (2015) and the journals *Online Information Review*, *Digital Creativity* and *ASAP*. She is one of the editors of critical computing blog https://enginesofdifference.org

Sophie Lewis is a freelance writer based in Philadelphia, and the author of *Full Surrogacy Now: Feminism Against Family* (Verso Books, 2019). Their essays on octopus eros, utopia, kinmaking, TERFs, antiwork philosophy, and social reproduction have appeared in venues ranging from *e-flux* and *n+1* to the *London Review of Books* and *The New York Times*. Lewis studied English Literature (BA) and Environmental Policy (MSc) at Oxford University prior to studying Politics (MA) at the New School for Social Research, earning a PhD in geography at Manchester University in 2017. Sophie's academic writings are published in journals such as *Signs, Frontiers, Dialogues in Human Geography, Paragraph* and *Feminist Theory*; their research is supported by patrons at patreon.com/reproutopia. Sophie is an unpaid Visiting Scholar at the Center for Research in Feminist, Queer, and Transgender Studies at the University of Pennsylvania. Their second book, *Abolish the Family: A Manifesto for Care and Liberation* is published by Verso and Salvage Editions in October 2022.

Nina Lykke is Professor Emerita of Gender Studies with special reference to Gender and Culture at the Unit of Gender Studies,

Linköping University, Sweden and Adjunct Professor at Aarhus University, Denmark. Lykke has participated in the building of Feminist Studies in Scandinavia and Europe more broadly since the 1970s. She is also a poet and writer, and has recently co-founded international networks for Queer Death Studies, and for Ecocritical and Decolonial Research. Her monographs include *Cosmodolphins* (2000), *Feminist Studies* (2010), and *Vibrant Death* (2022).

Mara Mills is Associate Professor of Media, Culture, and Communication at New York University, where she co-founded and co-directs the NYU Center for Disability Studies. Mills is a founding editor of the journal *Catalyst: Feminism, Theory, Technoscience* (winner of the 2020 4S STS Infrastructure Award). Most recently, she co-edited the book *Testing Hearing: The Making of Modern Aurality* (Oxford University Press, 2020) with Viktoria Tkaczyk and Alexandra Hui.

Astrida Neimanis is feminist writer and teacher interested in bodies, water and weather, and how they can help us reimagine justice, care, responsibility and relation in the time of climate catastrophe. Her most recent book is *Bodies of Water: Posthuman Feminist Phenomenology*. With Jennifer Mae Hamilton, she is co-convenor of the Composting Feminisms reading and research group. She is also a founding member of the Weathering Collective and Co-Director of the SEED BOX: A Mistra-Formas Environmental Humanities Collaboratory. She is Canada Research Chair in Feminist Environmental Humanities, learning and working on unceded syilx okanagan lands and waters, at UBC Okanagan.

Sarah Nuttall is Professor of Literary and Cultural Studies and Director of WISER (Wits Institute for Social and Economic Research) in Johannesburg, South Africa. She is the author and editor of many books including *Entanglement: Literary and Cultural Reflections on Postapartheid* and *Johannesburg: The Elusive Metropolis*. She has directed WISER for ten years.

Isabel Paehr, along with Ren Loren Britton, are MELT. They are arts-design researchers who work with games, technology and radical pedagogy. Tuning to the material-discursive conditions of tech infrastructures, they trouble patterns of agency in socio-technological systems with the methods of queer play, unlearning and leaking. Their work crumbles structures, unbounds materials, melts technology and makes collectivities. MELT has been shaped by (melting) Ice, Freezers, Software, Disability Justice, Trans*feminism, Signal, moving at trans*- crip- kinship- time, Black Feminisms, Materialisms, Post/De- Colonial thinking, Gifs, Climate Protests, Anti-Racism and Dancing.

Helen Palmer, PhD, is a transdisciplinary writer, performer and theorist, working as a Senior Scientist at the Department for Architecture Theory and Philosophy of Technics at Technical University Vienna. She is the author of *Deleuze and Futurism: A Manifesto for Nonsense* (Bloomsbury, 2014) and *Queer Defamiliarization: Writing, Mattering, Making Strange* (Edinburgh University Press).

Elizabeth Povinelli is a critical theorist and filmmaker. Her writing has focused on developing a critical theory of late settler liberalism that would support an anthropo-logy of the otherwise. This potential theory has unfolded across eight books, numerous essays and thirty-five years of collaboration with her Indigenous colleagues in north Australia including, most recently, eight films they have created as members of the Karrabing Film Collective.

CONTRIBUTORS

Marietta Radomska, PhD, is an Assistant Professor in Environmental Humanities at Linköping University (Unit Gender Studies), SE; founding director of The Eco- and Bioart Lab and Network; research team member of The Posthumanities Hub; and co-founder of Queer Death Studies Network. She works at the intersection of the posthumanities, environmental humanities, continental philosophy, feminist theory, queer death studies, visual culture and contemporary art; is the author of *Uncontainable Life*: *A Biophilosophy of Bioart* (2016); and has published in *Australian Feminist Studies; Somatechnics; Women, Gender & Research, Artnodes, Environment and Planning E*, among others. Web: www.mariettaradomska.com.

Filipa Ramos, PhD, is a writer and curator whose research focuses on how culture addresses ecology, with a particular interest in the relationships between humans and other animals. She is Director of the Contemporary Art Department of the city of Porto. She is Curator of Art Basel Film and founded the online artists' cinema Vdrome. She is Lecturer at the Master Programme of Institute Art Gender Nature FHNW Academy of Arts and Design, Basel.

Sophie von Redecker is a PhD candidate and lecturer in the Department of Organic Agriculture at Kassel University. Funded by a scholarship from the Rosa-Luxemburg Foundation, she is developing a new transdisciplinary field of (art-based) research: Agrarian Posthumanities, in which she investigates the human–nature relationship from a farming perspective, drawing on more-than-human ontologies and queer and postcolonial perspectives. First, she was taught by sheep and strawberries on her family's organic farm, then, she was professionally trained in theatre acting and received her state diploma in acting in 2012 from Schule für Schauspiel Hamburg.

Daryle Rigney is a citizen of the Ngarrindjeri Nation located along the lower River Murray, Coorong and Lakes in South Australia. He is Professor and Director of Research in Jumbunna Indigenous Nations and Collaborative Futures at the University of Technology in Sydney. Rigney is a member of the International Council of the Native Nations Institute at the University of Arizona, and a Board member of the Australian Indigenous Governance Institute. In 2020 he was appointed a Federal Australian Government Ministerial senior adviser for the co-design of an Indigenous voice at local, regional and national levels. Among his publications: he co-edited *Indigenous Australians and the Law* (with M. Hinton and E. Johnston, 2008); co-authored *Reassembling the Contact Zone: Negotiating Ngarrindjeri Nationhood within the Australian Settler-State* (with R. Hattam, S. Hemming, S. Berg, R. Boast, J. Matthews and P. Bishop, 2021).

Celia Roberts is a feminist technoscience studies scholar. She is currently a Professor in the School of Sociology at the ANU. Her current research is on reproduction during the bushfires and COVID-19, and on the translation of epigenetic science into ante-natal care. She has a long-standing interest in hormones, sex/gender and embodiment. She is the author, with Adrian Mackenzie and Maggie Mort, of a recent book on biosensing, called *Living Data: Making Sense of Heath Biosensing* (2019) and the co-editor, with Anders Blok and Ignacio Farías, of the *Routledge Companion to Actor-Network Theory* (2019).

Antoinette Rouvroy is a Doctor of Laws of the European University Institute (Florence), a permanent research associate at the Belgian

National Fund for Scientific Research, and member Research Centre Information, Law and Society, Law Faculty, University of Namur. She authored *Human Genes and Neoliberal Governance: A Foucauldian Critique* (2008) and, with Mireille Hildebrandt, co-edited *Law, Human Agency and Autonomic Computing* (2011). Her current research interests and book project revolve around algorithmic governmentality: the semiotic-epistemic, political, legal and philosophical ramifications of the computational turn and their implications on the modalities of critique.

Danielle Sands is Senior Lecturer in Comparative Literature and Culture at Royal Holloway, University of London. She is the author of *Animal Writing: Storytelling, Selfhood and the Limits of Empathy* (2019) and the editor of *Philosophy and the Human Paradox* (2020) and *Bioethics and the Posthumanities* (2021). She received a British Academy Rising Star Engagement Award for her project 'Posthumanities: Redefining Humanities for the Fourth Industrial Age', and is currently Co-I on the AHRC-funded network 'The Philosophical Life of Plants'.

Kay Sidebottom is a Lecturer in Education and Childhood at Leeds Beckett University. Her current research explores how teachers can work with posthuman ideas to facilitate meaningful and disruptive education spaces for our complex times. With a background in community and adult education, her pedagogical specialisms include radical and anarchist education, arts-based practice and community philosophy. Kay also leads an interdisciplinary degree in Social Change which is aimed specifically at activists and community workers; the first of its kind in the UK.

Jamie B. Smith works as a nurse and a research associate at the university of Edinburgh and

Charite Universitatsmedizin in Berlin. His PhD from Edinburgh explored nursing, philosophy and social justice and his Master's degrees was both in Nursing and Sociology. Jamie focuses on bringing strong critical posthuman theory to research using mixed methods of quantitative, qualitative and post-qualitative approaches to his work. His work explores how people, place and structures produce intimate relations and care.

Josephine Taylor recently completed her PhD at Royal Holloway, University of London where she held a Visiting Lectureship in Comparative Literature and Culture. Her research explores nonhuman narratives of energy, exploring the exploitation of different species in zones of extraction. She has published on science fiction, petrocultures, and the cultural myth of the zombie and its relation to extractive and decolonial histories. She is in the process of co-editing a special issue on transdisciplinary approaches to climate justice. She is also member of the beyond gender research collective, where they research, write, and publish on queer and feminist science fiction.

Omid Tofighian is an award-winning lecturer, researcher and community advocate, combining philosophy with interests in citizen media, popular culture, displacement and discrimination. He is affiliated with Birkbeck, University of London and UNSW. His publications include *Myth and Philosophy in Platonic Dialogues* (Palgrave 2016); translation of Behrouz Boochani's multi-award-winning book *No Friend but the Mountains: Writing from Manus Prison* (Picador 2018); co-editor of special issues for journals *Literature and Aesthetics* (2011), *Alphaville: Journal of Film and Screen Media* (2019) and *Southerly* (2021); and co-translator and co-editor of *Freedom,*

Only Freedom: The Prison Writings of Behrouz Boochani (Bloomsbury 2022).

Trixie Lok Ting Tsang studied medicine and studies comparative literature and cultural studies at the University of Hong Kong. She is a practicing psychiatrist.

Gry Ulstein holds a PhD from Ghent University in Belgium where she is a member of the project 'Narrating the Mesh', which studies representations of the non-human and climate change in contemporary narrative. Gry is particularly interested in contemporary weird narrative as an expression of ecological anxieties. While working on this entry, Ulstein received funding from the European Research Council (ERC) under the European Union's Horizon 2020 research and innovation programme (grant agreement No 714166).

Lauren Wilcox is Associate Professor of Gender Studies and Director of the University of Cambridge Centre for Gender Studies. Her first book, *Bodies of Violence: Theorizing Embodied Subjects in International Relations*, (OUP, 2015), draws on feminist theorizing that provides a challenge to the separation between human bodies and the broader political context to centre questions of bodies and embodiment for thinking about war and security studies. Dr Wilcox's current research project, War Beyond the Human, focuses on the political and technological assemblages of bodies that are both the subjects and objects of political violence to create an account of political violence that builds upon gender and sexuality theory to address the relationship between violence, desire, embodiment, race, sex, and gender in late liberal societies.

Elahe Zivardar, aka Ellie Shakiba, is an Iranian artist, architect, journalist and documentary filmmaker who was imprisoned by the Australian government in Nauru from 2013 to 2019. She was accepted as a refugee by the US in 2019 and currently lives and works in Washington DC. During her detention in Nauru she was highly active in using photography and video to document the horrific treatment and conditions endured by people seeking asylum and imprisoned offshore, she also used her skills to highlight the impact of Australia's border regime on the local population. Her footage was used by ABC Australia, The Guardian, CNN and the #KidsOffNauru campaign organised by GetUp, World Vision Australia which succeeded in pressuring the Australian lawmakers to release children and their families from detention in Nauru in 2018–19. Elahe continues to call for the freedom of the remaining detainees and for an end to offshore detention through her art, including her 'Border Industrial Complex' series of paintings and her documentary film *Searching for Aramsayesh Gah*, on the architecture of detention in Nauru. Zivardar is also an advisor to Amnesty International's Game Over Campaign as well as writing for The Guardian, Southerly, openDemocracy, Oxford Law Faculty's Border Criminologies blog.

Preface

In August 2020, when I first delivered this text, I spoke to Rosi Braidotti and her summer school co-teachers and students in the Netherlands from my kitchen table in Santa Cruz, in the midst of the COVID-19 pandemic, wishing I were present to work and play directly with my beloved colleague and her companions. At the time, it seemed a strange way to meet, but such touching from a distance is still necessary. Such touching is not nothing, partly because it teaches us to learn effective new skills and partly because it shows us what it feels like to be ripped apart by violence and disease, a lesson many in the world hardly need, but perhaps I did. Then as now, I long to speak in the flesh with my communities about the gathering storms of so many kinds. I need for us to talk with each other in our own halting voices. So again, in October 2021, I write from my desk in Santa Cruz to Rosi and her allies gathered in this glossary, to give and receive strength to imagine and perform more flourishing worlds.

Obviously, we are living through dangerous but also generative, transformational times at the confluence of multiple and ramifying emergencies. It is not simple or easy to refuse both facile hope in technofixes or any other doctrines and also despair at the depth of what we face. I need to think and feel with my comrades about concrete things in order to nurture knowledge and practices of many kinds for still possible futures rooted firmly in complex and often devastatingly violent naturalsocial pasts and presents. I need to learn how to face the strengthening whirlwinds together with human and more-than-human others. I – and we – need to learn how to inherit without denial and to live in thick presents even, or especially, when the sucking urge to despair seems to paralyze all of our limbs.

Forcefully on our minds is the COVID-19 pandemic. But I also think of the other diseases in both humans and non-humans that are rampaging through the living world. I am thinking of the plague of locusts that made so many hungry across the world in 2020. I think of the diseases of the forests, the diseases of the coral reefs, the fungi, the malarias, dengue fever, war-caused famines, the multiple pandemics that are enmeshed in extractionist and exterminationist ways of living, which make us into an epidemic and pandemic-friendly world. Such death work has put humans and non-humans in crisis in all the Earth.

PREFACE

But we are also simultaneously living in the midst of powerful emerging practices of collective care and refusal of death-denial and transcendentalism. I am thinking of simple things, only one example, like the organization of food delivery during the pandemic in the Navajo Nation, to people in very isolated places and houses in the Navajo Nation. The Diné, the People, came together to provide presence, companionship and sustenance. I think of the creativity of people who are intent on reinventing care comprehensively in the pandemic; we all know examples. We know how partial these efforts are, how deep structural changes must be, how strong the forces that oppose real change are. But the impossibility of doing nothing gives me – us –heart to do something, which turns out actually to make a difference, if only to hold open the space for staying with the trouble.

Another emergency forces itself on us all. It stands in relation to the first, of course, because all the parts of the raging and still gathering storms are intersectionally inter-related and entangled with each other. This emergency is racial capitalism and neo-fascism running rampant across our societies, across North and South America, across Europe, across Asia, the Middle East and Africa. The resurgence of racial, sexist, imperial and neo-colonial capitalism and fascism terrifies me. I thought I knew what racism, misogyny, class hatred and violent individualism in the US are and were; the last years have showed me that I hardly had a clue. Living in the United States right now, I am afraid that ever more exuberant sorts of authoritarian fascism will prevail after all. And not just here.

But I also know how powerful and creative those who build other worlds that deserve a future actually are. It is impossible not to recognize effective anti-racist, anti-sexist and Indigenous justice and care movements surging now in the context of worldwide economic and environmental crises. One of the most powerful is Black Lives Matter and all it stands and works for. Racial capitalism and neo-fascism are confronted at every turn with surging movements, often led by people of colour and Indigenous peoples all over the world. They know that economic and environmental crises are situated multispecies questions of justice and care.

And so, interlaced with these other two – pandemics and fascist ethnic nationalisms – we face the emergency of multispecies extermination, extinction and genocide in the web of climate injustice, extractionism and catastrophe capitalism. But I also think of the simultaneous global revulsion at notions of human exceptionalism and on-going extractionism and its commitment to growth without limits. Think of the mushrooming affirmation, all over the world, of the Earth and of earthlings of powerful kinds. Kim Stanley Robinson wrote *The Ministry for the Future* (Orbit, 2020) for a reason; he shows us that other futures really are imaginable and still possible. He also reminds us how necessary story telling is in the toolkit for staying with the trouble.

My last emergency for now has to do with the myriads of displaced and uprooted beings, both human and non-human. Forced migrations of all kinds swell and surge across the earth, fuelled by injustice and violence intensified by climate destruction. We are living in a world of refugees without refuge, as borders close with a vengeance just when needs are greatest. The world is in motion, with ever fewer homes, with ever less access to homes across species. Corridors should beckon travel and adventure, but we live in times of cruel, brutal corridors to nowhere. Taking care of those in motion, nurturing practices of justice and care linked to migration, is simply an obligation. Beyond obligation, such practices also generate liveliness and material hope. They make interlinked communities in motion. Emergencies are global, but they are not the same everywhere. The relentless specificity of all that earthlings face must never be forgotten in misleading universals. But again, think of all of the creative and forceful work for and with migrants that is everywhere, once we notice and once we join with the work. Hope emerges from practice; it does not precede practice. Doing something concrete with each other breeds getting better at it, perhaps in time to make a difference for untold numbers of living beings. Making kin with each other, making oddkin, grows with actually engaging with each other in situated practices of love, knowledge and rage.

It is clear that science and technology matter in every single one of these emergencies. Science and technology for the people – human and non-human beings – have never been more relevant. For my whole personal and professional life, I have been committed to engaging in sciences and technologies for the peoples of Earth, human and non-human. This is no time to stop. When mistrust of science seems global these days, caring for and with the mundane sciences and scientists that we need so desperately is crucial. In matters of knowledge practices as elsewhere, I am a cross-linked relationalist, not a sceptical relativist. We are all interlinked in power-charged ways; we are not all alone in self-justifying boxes. Knowing better together matters, and that requires not-knowing and taking risks to connect across chasms. The difficulty of that process – in the face of racial scientific colonialism, imperial suppression of so many ways of knowing and living, and much else—should be obvious. That is no excuse for not knowing more and better at the end of the day than in the morning – collectively, collaboratively.

Repeating myself, this is a time of unpredictable transformations, extreme danger and cascading catastrophes. But it is also a time when things might still be different, less deadly, more caring. The sky has not fallen, not yet. It matters to care and to engage with each other in staying with the trouble. The established disorder is no more necessary now than it ever was. It is simply the current state of affairs. It's past time to break the rule of the established disorder.

So, no more business as usual. These times may be more dangerous than ever, but there is also a real chance to make a difference now, if we come together, if we ask the old question of the Left and mean it: 'What is to be done?' This glossary is an attempt to provide navigational tools and imaginative props, the contributors positioned as modest witnesses to the discursive and practical difficulties we are confronting.

At moments like these, I turn to speculative fiction, a set of practices dear to my heart in order to imagine possibilities and perhaps make them real. I want to end my brief presentation by listing a few books I have recently read that I recommend for imagining ways through the gathering storms in these times of transformation.

The first is N.K. Jemisin, *The City We Became: A Novel* (Orbit, 2020). Winner of Hugo and Nebula awards among others, Jemisin is an African-American science fiction writer of great power. *The City We*

Became is speculative urban fiction about the boroughs of New York facing cataclysm and transformation. Each borough has an avatar, an ordinary person in the world, a person of colour, who materially becomes the borough, the city. That avatar must find and join with their siblings, the sisters and brothers, other persons of colour, from other cities. The avatar of Staten Island refuses the coalition; she cannot let go of the positionality of whiteness to become kin with her potential siblings. She is too afraid of letting go, of breaking the racial isolation and making racial coalitions and common cause with the dangerous generators of the cities that we may yet become.

As a parallel New York book, I recommend Kim Stanley Robinson's *New York 2140* (Orbit, 2017). The story is set in the near future, after global climate destruction results in the flooding of lower Manhattan. It is full of bumptious street people, in housing co-operatives and coalitions. It is about people bonding together to take over finance and banks, people who take over neighbourhoods, people who are scavengers, people who come together with innovative media workers and with some really interesting non-human beings. This book is about near-future catastrophism, but also a time of near-future possibility, for reimaging ways of making Earth together. Kim Stanley Robinson does his homework; he is knowledgeable about the structure of capitalism, of finance and about the nature of the underground of a city like New York and what happens when it is undermined by water. He takes very seriously the material structure and the detailed socialmaterialism of the cities we may yet inhabit together.

Laura Jean McKay's *The Animals in That Country* (Scribe UK, 2020) is set in Australia in a pandemic – called the 'zoo-flu'—in which infected red-eyed human beings lose *themselves* in terrifying ways. They don't die or even get all that sick, but they become acutely attuned to the bodies, and especially to the relentless messaging, of all the animals around them. The disease breaks human priority and self-possession definitively *for the humans*. A relentless semiosis develops between human and animal flesh. This is deeply disturbing for the people, because the messages are not what the human beings thought the animals would say or be. The main human character of the book searches for her granddaughter in the company of a hybrid dingo figure, the semi-wild, semi-domesticated dog of Australia. The character must move through becoming prey, though listening to the crows, through sexuality and sexual abuse and generation. Then, before any resolution is possible, a terrible, silencing cure is imposed that shuts off the humans' ability to hear the profoundly disturbing messages from the other living beings of the earth. The novel ends in the silence of a Cure, a cut into sociality and communication. This is all the more provocative in the light of the COVID-19 pandemic. Longing for the end of pandemic waves, we refuse to see or hear what the pandemic is teaching about coming together with each other in a world that is relentlessly entangled, replete with meanings we do not control or understand.

I close with children's books, especially Gloria Anzaldúa's *Friends from the Other Side/Amigos del Otro Lado* (Children's Books Press, 1997), which I use for teaching English as a second language with an immigrant. My student reads the English and I read the Spanish, as we teach each other. Beginning in the 1970s, Anzaldúa is an important feminist lesbian Chicana writer, best known as the author of *Borderlands/La Frontera: The New Mestiza* (new edition, Aunt Lute Books, 2012). An astute scholar as well as a figure of wisdom and presence, Anzalduá is central to the history of capacious, risk-taking concocimiento (consciousness). *Friends from the Other Side/Amigos del Otro Lado,* is set on the Mexico–Texas border. It is the tale of two youngsters coming together, one on the Mexican and the other on the Texan side of the border, taking care of each other across the border in harsh times. I recommend this book for the beauty of the illustrations, but especially for the beauty and specificity of the language, which is not just any English or any Spanish: it is Texan-Chicana English, written in a particular regional Texan-English and a particular regional Texan-Spanish. It is a simple, powerful story that teaches what it means to come together across this border in times of great danger. It is the story I need now.

These speculative narratives drive home an important truth: academic knowledge production – like this glossary – needs to be a mix of critical and creative, analytic and normative insights. It has to be practical and profound, helpful and inspiring at once. Tracking the path of the incoming storms, but also raising prospects of hope along the way. Indeed, what is to be done?

A retired professor from the University of California Santa Cruz, Donna Haraway is a lover of biology, literature and arts, feminism, and all sorts of living and dead humans and more than humans. She continues to write, speak, agitate and dream of transformative change for earthlings in dangerous times.

Donna Haraway

Acknowledgements

This complex but necessary project could never have come into being without the vision and the support of our publisher, Liza Thompson of Bloomsbury Academic. Considering that most of the drafting and editing was done during the long, dreary months of the COVID-19 lockdown, Liza's unfailing enthusiasm about the glossary was a precious source of energy and inspiration for the editors: we thank her whole-heartedly. We were also greatly helped by two very talented and motivated editorial assistants: we thank Max Casey for coordinating the volume entries and for help in the final editing of the manuscript. And we also express our gratitude to Onessa Novak for getting the project started and setting up the basic structure of the volume organization.

We were delighted to secure yet another stunning picture by photographer Natasha Unkart for the book cover, which connects visually to the previous volume of the posthuman glossary. We thank her warmly.

The three co-editors acknowledge that it was a true pleasure to work together and that much was achieved, with the minimum effort and the maximum output. When efficiency meets joy, everything becomes possible: thank you all round for a great team effort!

Introduction

ROSI BRAIDOTTI, EMILY JONES AND GODA KLUMBYTÈ

While the *More Posthuman Glossary* is being published only four years after its predecessor, it is moving in a very different world. The world we live in now is increasingly polarized, torn between huge technological developments and accelerating ecological devastation, staggering financial growth and cruel socio-economic disparities. It is a world plagued by a pandemic that exposes the inner fractures and the structural inequalities of an unsustainable social, environmental and psycho-affective system, and various global and local conflicts and wars that intensify these fractures. In such a context, the scope and scale of posthuman scholarship has changed dramatically – both qualitatively and quantitatively – since the first, best-selling glossary was published in 2018. A number of significant changes in the field can be observed, and these shifts have shaped the present volume.

For example, back in 2018, the editors still felt the urge to define and defend the field of posthumanism against indifference and hostility. Given its timing, being written and collated as posthuman theory was still forming, the first glossary ended up being a much more theoretical and speculative volume than the present one. Now, writing in 2022, the field has moved well beyond the defining stage into a new era of confident and pluralistic growth. Reflecting on this progress, it seems fair to state that posthumanism as a field has expanded into a steady flow of publications, academic events, curricula, websites, international networks and research projects. The speed of this shift is remarkable, but it also reflects the present moment. Posthuman theory, with its strong focus on technological and scientific development, on questions of the human and who is included and excluded from the category of 'humanity', and its focus on the need to urgently re-think human connections to the environment, is deeply pertinent in the current times. After all, these are troublesome times, as Donna Haraway so rightly puts it in the preface to this volume; times of a planetary pandemic that has disproportionately impacted the disadvantaged, times where Indigenous populations and activist groups globally are beginning to declare a climate emergency, times where anti-racist work through the Black Lives Matter movement has gained vast global momentum, and where multiple feminist and LGBTIQ+ movements are increasingly active the world over. In our times, human relationships to technology are unfolding in the context of the Fourth Industrial Revolution and the Sixth Extinction, bringing new paradoxes and conflicts to the foreground. They need to be examined further, in a more complex intersectional manner that takes into account multiple social variables, including class, race, age and gender. While populist parties on both the Right and the Left of the political spectrum turn against science, intellectual enquiry and academic scholarship, we embrace them more than ever, in a critical and creative spirit. There is an urgent need to think differently and to find new solutions to unresolved problems and to emergent challenges. Posthuman theory has allowed a thinking through with, and sometimes even beyond, the traditional humanities and the conventions of critical theory, allowing for more adequate reflections on the predicaments of the current times.

Another vitally important shift that can be observed in the field is that, not only are there more individuals now working in the realm of posthumanism, but posthuman theory has, itself, expanded across a greater number of disciplines. This volume also reflects this shift, with a strong representation of entries from the humanities, as in the first edition, but also with the addition of new entries that are situated across a wider array of disciplines. These include multiple sub-disciplines within the humanities but also pedagogies, law, biology, policy, nursing studies, computer science, engineering and beyond. More importantly, they also entail growing convergences within, amidst and across these fields and disciplines, thereby adding a new level of complexity to both the fields themselves and to posthuman theory. This broad inter- and intra-disciplinary spread means that new terminologies are entering the field, more innovative neologisms, 'new weird' ideas and more methodological experimentations. There are, for example, more experimental styles of writing and thinking here than in the first volume, and more poetic licence is deployed overall. Art practice – the singular touch of many 'cosmic artisans' and the multi-layered complexity of 'posthuman aesthetics' – is not only recognized as a valid research tool, but also practically applied in several fields and areas of expertise. Moreover, a distinct meta-methodological tendency runs through the collection – with many contributors reflecting on their own knowledge practices. This approach alone is a game-changer that expresses the confidence and intellectual maturity of the field of posthuman scholarship.

Conceptually, the volume is quite consistent. The approach inspired by new materialism has not only taken root, but has flourished in a number of cross-pollinating directions. For instance, there is more attention now to the elements – earth, air, water, fire, but also much more emphasis on their perennial inter-mingling and on the energy generated by their constant exchanges. Bodies are embedded, relational, affective and heterogeneous. Human and non-human bodies are multi-layered: they are breathing, fermenting, resonating, hormonal, gestative, melting and more. They are bodies of soil and water, of code and algorithms – and they live and die together. A great deal of entries in this second glossary address illnesses and ways of dying that match the complexity and the contradictions of the posthuman convergence. The posthuman convergence redefines both biopower and necropolitics.

The unusually high scale and speed of growth also allows for a shift in practical perspectives. The posthuman is now being applied in practice, as a navigational tool, a method and a leading concept in a wide spectrum of scholarly and professional fields. We, as editors, find this to be deeply inspirational, yet there are so many applied cases that we have found it impossible to fully index each and every one of them in the way that the first volume sought to do. As a consequence, this volume is smaller in scope and size than the first one, because it functions on a different principle: we have selected samples of this explosion of new posthuman knowledge from different fields in the aim of providing an overview of the field as opposed to an extensive mapping. This affects the way the volume is to be read: each entry is a probe sent out into the world, to bring us a measure of what is happening. They are accurate, but more akin to weather-maps than definitive cartographies.

At the same time, the stronger focus on practice in the *More Posthuman Glossary* has also resulted in a series of entries that are informed by the knowledge of lived experiences. By giving centre stage to creative minds and public intellectuals such as Behrouz Boochani and Elaine Zivardar (also known as Ellie Shakiba), this volume acknowledges the intellectual labour that unfolds across literary, activist, artistic and other domains outside of, and traversing that of academia. Some entries in this volume will read as manifestos, complaints, poetic and political contemplations – the multiplicity of formats of thinking and writing are needed to find ways to adequately account for the complex present. This exuberant growth is both encouraging, as it stresses the relevance of a posthuman approach, and it is challenging, as it defies classifications and overarching syntheses.

The volume therefore offers a striking range of implementations and of experiments with terms and imagery that reflect both the breadth of the current expansion of posthuman scholarship, and its increasing depth of specialized application. This paradoxical combination makes the volume less linear and predictable, as a reading experience, than the first glossary. Given the alphabetical organization of the material, at times the transition from one entry to the next can be abrupt, and may strike the readers as a non-sequitur. We, the editors, are well aware of this feature and have deliberately taken the risk of non-linearity in order to respect the paradoxical mix of breadth and depth, as well as the diversity of the field. In this respect, the volume encourages a strategic 'defamiliarization' of our reading habits. We value this methodological shift as an integral part of the posthuman approach.

While this glossary is entering into and therefore represents a radically different posthuman world to its predecessor, we are wary, at the same time, of the politics of posthumanism. The expansion of the field has not served to unify it. Rather, if anything, nowadays a thousand more posthumanisms exist. This, as noted above, is a positive thing for many reasons, but it is also essential to note that posthumanism, while no longer being marginal, is also not always particularly radical in orientation. Differing political orientations and ethical concerns are reflected in the various communities that constitute the field of posthuman scholarship at present. For the most part, the editors of this volume have sought to select entries which reflect the definition of critical posthuman theory that was given in the first glossary. That is defining posthumanism as positioned between the convergence of posthumanism, based on post- and anti-humanist critiques of the subject on the one hand, and post-anthropocentrism on the other. This approach is vitally important to us as editors, as we have each long been engaged in intersectional feminist work which has persistently addressed the question of the exclusionary subject of the human. Our approach ensures that vitally important questions around the position of the human are centred, including questions around the status of non-human entities as valid subjects, while at the same time retaining a critical focus on the persistent reality of inequalities between different humans. We believe that it is crucial to always hold these two aspects alongside one another when undertaking posthuman work. There are many theories that are sometimes labelled as being posthuman theories that unequivocally fail to hold these two important political positionings together. Transhumanism and object orientated ontology, for example, explicitly reject the critical function, the importance of re-thinking subjectivity and the political function of epistemology and the critique of knowledge production. They have both been widely criticized precisely because they broadly do not pay attention to human inequalities and processes of dehumanization and are subsequently flawed in their world-view (Braidotti 2019; Parr 2022).

But the world into which this glossary is released has changed in other, more painful ways, too. As many entries argue, the COVID-19 pandemic is a human-made disaster, caused by the flawed relationship between humans and the ecological balance and lives of multiple species. The paradox is that this planetary contagion has resulted in an increased use of technology – both digital information technologies and vaccines and biomedical technologies. We are left wondering what is really at the heart of the social and environmental ecological upsets that have resulted in intensifying our collective reliance on the very high-tech economy of cognitive capitalism that caused the problems in the first place. This combination of contrasting elements in relation to the Fourth Industrial revolution and the Sixth Extinction is the trademark of the posthuman convergence (as defined by Braidotti 2013; 2019; 2022).

The pandemic involves complex and internally contradictory alternations of affects and emotions: a deep sense of suffering alternates with hope, fear merges with resilience, boredom with vulnerability. We are all struck by the huge costs and damages inflicted by the current context, on both the human and non-human inhabitants of this planet. This uncommonly high degree of affective involvement intensifies the challenges for researchers in the field and also encourages their reliance on artistic and creative practices, to supplement academic methods. In some ways, theory may not be the best tool to deal with what is happening right now. Affects run deep and it is not easy to address them. Words, in so many ways, fail.

How to find the right tone and the adequate language to approach the cluster of issues around the human/non-human interaction in a world plagued by disease, pain, war and loss has become far more acute now than it was a few years ago. It would be unethical to theorize about the ongoing epidemiological catastrophe or about ongoing wars and conflicts, or use these events as evidence to prove the validity of some philosophical position. While relying on theoretical cartographies to find our way across the growing amount of excellent scholarship in the field, and devoting several entries in this glossary to the COVID-19 epidemic and to issues of armed conflict, we do not think this is a time for grandiose theorizing, but rather, for collective mourning and for practices of resistance and regeneration. Over and above all else, we also need to develop different ways of caring for and with the world, a more transversal, relational ethics that encompasses humans and non-humans. Several issues in this glossary address this aspect of our predicament, offering insights and alternatives. Many of them read as fragments of meditation upon the sorrowful state of the present, others as invocations of hope.

A pandemic exposes, exacerbates and creates inequalities and their structural formations. Viruses born of human interference with animals and environmental sources end up, then, following human patterns of discrimination as they become mediated through human structures, knowledges and interactions. They act as indicators of global social inequalities, including racialized and gendered inequalities, unequal social-economic structures that dominant neoliberal political classes are persistently intent on, at best, disregarding, at worst, denying. Public health is, more than ever, an intensely political issue and neoliberal governance has laid the foundations for the spread of the contagion through exacerbation of the socio-economic power differences. The fact that wide swathes of the world remain without access to vaccines while people in the Global North receive multiple boosters, exemplifies that fact that the unequal spread of health care and access to biotechnology is by no means over. Rates of contagion and uneven vaccine distribution make it painfully evident that not all humans are equal: the human is not and never has been a neutral category. The human, rather, is a normative category that indexes access to privileges and entitlements. Humanity is a quality that is distributed according to a hierarchical scale centred on a humanistic idea of Man as the universal measure of all things. This dominant idea, however, has never been as universal as it proclaims to be, but is situated and culturally specific: it is based upon the assumed superiority of a subject that is masculine, white, Eurocentric, practicing compulsory heterosexuality and

reproduction, able-bodied, urbanized, speaking a standard language (usually English). This subject is the 'Man of reason' (Lloyd 1984) that feminists, anti-racists, Black, Indigenous postcolonial and ecological activists have been criticizing for centuries (Viveiros de Castro 2015).

Exposing the limitations of this hegemonic image of a dominant category of the human also results in revendicating the human-ness of those who do not fit this image. These are the less-than-human others, dehumanized or excluded from full humanity. Historically, they have been the sexualized and gendered others, such as women and LGBTIQ+ people; the racialized others, e.g. people of colour, people of the Global South and Indigenous peoples; and the naturalized others, such as animals, plants and the Earth itself. In a concomitance of events that define our times, the revendications of these marginalized others are exploding all around us. At the COP26 meeting in Glasgow in 2021, the Indigenous People's alliance spoke uncomfortable truths to the Western world, holding it responsible for the devastation of the environment. Many Indigenous epistemologies and cosmologies, many strands of postcolonial and decolonial thought and multiple philosophies of the Global South refuse the separation of nature from culture that is foundational to Western science. Many of these bodies of knowledge and cosmological visions have long stressed the agency of non-human forces and the crucial importance of Gaia as a living, symbiotic planet. They have been speaking loud and clear, we have not been listening.

At the same time, as noted before, a global revolt against endemic racism has exploded, with the global Back Lives Matter movement leading the way in contemporary times. This glossary explicitly speaks to race and colonialism; and these perspectives are increasingly developing within the field of posthumanism, a turn which is long overdue and which we greatly welcome. This glossary thus goes further than the first one in reflecting concerns, objections and new perspectives emerging from the scholarship. Posthuman theory has been critiqued in the past for being too white, and too Eurocentric. While there have long been voices working to bridge issues of race, colonialism and the posthuman, the expansion of the field here is evident. There are now more scholars of colour working on posthuman theory, most scholarship which brings a postcolonial lens to the field, and more work on the links between posthumanism and Indigenous thought. This expansion is both important and necessary and we are proud to have been able to include some of the brilliant scholars working in these vastly developing fields.

The ethical dimension runs throughout the volume, trying to strike a balance between the planetary nature of the posthuman convergence, and its highly localized instances. How to think about our being ecologically interlinked through our terrestrial – but also hydro, meteo, geo and zoe milieu, and the extensive technological mediation, and yet also fractured by profound differences in power and access, is the challenge. The shared horizon of hope, however, remains the same: we need to acquire adequate insight and knowledge of our current predicament, but also resist with equal lucidity the pull of apocalyptic thinking on the one hand and the abyss of despair on the other. The current crisis can enable subtler and more complex cartographies of powers and discourses at work in our societies, that is to say a more adequate rendition of where we are at. These accounts must begin through a questioning of who 'we' might be to begin with, and whose anxiety is taking centre stage in public debates about the posthuman predicament.

A pandemic on the scale of COVID-19, brings home to the Western world an ancient truth: that 'we' are all in this planetary condition – this 'syndemic' – together, whether we are humans or others. But it is also high time for this heterogeneous and collective 'we' to move beyond the Eurocentric, gendered, ableist, classist, heterosexual humanistic representational habits that have formatted it, dislodging also the philosophical anthropocentrism they entail and enforce. This shift of perspective inaugurates critical posthuman thought, yet it does not move in one single direction. Rather, it, and subsequently the present volume, points in multi-directional ways to a range of possible vectors of becoming posthuman.

In assembling different situated perspectives and selected probes in this volume, our hope is to intensify the connections and cross-references in this fast-growing field of scholarship. Increasing our relational links, our transnational, trans-cultural, trans-species solidarity, while knowing all along that, although 'we' may be in the same gathering storms together, we sure are not all in the same boat.

A

ACTING AS COUNTRY

Aboriginal sovereignty is not accommodated by Western political frameworks that prioritize independence, autonomy and territorial possession to define the operation and limits of power as a form of mastery and exclusive right. Instead, it is common for Indigenous peoples to articulate our sovereignty in relational terms of ecological and ontological interdependence; Aboriginal sovereignty is performative and chiefly involves 'acting as Country'. Although the world's Indigenous peoples are diverse, having distinctive cultural practices developed over aeons of time in specific locations, Indigenous peoples globally can be considered united in their efforts to represent and protect their interests and rights in the traditional lands and waters that define Indigenous Being as such. In this sense, 'acting as Country' defines a universal goal and character of Indigenous sovereignty. This conceptualization of sovereign being advances a cultural understanding of the relational nature of power, which contrasts with dominant Western notions of sovereign dominance, possession and exclusivity and resonates strongly with posthuman principles of relationality (see Bignall, Hemming and Rigney 2016).

In settler-colonial situations such as Australia, where First Nations peoples are overwhelmingly subjected to the legal, political, socio-economic and cultural forms imposed by colonizing authorities, practices of acting as Country define a distinctive quality of Aboriginal sovereignty. The notion that Aboriginal self-governance involves acting as Country offers a novel conceptual resource for Indigenous politicians struggling to reclaim political authority after colonization. Reclaiming Aboriginal sovereignty involves rebuilding an effective capacity to act as Country through the cultivation of positive relations in support of life-affirming ecologies. Acting as Country is, then, the continuing exercise of Indigenous sovereignty through an ongoing duty of, and responsibility for, protection of Country. This duty binds Aboriginal peoples with their traditional territories in accordance with a system characteristic of Indigenous Law, which links the human and natural worlds and thereby specifies complex interrelated conditions of human right and environmental obligation. The interconnected right and responsibility to 'act as Country' is vital for Indigenous authorities as the Traditional Owners and original custodians of ecologies under threat from unsustainable and potentially destructive industry, development and population growth. Furthermore, the capacity to act as Country is crucial for the health and well-being of Indigenous nations, whose identity and existence as such is inseparable from the environmental health of the lands and waters that constitute and support Indigenous Being (see Hemming et al. 2019).

'Nation rebuilding' describes key aspects of the process Aboriginal Nations can undertake to recover their sovereign capacity after colonization. Proceeding through phases of Identification, Organization and Action, Indigenous nation rebuilding is key for Indigenous community development and self-determination after colonization and supports the sustained efforts of First Nations to reclaim and exercise governmental agency (Cornell 2015). As a process of recovery, Indigenous nation rebuilding strengthens the political subjectivity and effective institutions required for the self-governance of Indigenous nations. Self-determined political identity, organization and action, are essential existential tools for Indigenous communities as they strive to reclaim political authority and the right to self-governance after colonization. Indigenous Nation rebuilding for self-governance is a strategic and structured process of political revitalisation that Indigenous leaders can mobilise to effectively practice Aboriginal sovereignty in 'acting as Country'.

Connection to other entries:
Eco-Law
Ex-colonialism
Posthuman Agency
Relational Sovereignty

Daryle Rigney

AGRARIAN (POST-)HUMANITIES

The Agrarian Posthumanities are an idea, a concept, a field of study and a way of thinking of the land with, across and beyond disciplines. While the term, itself, is new, the programme of research that the term may offer draws on and is related to a wider array of theories that can be found in various academic, artistic and activist contexts.

The Agrarian Posthumanities can be seen as the third wave of studies that seek to connect the Agricultural Sciences with the Humanities, the second wave being the field of Critical Agrarian Studies, which stands itself in the footsteps of its own fore-bearer, Peasant Studies. Broadly, the Agrarian Posthumanities, like its forebearers, seek to bring the discipline of the natural science of agriculture to the humanities. However, unlike Critical Agrarian Studies and Peasant Studies, the Agrarian Posthumanities also take account of shifts from within the humanities towards the posthumanities. This interdisciplinary turn, by bringing together multiple disciplinary perspectives, allows for a more adequate account of many of the central issues at stake in the field, including: environmental devastation, food in/justices, the migration of seasonal workers, the 'slow violences' (Nixon 2011) committed on land and bodies, inequalities in relation to gender and sexuality in the food industry, care-relations with soil (Puig de Bellacasa 2015), and the need to better understand non-human–human encounters while farming. Yet, the Agrarian Posthumanities are not simply concerned with social questions in agricultural contexts but propose a new understanding of 'the social'.

While the forebearer of the Agrarian Posthumanities, Critical Agrarian Studies, was developed through Marxist traditions and focused on systemic and institutional analyses, the Agrarian Posthumanities shifts the focus towards poststructural accounts of the world. They are therefore, based on a completely different ontological view, challenging Critical Agrarian Studies as well as Peasant Studies by seeking to move beyond the anthropocentrism inherent in these approaches. Thereby, the Agrarian Posthumanities deconstruct the traditional assumptions of the humanities (these assumptions are often found in the sciences too), such as patterns of thought based around the nature/culture and human/nature binaries. The Agrarian Posthumanities thus bloom from the idea that farming is an enactment of a posthuman becoming, since farming is, to draw on posthuman theory from outside the Agrarian field, always a 'becoming-with' (Haraway 2008), namely with what 'the human' wants to think of as 'the other'. In farming, we need non-human–human-working groups, to use Jane Bennett's phrase (2010). Thus, agriculture, refigured as *agri_culture*, shows in an affirmative and literal way that 'we simply can no longer stand for the modern divide of non-human and human, nature and culture, and we can no longer up-hold the division of labour where "nature" is left to the science and "culture" to the humanities.' (Åsberg and Braidotti 2018: 2). Agri_culture is positioned between nature and culture and thus stirs up and challenges hegemonic dichotomies.

The Agrarian Posthumanities shed light on what farming practices are able to teach us about the complex issue of thinking with nature. For example, Michelle Murphy (2017) has examined how toxic and carcinogenic chlorine compound PCB used in industrial agriculture as a carrier for insecticides and for the disinfection of stables, materializes in human bodies. Such examples demonstrate how 'nature' and 'culture' are inseparably entangled in a naturecultural continuum. Hence, the project of the Agrarian Posthumanities is not to obliterate the differences between categories, but to add complexity to them,

drawing attention to the manifestations and implications of these intimate and complex entanglements and assemblages.

However, the Agrarian Posthumanities also call on the agricultural sciences to rethink their foundations. For example, Gabriela Méndez Cota examines connection of posthuman thought and agriculture, underscoring the need for a *Wissenschaftskritik* ('critique of science') that includes 'a critique of humanism on an epistemological, ontological and ethico-political level.' (Méndez Cota 2011: 15). It is also clear that further research is needed on the origins and history of institutionalized agricultural education. The history of European agricultural sciences is not only replete with colonial and capitalist exploitations but also full of blind spots – agricultural sciences as taught in European universities should clearly be named 'white western agricultural sciences' to underline their focus or limitations. The Agrarian Posthumanities challenge the way that alternative genealogies of agri_culture are made invisible. These alternatives can be found, however: they can be found by listening to activist Leah Penniman (2018) about the Black roots of Organic Farming, or by taking seriously the slogan from the Women's Earth Alliance and Native Youth Sexual Health Network that 'Violence on land is violence on our body,' or by accepting the wisdom of the Potawatomi language of the ancestors of Indigenous scholar Robin Wall Kimmerer, in which 'there is no "it" for nature' (Kimmerer 2017). The Agrarian Posthumanities endeavour to let these new foundations for the agricultural sciences flourish by composting the economic and colonial roots of the discipline. This means engaging responsibly with the genealogy of agricultural sciences, working to decolonize the curriculum, to question hegemonic narratives (such as the one that we need to grow more to feed the world), to listen to alternative voices (such as La Via Campesina who fight for food sovereignty instead of food security), using these reflections in an affirmative way, a way to research otherwise.

At the same time, the Agrarian Posthumanities are deeply rooted in the material practice of farming and stand in solidarity with peasants protesting all over the world. Starting from there, we will find more affirmative forms of agri_cultural sciences, forms that acknowledge that current dominant practices are rooted in monoculture histories of plantationocenes (Haraway et al.2016) while also noting the ability to create spaces for more sustainable flourishing (Redecker and Herzig 2020). The Agrarian Posthumanities are thus a radical way of un/learning that is still in the making, an area that may not only transform the Agricultural Sciences but may also enrich 'the Humanities' with the knowledge of the 'traditional' Agricultural Curriculum.

Connection to other entries:
Composting
Critical Posthuman Theory
Geontopower
Humus Economicus
Toxic Embodiment
Traditional Agricultural Sciences

Sophie von Redecker

ALGORITHMIC GOVERNMENTALITY

Algorithmic governmentality is the actualization of a shift in governmentality towards a cybernetic mode of government that is no longer linked to law, discipline or biopolitics. It designates the actualization of the Foucauldian premonition of a post-disciplinary, post-normative and highly speculative society in the contemporary context of neoliberal digital capitalism through a series of shifts in techniques of signification, techniques of power and technioques of the self after the computational turn. The metaphor of the 'computational turn' evokes a radical transformation of the 'linguistic turn' insofar as the unit of perception, interpretation and comprehension of the world are no longer the sentence, the word, the interpretable sign and contestable representation, but digital data functioning as pure signals computable in real time. Algorithmic governmentality fits 'the image or idea or theme of a society in which there would be optimization of systems of difference, in which the field would be left open to oscillatory processes, in which there would be tolerance for minority individuals and practices, in which there would be action not on the players of the game, but on the rules of the game, and finally in which there would be intervention not of the type of internal subjugation of individuals, but intervention of an environmental type' (Foucault [1979] 2008).

Propelled by imaginaries of innovation, agility, efficiency, objectivity, endogenous modulation rather than heteronomous and rule-based government, bypassing institutional, conventional, legal, normative design, the new rationality of government informed by digital data (data behaviourism), instils a logic of speculation and pre-emption, instead of prediction and prevention, at the core of governmental rationality (Konings 2018). Machine learning algorithms (the technical strata of algorithmic governmentality) replace stable conventional statistical categories, institutionally, legally, culturally pre-established norms by plastic systems of differences (ranking, scoring, pairing, profiling) presenting a dynamic picture of risks and opportunities, of inferred behavioural propensities, that does not require the reductive mediation of a norm or statistical benchmark, let alone a human evaluator (Shapiro 2021). Pre-semiotic data – the main instrumental unit of algorithmic governmentality – is stripped of intentionality and collected at the infra-individual level, then aggregated into supra-individual patterns, circumventing the reflexive human subject as well as collective forms of engagements (Rouvroy and Berns 2013). On a technical level, this allows for what Robinson calls a 'vital network' (Robinson 2016) – an algorithmic milieu of communication and control that acts based on algorithmic, that is to say, non-human, modes of sense-making. At the same time, this also enables a kind of 'data behaviourism' (Rouvroy 2013) – a mode of knowledge production that evades the subject and that is operationalized towards pre-emptive control (Rouvroy 2020). As the logic of prediction shifts towards the logic of pre-emption through algorithmic modelling of reality, algorithmic governmentality here aims not so much at eliminating risk or uncertainty as at neutralizing the contingency, indeterminacy, radical uncertainty that are not conducive to capital accumulation while generating new sources of potentially profitable contingencies.

Pre-emptive rationality of algorithmic governmentality is a key point of its operations. The aim here is not to 'exclude anything that does not fit the average' (Rouvroy and Berns 2013: 8) but, on the contrary, to render power agile through the detection and leveraging of particularities away from large numbers. In a sense,

algorithmic governmentality seeks to foreclose the to come (à venir) (Derrida 2010) by pre-forming the future in a speculative yet actionable set of patterns.

Aware of its own speculative foundations, algorithmic governmentality is not a mode of government relying on discourses of truth, nor does it presuppose the (functional fiction of) the liberal subject capable of understanding and will. Rather, it is a mode of government relying on inferred statistical reliability without truth and leveraging radical uncertainty or contingency rather than normalizing behaviours or reforming individual psychisms as to make them embody the norm. Algorithmic governmentality does not function by fitting the bodies to the norms but rather – simulating the endogenous normativity of life itself (Canguilhem 1978) – by attuning the norm to the movements of life. In this imaginary of algorithmic governmentality, '[E]ach hyperindexed individual is effectively a multitude, but a multitude without others since in these dispositifs each individual becomes his or her own statistical reference' (Rouvroy and Stiegler 2016). This hyperpersonalized in/dividual* is at the same time plasticized and segmented, connected to statistical patterns of behaviour, susceptible to being called forth as any number of constellations of meaningful variables without performing any kind of 'wholeness', 'consistency' or singularity, disconnected and abstracted as it is from the organic, social and symbolic dimensions of existence. In that sense, algorithmic governmentality thus precludes processes of subjectivation or individuation, running on connective rather than conjunctive processes, producing surface level connections and modular,

* On "dividual" as opposed to "individual", see Deleuze 1992.

temporary aggregates or concretions, rather than conjunctive concatenations, or emergences, events, singularities (Berardi 2015).

Such governmentality opens it up to non-human forces of thought and affect, but equally also to forms of neoliberal exploitation and leveraging of contingency that short-circuit individuation. Indeed, this de-articulation of governmentality in relation to law, discipline, and even biopolitics appears to free individuals from the yoke of representation but also comes at the cost of an infinite thirst for credit as stable metrics for the evaluation of merits, needs, desirability or dangerosity give way to absolutely plastic and opaque ones, dependent on the behaviours of all individuals. This imaginary dis-institution of society also disallows collective participation in the determination of common 'meanings' and collective strategies to face uncertainty.

One of the roles of the political action in algorithmic milieu becomes the identification and fostering that which cannot be captured by digitalization and algorithmic processing, such as the unrealized. Reinvigoration of the collective, the relational, the social, the people to come, is also crucial to creating spaces that offer lines of flight. This will require both collective experimentation and institutional creativity to generate new forms of collective enunciation, new commons (Rouvroy 2020).

Connection to other entries:
(De)Constructing Risk
New Materialist Informatics
Ontologized Plasticity
Pattern Discrimination
Postcolonial and Decolonial Computing
Posthuman Data

Antoinette Rouvroy and Goda Klumbytė

ART AND BIOETHICS

The emergence of converging biotechnologies that use human biological material or mimic parts of the human body raises fundamental ethical and philosophical questions that are integral to the posthuman condition. Examples include the rise of organoid technology, tissue engineering, stem cell research, synthetic biology, genomics and 'genetic engineering' (Boers et al. 2016). These biotechnologies have a far-reaching impact on established values, norms and relationships as they touch upon basic notions of personhood, identity, humanity, our corporeality, autonomy (see also entry 'Organoids'), and on how we want to shape biomedical research, medical care and governance (van der Burg 2009; Jongsma and Bredenoord 2020). To cope with these fundamental ethical questions a different bioethics is needed that allows for experimentation with how different communities want to and can shape themselves as humans and their lifeworld in relation to biotechnology (Verbeek 2010).

Arts practices play an important role in this quest (Sarah N. Boers 2019; Roeser, Alfano and Nevejan 2018; Couture et al. 2017). A dialogue between arts and ethics traces back to Aristotle, of course, but lately novel art disciplines have emerged, such as bio-art and biological art. They experiment with biotechnologies in art forms varying from traditional art expressions to practices which integrate living biological systems or biotechnologies into the art work (Pentecost 2008). Artistic practices can be employed to stimulate moral reflection on advanced biotechnologies among different audiences, including bioethicists, developers, policy makers, citizens and patients. Accordingly, art practices stimulate the participatory bioethics that is advocated in 'ethics parallel research' (Boers 2019; Roeser, Alfano and Nevejan 2018; Jongsma and Bredenoord 2020; Couture et al. 2017). Art practice allows for experimentation with the uncertainties and ambiguities inherent to emering biotechnology, for example, through exploring different time scales and future scenarios, while playing with the potential effects of technology on human identity, personhood and society. They also elicit emotional, sensory and imaginative experiences.

My own experience bears witness to the positive force of art as research practice, notably in stimulating dialogues between bioethicists and broader audiences, through active collaboration with fine artist Rosa Sijben. In 'A Sculpture Like You and Me', a complementary performance and publication, my collaboration with Sijben resulted in a joint investigation of the ambiguous nature of objects and the interchangeable roles of human persons and non-human things (https://vimeo.com/174536993/bfc270e94f). The performances (in different locations in 2016–2017) took place in a white cube in which the audience and sculptures made by Sijben were situated. My contribution as a bioethicist consisted in giving a public lecture and initiating a monologue on the ethics of organoid technology. I emphasized especially questions regarding their moral value and their commercialization. During my monologue, Sijben started to manipulate me by instructing me to repeat certain sentences and change positions. As a result a choreography emerged in which my text began to relate to the sculptures made by Sijben and to the audience. In the publication the script of the performance was coupled with images of the perform-

ance sculptures and of daily objects that served as their source of inspiration.

The art project changed both the *process* and the *outcome* of my moral reasoning, while using an approach called Wide Reflective Equilibrium (RE) (van Thiel and van Delden 2010). In RE the reasoning process goes back and forth between beliefs stemming from practice (morally relevant facts and intuitions) and from theory (principles and background theory). The thinker attempts to achieve a state of RE in which these different types of input are moulded into a coherent moral view. The art project helped me to broaden the initial input for moral reflection, as I could include the perspectives of different audiences, Sijben, and her colleagues. Additionally, my moral intuitions regarding organoid technology deepened through a direct emotional engagement with the topic while making and executing the live performance. Most importantly, the project allowed me to experiment with the ways in which organoids challenge the subject–object distinctions that still underlie dominant bioethical discourse and regulation of tissue donation and commercialization. In her artwork, Sijben experiments with object- and personhood making use of sculptures, installations and performances. Our collaboration enabled me to recognize the blurring lines between subjects and objects in multiple contexts, including discussions of gender and race. In our weekly labs and the performances I could playfully associate with the multiple meanings and values associated to organoids: how they came into being and transformed in a complex network of exchanges. I physically felt this blurring line when acting as a performer, where I was both my human self and a sculpture as part of the performance, directed by Sijben. Insights from these experiments fed directly into a conceptual paper on the moral value of organoids (Boers, Van Delden and Bredenoord 2019). I came to recognize organoids as hybrid entities that defy established categorical distinctions between human and non-human entities. Organoids are hybrid transformations of human bodily tissues by technology into new entities. The process is intrinsically significant for science, but also generates instrumental and commercial exchange values (Boers, Van Delden and Bredenoord 2019). Lastly, the project allowed different audiences to explore questions regarding moral value and commercialization raised by organoid technology and the complexity concerning subjecthood, objecthood and corporeality. The audience became part of the hybrid world of organoid science and art practice. They experienced what it is like to become a non-human sculpture in a performance, and speculate about how their organoids might circulate in the world, both as a personal tool for healing and care and as a market good.

In sum, the active engagement of bioethicists with the arts is fruitful, because in doing so their moral reflection transforms from an *individual, formal, and mental* experiment to a *free, creative, sensory, and external* ethics lab in dialogue with different interlocutors (Boers 2019 2018). Particularly when dealing with complex technologies, such as the organoids, it enables bioethicists to actively experiment with different scenarios and experiences of corporeality, personhood and identity (Roeser, Alfano and Nevejan 2018). It enables bioethicists and broader audiences to have an embodied experiment and experiences of what it can mean to become human/posthuman fully immersed in technology.

Connection to other entries:
Defamiliarization
Organoids
Posthuman Care
Posthuman Feminist Aesthetics

Sarah N. Boers

C

COLLABORATIVE POLITICS

Gilles Deleuze characterizes 'societies of control' in terms of a neoliberal tendency towards social fragmentation and the radical splintering of collective life. This exacerbates as processes of individualization extend to technologies of 'dividualization', when subjects become commodified data dispersed through vast information networks. According to Deleuze (1992: 5), control society 'presents the brashest rivalry as a healthy form of emulation, an excellent motivational force that opposes individuals against one another and runs through each, dividing each within'. As Frida Beckman (2016: xxii) has remarked, this feature complicates a viable programme of resistance to the politics of control, since 'control society incorporates opposition and critique within itself'. Rather than direct opposition, then, resistance to contemporary political formations of control will require a strategic use of the force Agamben and Wakefield (2014) refers to as a 'destituent power', with the potential to render control systems 'inoperative' by replacing their generative conditions with creative substitutes that can materialize alternative kinds of social and political structure. If the 'constituent' logic of control society includes 'the brashest rivalry' – normalized by a neoliberal culture of conflict and competition built through colonial and capitalist technolo-gies of alienation, racist dehumanization, dislocation and division – then an alternative logic of collectivization and collaborative alliance sets a new agenda for posthuman politics.

Deleuze's influential early interpretations of Spinoza and Nietzsche has left a marked legacy in the contemporary emphasis on affective politics, characteristic of posthumanist philosophy. Rather than stressing the sovereign character of power as a quality possessed, and wielded as a force of domination over others, posthumanism understands power chiefly in relational terms as the capacity to affect and to be affected. Likewise, liberty is conceived as a dispositional practice of exercising governmental capacities to influence the political relations in which one is constitutively enmeshed. The affect of joy results when bodies enter into relations that increase their powers of acting and thereby enhance their potential for experiencing a maximum possible freedom within the relations that define their existence as such. For Deleuze's Spinoza, the motivating affect of joy corresponds with an affirmative ethics and a collaborative politics through which existence affirms itself and others, as a power of individuation made possible through an active process of relational constitution: 'The logic of real distinction is a logic of coessential positivities and coexistent affirmations' (Deleuze 1988: 95).

Posthumanist styles of political engagement influenced by this Spinozist understanding of existence and social purpose will therefore be carefully collaborative and associative, guided by an affirmative ethics of joyful interaction. Enriching this line of thinking in connection with feminist theory, Rosi Braidotti (see, e.g. 2019a; 2019b) insists upon the urgent need for an affirmative approach to politics and the positive activation of transformative and critical mode of thinking. This supports the production of posthuman knowledge able to sustain a critique of the present moment in which we find ourselves – at a point of social and environmental crisis caused by the imperialist humanist legacy of modern Western anthropocentric-colonialist-capitalism – while enabling new configurations of collective life to emerge. For Braidotti, the Spinozist ontology of immanence evident in Deleuze's philosophy corresponds with a materialist, collective, vital, embodied and relational ethics. Affirming the relational nature of existence, we must accept we are always already enmeshed in power relations and at least partly constituted by the knowledge others have formed of us; this powerful edifice can constrain our powers of self-determination. However, this should not entail passive acceptance of a state of general powerlessness and paralysis, but rather challenges us to attune more actively to the complex potentialities that emerge during processes of relational co-constitution. Over time, cohabiting powers can learn to appreciate and affirm those aspects of their coexistence that bring mutual benefit (even if these are overall or by comparison very few or minor in nature), and to avoid or minimize interactions where disagreement is trenchant and irresolvable. From selective engagements that bring positive affections and shared enhancement, further benefits might actively form over time. An approach to political identity as open, complex and shifting – and to social relations as partial, selective and piecemeal – gradually enables the incremental transformation of widespread hostility towards more amicable forms of sociability built from alternative dispositions and joyful forces of agreeable constitution (Bignall 2010).

Emphasis on an affirmative and collaborative politics of relational co-constitution sets Spinozist posthumanism apart from the negative dialectics associated with contemporary strains of post-Hegelian and post-Marxist revolutionary politics of negation, observed for example in the Frankfurt School. In its affirmative focus and collaborative mode of transformative strategy, Spinozist posthumanism likewise differs from the critical politics of competitive agonism we find, for example, in the Lacanian Marxism of Laclau and Mouffe; and from poststructuralist philosophy after Derrida that prioritizes the critical movement of deconstruction and attends closely to instances of aporia and subjective inadequacy. Rather than engaging in an ethics of self-dissolution, or in a divisive and oppositional politics of combative resistance, partners in a posthuman programme of transformation will strive for shared reward through respectful practices of mutual affirmation and selective agreement, which they will seek actively to orchestrate collectively and institutionalize as the sanctioned structures of a public culture and society-in-the-making.

Connection to other entries:
Feminism and Oceans
Norms
Posthuman Agency

Relational Sovereignty
Rights of Nature

Simone Bignall

COLLAPSE

After centuries of intense activity at the behest of *some* humans in the Minority World, we seem to be witnessing the collapse of the climate and ecosystems that defined the stability of the Holocene epoch. The multi-scalar tangle of relationships that compose the complex adaptive systems of our biosphere might far exceed our capacities for objective accounting, yet this hasn't stopped scientists from mobilizing an unprecedented amount of effort and infrastructure to model the dynamics of these relationships as they shift and unravel. This has made it possible to define the thresholds of large-scale collapse as 'tipping points', where 'a tiny perturbation can qualitatively alter the state or development of a system' (Lenton et al. 2008). In their most recent iteration, these thresholds have extended into 'large scale sub-systems', or 'tipping elements' of the earth system that are at risk of collapse (Wunderling et al. 2021), mounting evidence showing that multiple thresholds have been breached (Heinze et al. 2021; Ripple et al. 2021). As a consequence, we face ranges of environmental variability unprecedented in human history, now projected within the lifetimes of present generations. Collapse has thus become a *predicament* that envelopes everybody, human and non-human, in ever particular, yet uncertain ways.

The nascent field of 'collapsology' seeks to understand what immanent, non-linear shifts in planetary sub-systems entail for human societies. This highly interdisciplinary field adds to the topic of collapse a movement, raising the uncomfortable and under-acknowledged prospect of 'civilisational collapse', understood as 'the process at the end of which basic needs (water, food, housing, clothing, energy, etc.) can no longer be provided (at a reasonable cost) to a majority of the population by services under legal supervision' (Cochet 2011). Avoiding millenarian binaries, the 'collapsogues' situate their work in a 'mosaic of collapse' (Servigne and Stevens 2020: 167), where manifold possibilities of collapse are inhabited with/in the framework of a 'post-normal Science' (Servigne, Stevens, Chapelle 2021: 90). This framework is tended on the assertion that our agency cannot be understood outside the possibility space of environmental collapse; evoking a non-neutral space in which the work and life of academics is fully implicated (Bendell and Read 2021).

Both in the domains of nature and of culture then, collapse appears as the threshold of 'life as we know it', tracing the uncertain outlines of the 'Anthropocene boundary event' (Haraway 2016: 100) in which we find ourselves. With Yves Citton, we might approach collapse then 'as a horizon' (Citton 2020) of our naturalcultural agencies, handling it both as a predicament *and* as a heuristic. As a means and an ends, collapse might paradoxically help us to handle the uncertainty of our shared worlds in an effort to hold them together. This is, if anything, a posthuman challenge, to 'try to take seriously the necessary sharing of our inescapable incompleteness … build[ing] upon our relationality to accept the double limitation of our impossible self-sufficiency and of our inescapable reciprocal inter-possession' (Citton 2020: 98–99). Such exploration of reciprocal boundaries among dis/appearing lifeworlds exceeds the interiority of the creative intellect we inherited from modernity. The probabilities of collapse imply a diffraction of our sense of agency, multiplying its vectors as we move ever deeper into posthuman territories.

These territories might include the work of Ilja Prigogine on thermodynamics, showing how the ambiguity of collapse extends 'all the way down' to the irreversible transformations of physics into life. With Isabelle Stengers, he situates collapse in a microscalar environment where the 'deterministic, reversible processes' of physics transform into the 'stochastic and irreversible ones' of biochemistry (Prigogine and Stengers [1984] 2017: 232). Grasping entropy as an 'evolutionary paradigm' (297) in 'purely local' terms (205), they demonstrate that living systems are not reducible to a function of their outcomes in terms of a 'purposive development' (idem.), but rather show us how to 'see ourselves as part of the universe we describe' (300). Their paradigm opens up an uncertain agential space among the probabilistic 'bifurcation regions' (206) by which unstable dynamic systems in far-from-equilibrium conditions are open to structural change. This is 'both a hope and a threat' (313), affirming our generative capacity as 'macroscopic beings in a world far from equilibrium' (300), 'since even small fluctuations may grow and change the overall structure', while simultaneously raising the prospect of collapse, as 'in our universe the security of stable, permanent rules seems gone forever' (313).

Gregory Bateson situates agency in non-linear systems as an index of survival, where 'the overall flexibility of a system depends on keeping many of its variables in the middle of their tolerable limits' (2000: 510). Here, threat of collapse

emerges when ambiguity ends and agents start to *purposefully* select for single or closed sets of variables: '[p]urposive consciousness pulls out, from the total mind, sequences which do not have the loop structure which is characteristic of the whole systemic structure' (Bateson 2000: 440). Félix Guattari reconciles the cybernetic loops of Bateson's 'total mind' with Prigogine and Stengers' irreversible processes in his *The Three Ecologies* (2000). As material and local phenomena, his transversal agencies do not relate to an environment given 'as an in-itself [*en-soi*], closed in on itself, but instead as a for-itself [*pour-soi*] that is precarious, finitized, singular, singularised, capable of bifurcating' (Guattari 2000: 34). Rather than being reduced to a function of our purpose, transversal agents thus become a *result* of their environmental engagements: 'the existential taking on of context is always brought about by a praxis which is established in the rupture of the systemic "pretext", such that their consequences might prove to be either 'habitable' or 'deathly' (Guattari 2000: 36). What happens when such a praxis must operate in conditions of collapse?

Aligned with Guattari's existential practice, Karen Barad's intra-active account of measurement establishes an agential principle common to sub-atomic and ecological scales. Their resolution of the wave-particle duality in quantum physics – finding 'no indication ... of physical collapse, only cuts' (Barad 2007: 343) – renders self and environment mutually constituted in a diffractive 'cutting together-apart (one move)' (Barad 2014: 168). Barad's enactive notion of agency is extended by Stacy Alaimo to 'a trans-corporeal space, where "body" and "nature" are comprised of the same material' (Alaimo 2008). With it, Alaimo acknowledges the intimacy of collapse for 'all of us inhabitants of toxic, transcorporeal, material places' (idem.). Diffracting collapse, Alaimo suggests the precautionary principle to hold 'epistemological space as ethical space' (2008: 261) and elaborate a posthuman sense of agency in which 'we' never get the first move: '[w]hen an activity raises threats of harm to human health or the environment, precautionary measures should be taken even if some cause and effect relations are not fully established scientifically' (quoted in Alaimo 2008). With it, she renders response-ability as a multiplication of vectors of solidarity, showing how, in conditions of collapse, the posthuman challenge might lie both in emancipation and in co-habitation, in grasping that which comes before the human.

Connection to other entries:
Convergences
Disappearance
Posthuman Agency
Relational Sovereignty

Christopher F. Julien

COMPOSTING

'Composting' began as a feminist reading group in Sydney in 2015. Our desire was to cultivate a forum where ideas in the hot 'new' field of environmental humanities could be critically examined from a feminist perspective. Partly inspired by Haraway's commitment to earthy justice that invites us to imagine ourselves as 'compostists' (2016) the proposed alchemy of our method was relatively straightforward: what happens when we read feminist

texts alongside environmental scholarship? How are (or aren't) feminist scholarly labours composted into or with contemporary environmental ideas? We knew that longstanding feminist concerns about difference, desire, affect, care, kin, embodiment and labour (to name only some of feminisms' core concerns) could offer vital resources for rethinking human relations to the more-than-human world.

Garden composting is a practice of repurposing the old (kitchen scraps, nail clippings, hair trimmings) in order to make new things grow. A working compost pile is carefully tended. Just as composting is not evenly practiced by all householders, environmental humanities scholars do not necessarily commit to the labour of enriching their emergent intellectual substrate with ready-to-hand nutrients. We discovered that while environmental scholarship had many feminist scraps in the pile, most were poorly-digested by this muddy multispecies metabolism. In some cases important feminist insights had been incorporated without any attention to their genealogies; in yet other instances feminist possibilities for socio-ecological transformation remained untapped, as latent energies (Hamilton and Neimanis 2018).

Our reading group still continues more than six years and fifty meetings later. A shifting group of scholars, artists, activists and community members have met approximately monthly to probe environmental questions and their connections to intersectional feminist thought and praxis. But from the departure point of our initial critical project, our composting sessions have blossomed with a more reparative character. What new alchemies are enabled through a feminist-compostist attention to weird admixtures and their resulting possibilities?

In thinking together in difference, composting has thus become a more general and generous feminist methodology for analysing and acting in these times. While encouraging an experimental inquisitiveness about what feminist composting can be, we remain committed to five core principles:

1. **Composting is fiercely and persistently feminist:** Echoing Haraway's concern with the breathtaking swiftness with which feminist labours can be disappeared (Terranova 2017). composting encourages vigilance: old constructions of power can easily strangle new shoots. While jubilantly experimental, composting ensures that self-reflexive, intersectional and inclusive feminisms flourish. The feminism never gets weeded out.

2. **Composting is DIT ('do-it-together'):** DIT is a feminist modality proposed by Hayley Singer, Stephanie Lavau, Anna Dunn, Tessa Laird and Blanche Verlie. In a desire to 'unpick the ramifications of "DIY or die" stories for the nature-cultures that make up Earth's contexts and relations,' Singer et al. issue a rallying cry for 'DIT', or Do-It-Together as an alternative guiding imperative (2019). Composting exuberantly subscribes to this ethos, celebrating co-doings, co-thinkings and critical cross-fertilizations of many kinds. As a radical extension of a feminist politics of citation (Ahmed 2017), composting refuses the fallacy of a self-sufficient body; it always asks 'what labours enabled this labour?' As a mulching method, it is also a celebration of the joyful, sweaty and complicated work of collaboration.

3. **Composting is attentive to resistance:** Composting recognizes the complexities of growing unfamiliar things from awkward encounters. Not everything can be thoughtlessly mashed up in an amorphous pile. Even as unexpected worlds sprout from strange salvagings, histories require careful tending, and origin stories (in all their queerness) should be honoured. Composting's feminist ethics and politics of citation thus resist extraction of ideas and violent co-optation. This is particularly relevant when we look at white feminism's own erasures and appropriations of Black feminist and Indigenous feminist labours. As Singer et al. provocatively ask in relation to DIT, 'what does it mean to strive for collective action when queer, Indigenous, anticolonial and posthumanist artists, scholars and activists have so deeply problematised the anthropocentrism underpinning taken-for-granted colonial understandings of both collectives and agency?' Composting responds by tending to togetherness carefully.

4. **Composting is more-than-metaphorical:** Composting is a direct descendant of a feminist insistence on the inseparability of theory and praxis. It avers that all 'thinking work' emerges from and contours the world around us: how we *think*, *speak and write* the world shapes how we *act* in it and *make* it. 'Actual' composting is a hope that cumulative effects of small-scale actions can help sustain the planet but it also involves the scraps of unpaid domestic labours. It reminds us of prior struggles to transform the reproductive economy, reclaim and revalue mothering, rethink the heteronormative nuclear family, and remember other (classed, racialized,

colonized) bodies and labours upon which white social reproduction is built. Even if composting as described here may traffic more in metaphors than in mucky backyard matters, it is no less engaged in seeding material futures.

5. **Composting is energy-saving:** Composting is an explicitly feminist response to climate emergency, inseparable from the crises of white supremacy, misogyny, colonialism and late capitalism that fuel it. This feminist politics of citation is not about name-dropping or check-listing, but about honouring many material feminisms that have come before because of their value to ongoing world-building. As a response to environmental crises, composting is also a specifically feminist response to an academy bent on the superficial sparkle of bright shiny newness. The last thing we want to do is to use the final bursts of energy from the fossil-fuelled Anthropocene academy to relentlessly posit the next big idea (after all, we are 'writing the Anthropocene' in both figurative and material ways) (Boes and Marshall 2014). Without doubt, just as an apple core mixes with worm casings to revitalize the soil, composting as method has a transformative mandate. Yet any innovation must also counter a regime of disposability. The earthy justice that composting prioritizes is energy-saving: reduce, reuse, recycle, retrofit, compost.

Composting's logics are not new. Like both the scrappy domestic practice and the earlier social justice struggles that inspire it, composting involves messy and under-valued work. But this is the work required to live with climate catastrophe today.

Connection to other entries:
Convergences
Critical Posthuman Theory
Emergent Ecologies
Hydrofeminism
Transcorporeality II

Astrida Neimanis and Jennifer Mae Hamilton

CONVERGENCES

Convergences is the process by which posthuman knowledge practices – the Posthumanities – intersect, intermingle, split and recombine in a transversal and transdisciplinary manner within and across the academic Humanities. This process blurs disciplinary and other categorical distinctions and redesigns traditional debates about what used to be called the 'two cultures' (Snow 1959) of the Humanities and the Sciences, or what is in nowadays terms the 'three cultures' (Kagan 2009) of the Humanities, the Life and Techno-Sciences and the Social Sciences. The shifts introduced by convergences are thematic, conceptual and methodological.

Thematically, the objects of study for the converging Posthumanities are heterogeneous, focusing on a mixture of human and non-human subjects, postnatural and meta-cultural objects that include animals, hyper-objects, algorithms and speculative futures. The process orientation also introduces changes in the scale and speed of their inter-relation, engendering complex object-assemblages, which define transversal research fields that stretch across and beyond the humanist and anthropocentric agendas of the past. Examples of these fields are: the environmental humanities, digital, medical, neural, geo, global and other 'new' humanities. They often overlap, but keep their specific angles, intellectual genealogies and often diverging practical applications. Stressing the converging aspects of their encounters is a way to respect their specificity, while avoiding the segregation of their respective knowledge claims.

Theoretically, convergences situate the Posthumanities within the field of critical thought. Many of the convergences build upon the legacies of the institutionalized counter-knowledge production practices introduced by critical 'study fields', such as: feminist, gender and sexuality studies, disability studies, Black studies, postcolonial and decolonial studies, and many more. Some of those 'studies' focused on non-human objects of inquiry and looked to the natural and technical sciences – for instance, environmental studies, animal studies, media studies, science and technology studies. They interacted productively with feminist theories, especially ecofeminism and neo-materialist feminism. They also resonated with more Indigenous philosophies that reject the distinction between humans and non-humans and stress the immanence of living matter (Rose 2004; Viveiros de Castro 2015). Convergences as a posthuman approach provides a generative meeting ground for these fields of research.

A second theoretical feature of the epistemic process of convergences concerns the structure of subjectivity, a topic often neglected or dismissed in mainstream posthuman scholarship. The converging effects of posthuman knowledge expand understandings of contemporary posthuman subjects – as materially embodied and embedded entities defined by dynamic and transversal interconnections across multiple organisms and rela-

tions. These material coordinates stress the continuum with the diversity of living matter which, in its organic and technological variables, is anything but the exclusive prerogative of humans. The human is just one of the material formations currently being reconfigured in the posthuman convergences.

These ongoing developments confirm another theoretical insight, namely that the human is not a neutral category, but rather one that indexes access to power and entitlements. This leads to question the idea of the 'human' as the proper subject and the privileged object of study in the Humanities (Braidotti 2019). The recent theoretical turn to neo-materialism supports this critical shift (Alaimo 2010), by asserting the primacy of non-human life, in a materially grounded but non-hierarchical manner that acknowledges the differential intelligence of matter and the respective degrees of ability and creativity of all organisms. It also adds to this analytical frame the ubiquity and pervasiveness of technological mediation, as well as the escalation of environmental damage and species extinctions. The intersection of the computational with the environmental and ecological, coupled with a recurrent concern for social and environmental justice, requires such a critical turn (Guattari 2000).

The transversal methodology of convergences connects heterogeneous categories, locations and objects, introducing hybridity at the core of the research process. It stresses primarily the importance of non-humans as agents and co-constructors of transversal thinking and knowing. This post-anthropocentric turn by extension means that thinking and knowing are not the prerogative of humans alone, but take place in the world, defined by the coexistence of multiple organic species, computational networks and technological artefacts alongside each other.

Methodologically, the convergences facilitate links to animality, to algorithmic systems, to planetary organism, on equal, but rhizomic terms, that involve territories, geologies, ecologies and technologies of survival. They introduce an enlarged form of empiricism. This meta-methodological turn that inserts transversality as a ruling principle and transdisciplinary as a standard practice, allows transgressive scholars to display their expertise and know-how, although they may not (yet) be recognized as experts, or in spite of what they may know about the limitations of their disciplines. In other words, it empowers marginal knowledges.

Convergences affect many emerging fields by effectively combining new theories with alternative practices, drawn from the academic world, but also from a wide range of professions, the art world and activism. As a methodology they are generative of new instruments and thus point out that the contemporary Humanities as SHAPE – social sciences, humanities, arts for people and the economy – move across old socio-economic partitions. Some examples of these convergences include: intersections between environmental studies, computation and Indigenous philosophies, or life sciences, art and technology studies; critical algorithm studies, new materialism, human–computer and human–robot interaction and systems design; medical humanities, necropolitics and neurohumanities, and others, which go beyond the by now established fields of environmental, digital, cognitive/neuro and medical humanities.

These thematic, theoretical and methodological changes entail consequences for the organization of the (sub)disciplines that compose the Posthumanities.

Convergences as a practice can assist in the institutional re-organizations of the Humanities Faculties, by questioning the principles of neoliberal governance, or repurposing them for the sake of transversal interconnections, leading to yet more convergences. Convergences are ways to address the missing links in the current re-organization of knowledge production in the academic Humanities, notably in terms of social and environmental justice, marginal knowledges and the materially-grounded perspectives of marginal subjects. Convergences become therefore sites of experimentation with creative solutions for the major social, political and environmental challenges of our times, thereby contributing to the next phase of posthuman citizenship negotiations.

Connection to other entries:
Critical Posthuman Theory
Defamiliarization
The Distributed University
Emergent Ecologies
Transcorporeality II

Rosi Braidotti, Emily Jones and Goda Klumbytė

COSMIC ARTISAN

During this period of advanced capitalism and intense ecological predicament, philosophy provides vital acceleration points to further understandings and opens up spaces for new ways of exploring the complexities of our times. Rather than ideas to be decoded and analysed to extract meaning, Massumi (1992: 8) suggests that Deleuzian philosophical concepts can be activators, which readers can put to work in order to '... re-inject after-images of their dynamism into still other lives, creating a fabric of heightened states between which any number of connecting routes would exist.' By focusing on movement and potential, educators can use concepts to traverse disciplinary boundaries, offering new insights and enabling new activist formations; much needed to address our ecological and democratic crises.

Such a concept is Deleuze and Guattari's (1987) notion of the Cosmic Artisan. In this entry I draw on jagodzinski's (2018) ideas about the potential role of cosmic artisans in anthropocentric times, whereby critical educators and activists put the concept to work in order to re-energize and frame their practice as a means of affirmative and collaborative endeavour. Two specific examples from my own teaching practice will be shared, demonstrating how the concept can be used to disrupt hegemonic understandings of education and encourage thinking outside the limiting constraints of familiarity.

An artisan, for Deleuze and Guattari, is someone who is determined to '... follow the matter-flow as pure productivity' (1987: 479) where the matter, or material itself, intra-acts with the creator; not as an 'out of world' experience, but one firmly situated and embedded in the present moment. The theorists call at various points in their works for a new earth and a new people; and the cosmic artisan is seen as being pivotal in this process of harnessing unworldly forces. A new earth does not represent a utopia, but a means of revealing possibilities that are always already present. As Sholtz (2015: 36) describes them, 'Cosmic Artisans exist at the limit, are fabulators in the sense that they actualize lines of flight, potentials that exist immanently, virtually, intensively.'

'Becoming cosmic-artisan' through homemade artistic and story-telling creations can therefore enable teachers and activists to re-imagine education situations as they are or could be. By channelling and connecting with a range of forces via *potentia* power – that is, natural, relational, communal power outside formal structures – Deleuze and Guattari suggest that the artisan becomes 'cosmic' and infused with vital transformative energy; 'a homemade atomic bomb' (1987: 401).

In the first example of 'becoming cosmic-artisan', drawn from my own pedagogic practice, students (a group of trainee teachers) explored their relationships to education by creating artistic and poetic responses to daily experiences of life in the classroom. Paying attention to embodied responses, affective atmospheres and entanglements of human and non-human agents resulted in raw creations that resembled Art Brut; where the emphasis was not on creating art for itself, but being creative in order to gain new realizations of what schooling does, and can be. By bringing 'outsider' practices into a formal academic curriculum, students were able to explore and disrupt understandings of education-as-usual and subsequently reflect on the implications of this for their own future teaching roles.

My second example involves practice on a Childhood Studies programme in which students explored intersections of youth and gender. Drawing on critical human and spatial geography practices, we took an approach which aimed to encourage transdisciplinary habits of mind, shifting space both metaphorically and physically as we moved outside the classroom to explore the university campus. In this wandering, students were invited to pay attention, not only to the walk's physical features, non-human aspects and layout, but also to their bodily and affective reactions to space and place as situated and located (young, female) subjects. Collaborative maps were then assembled, using sketches and sticky notes to develop a new kind of creative 'campus cartography' which subsequently provided insights and ideas for future affirmative and activist projects.

These examples demonstrate that – despite the creeping instrumentalization of neoliberal educational practice – there remain opportunities to acknowledge and take lines of flight to move outside the constraints of formal curricula. These moves work to disrupt educational business as usual, shifting educators and students from despair to hope through affirmative creative practice. They may also be diffractive; a method neither critical (about 'them') or reflexive (about 'me') (Van der Tuin, in Braidotti and Hlavajova 2018: 99–101), but about new patterns and insights emerging when texts and artefacts are read or created through one another.

Within Higher Education, a further way in which to activate the role of cosmic artisan is to work with a slow ontology (Ulmer 2017); slow, not in the sense of working at a more leisurely pace, but as being scholarly in a different way. This way of working to rhythms of enquiry 'where scholars choose to live writing and research through locality, materiality and artisan craft' (2017: 201) disrupts usual academic paradigms which focus on speed and efficiency and prioritize outputs over creativity. 'Becoming cosmic-artisan' thus requires a sensitivity to the affective nature of teaching and learning; a heightened awareness of the social forces or intensities that work across bodies, and a willingness to follow these flows to their limit.

As an act of affirmative ethics, employing art in this way both defamiliarizes (renders the everyday hegemonic ways of being strange) and elevates minoritarian thinking. Cosmic Artisans draw on a sensitivity to affect and the different rhythms of learning; riding waves of *potentia* energy in order to connect with other bodies (both human and non) via creative means. In this way, as Sholtz (2015) suggests, art practice can move us beyond our own subjectivity through a connection with flows and intensities which transform what it means to be human. Cosmic Artisans thus render art both impersonal and communal; seizing moments of heightened affect to instigate the transdisciplinary practices required to instigate a new educational imaginary.

Connection to other entries:
Art and Bioethics
Convergences
The Distributed University
Posthuman Feminist Aesthetics

Kay Sidebottom

CRIP THEORY

Crip theory accounts for unjust enactments of disability that emerge within relations of ableism, medicalization, ongoing forms of eugenics and scientific racism, and practices of debilitation, maiming, violence and neglect, institutionalization, and structures of indifference. These unjust enactments overwhelmingly dehumanize disabled people. Critical and feminist posthumanism contributes to crip theory by marking the contingent relational doings of mattering and meaning that come to constitute disability, such as through the entangled and intimate interdependencies of disabled people with technologies, animals and environments. In turn, crip theory advances critical and feminist posthumanism by politicizing the agential world-dismantling and world-building role of disability culture and disability justice. Against the repudiation of disability, crip theory desires disabled thriving, a joyful positioning of disability that frictionally displaces disability as tragic medical condition that always needs to be overcome or cured, instead highlighting how crip kinship, care and access create disabled lives worth living.

Over 15 per cent of the global human population is disabled. Of the roughly 1.5 billion disabled people worldwide, 80 per cent are estimated to live in the Global South (UNDP 2018: 3). Globally, disabled people continue to experience barriers including a lack of access to healthcare, medical equipment and assistive technologies, low rates of employment, insufficient access to adequate living conditions including accessible housing and sanitation, personal support for care, as well as basic needs such as food and water. Such barriers are evidence of the deeply rooted forms of ableism embedded within the universal humanist project of the secular, disenchanted, rational, independent individual, as well as through transhumanist fantasies that seek to transcend the limits of the human condition through technological innovation rather than social struggle.

Our shared non-human world itself is increasingly disabled because of human-driven climate change, environmental extraction, and ecological exploitation and destruction. Rather than abandoning the world as broken with no cure readily available, critical and feminist posthumanism,

in conversation with crip theory and queer inhumanisms, engages an ethics of the more-than-human to open transmaterial spaces that document damage and persistent copresence so as to 'read up from particular situations' (Luciano and Chen 2015: 189) via an expansive range of methods, scholarly and activist interventions, disciplinary and community-based sources, and political commitments to disability, queer, trans, racial and ecological justice.

As crip theory generatively positions disability as relations we participate in rather than as an individualized and naturalized medical problem, disability and ability emerge as contested and frictional social, political, economic, cultural and ecological relations whereby disability disrupts, confronts, and transforms the normative order of things. Crip is a 'non-compliant, anti-assimilationist position that disability is a desirable part of the world' (Hamraie and Fritsch 2019). Crip theory challenges what Ellen Samuels calls 'the overwhelming fantasy of modern disability identification,' namely that disability 'is a knowable, obvious and unchanging category' (2014: 121). Crip theory is committed to disturbing ableist relations that impede the flourishing of disability culture and justice. This is, in part, due to the ways in which crip theory emerged from activist and artistic locations, marking a 'radical alternative to an assimilationist or reformist disability politics' (McRuer 2016: 119). Crip theory is a capacious way of forging a radical politics among not only those labelled with physical, mental or sensory impairments but also among broken environments, and those who behave in non-normative ways, experience chronic pain or illnesses, endure forms of debilitation, or otherwise embody ways of being that may be 'in excess of the able-minded or able-bodied/disabled binary' (McRuer 2016: 122).

Crip theory has its roots in 'a flamboyant sense of collective identity' (McRuer 2016: 119), characterized not only in defiance to nondisabled norms and values but also by 'crip jokes' (Clare 1999: 68) and a 'wicked humor, including camp' (Sandahl 2003: 37). This sense of humour is reflected in the neologism crip itself, derived and reclaimed from the English word 'cripple' which has been historically deployed to demean, stigmatize and pity disabled people. However, as crip theorist Robert McRuer notes, 'Collective reclamations of words are never simplistic reversals. They do not offer a one-to-one replacement (a singular positive meaning for a singular negative one). Instead, as collective revaluations, they simultaneously allow for the germination of multiple, unexpected meanings that can be "worldmaking"' (2016: 120).

Crip theory is both a key site of critique, marking the ways compulsory ability, capacitation, and enhancement function (McRuer 2006; Fritsch 2016), but simultaneously is also in the service of building more accessible futures that enable disabled people to thrive. Crip worldmaking anticipates disability here and now and imagines disabled futures, attending to the material and discursive formations of disability and ability. Crip worldmaking includes explorations of, for example, crip futurity and crip time (Kafer 2013; Samuels 2017), crip technoscience (Hamraie and Fritsch 2019), crip community, kin, care, and affects/emotions (Mingus 2010; Kafer 2019; Eales and Peers 2020; Forrest 2020), cripistemologies (Johnson and McRuer 2014), crip sexuality (Martino 2017), crip art (Chandler 2017; 2018), and crip culture

(Wong 2020). Aligned with posthumanism, crip theory disrupts the universal humanist ideal of 'Man' as well as takes up non-human and inhuman relations of disability in, for example, its explorations of cyborgs and technology (Murray 2020; Kafer 2013; Hamraie and Fritsch 2019), animacy and toxins (Chen 2012; 2015), non-human animals (Taylor 2017; Price 2017), and settler colonial ableism, Indigenous theory, and activism (Cowing 2020; Jaffee and John 2018).

Crip theory is closely aligned with queer theory not only for the ways it unsettles, makes strange and twisted, but also through the entangled histories of queer and disabled people being pathologized, criminalized, medicalized and institutionalized. Queer and crip 'flaunt the failures of normativity' sharing 'a striking range of political and imaginative affinities' (Fritsch and McGuire 2018, vi). Queer/crip provokes 'an unstable yet fruitful site of interdisciplinary, relational, and interspecies exposure and exchange' (Fritsch and McGuire 2018: vi) that has the possibility to 'remake the world' via novel forms of 'crip/queer solidarity' (McRuer 2012: 1). As Eli Clare (1999: 70) puts it, 'Queer and Cripple are cousins: words to shock, words to infuse with pride and self-love, words to resist internalised hatred, words to help forge a politics' that can undercut the 'power of those who want us dead' (1999: 93).

In this way, crip theory and crip worldmaking is needed as much as 'access, healthcare, housing and employment' for these become the ways 'by which we can live with disability. These are, in other words, the specific practices, sensibilities and discourses that imbue disability, not only with possibility, but with transformative meaning, value and desirability' (Fritsch and McGuire 2019: 49). Engaging crip theory enables both the 'disability to come' and 'the disability already here' to be something more than individual overcoming and rehabilitation (Ben-Moshe 2018). Indeed, 'As long as disability remains an untenable way of being, disability will not only continue to haunt us as an object of dread but will also be selectively weaponised against us to support the targeted debilitation of particular – and often already marginalised – populations' (Fritsch and McGuire 2019: 48). Instead, crip theory opens up possibilities not only 'for building more accessible futures and improving the life chances of historically oppressed people' (Fritsch and McGuire 2019: 50) but also for damaged environments.

Connection to other entries:
Endomaterialities
The Meltionary
Posthuman Agency
Posthuman Nursing
Toxic Embodiment
Transcorporeality II

Kelly Fritsch

CRITICAL POSTHUMAN THEORY

Critical Posthuman Theory develops at the convergence between posthumanism and post-anthropocentrism, seeking to dismantle hierarchies between humans, such as gender, race and class but also to debunk the idea that the human sits in hierarchical supremacy over other subjects – including the environment and non-humans (Braidotti 2022). This body of work thereby brings critiques of human-

ism as found, for example, in intersectional feminist theory, postcolonial, queer and race theory, ecofeminism and critical disability studies together and alongside critical animal and environmental studies and science and technology studies, among others. It positions itself both thematically and methodologically at the conjunction between these areas, to provide a transversal and transdisciplinary framework to critique the exclusionary nature of the specific vision of the human subject situated at the centre of the Western social, symbolic and discursive order.

Not all posthuman theory, however, is critical. Posthumanism now has many branches and has become an 'umbrella term' for a diverse range of theories including transhumanism, new materialisms, anti-humanisms, 'agential realism' (Barad 2007), the Anthropocene and the 'ahuman' (MacCormack 2020a). Braidotti (2013: 38) outlines the various origins and strands of posthuman theory, describing:

> ... three major strands in contemporary posthuman thought: the first comes from moral philosophy and develops a reactive form of the posthuman; the second, from science and technology studies, enforces an analytic form of the posthuman; and the third, from my own tradition of anti-humanist philosophies of subjectivity, proposes a critical post-humanism.

The first type of posthumanism is actually a neo-humanism, typified by the work of scholars such as Nussbaum (2006), who defends humanism, rejects the suggestion of its historical decline and stresses its increasing relevance in relation to the disruptive changes induced by globalization, technological advancement and environmental issues. This results in reinstating an updated form of liberalism, built on Nussbaum's 'capabilities' approach

(2011), namely the idea that we should all be equal and this should be achieved through giving everyone equal capabilities and opportunities. Much as she shares the aspiration to equality, Braidotti critiques the foundational notion of moral universalism that underscores this strand of posthumanism. She opposes to it a situated and relational posthuman ethics of affirmation (Braidotti 2019; 2022).

Braidotti also critiques the second strand of posthumanism which comes from science and technology studies, noting that, while this strand engages strongly with contemporary developments in the field, it often upholds universal humanistic values, with little critical analysis of the possible perils of doing do. Transhumanism perhaps best exemplifies this mode of thought. There are multiple transhumanisms today. Some are quite radical and aim at a democratic use of technologies to enhance social justice and economic access (Ferrando 2019). Other transhumanists, on the other hand, are compatible with and even supportive of cognitive capitalism (Bostrom 2003; 2005; 2011). They seek to move humans beyond their current physical and cerebral limitations, by drawing on a mixture of human–machine, neural and biomedical enhancements. Transhumanist human enhancement expands to practices that prevent the ageing process and aim to create stronger, faster and more efficient human beings. By pursuing an ideal of human perfectibility framed by the humanist Vitruvian model, transhumanism reiterates the European and Eurocentric Enlightenment vision of the Man of Reason (Lloyd 1984; Wynter 2003). It thus proposes a form of 'ultra-humanism', (Ferrando 2019) that ends up reifying 'a particular normative version of humanity that enables distinctions between more or less worthy forms of life.' (Wilcox 2017a: 5). This approach differs from the critical posthuman stance in that, not only does it ignore inequalities between humans but also, by seeking to create a super-human form of intelligence, it actively works to strengthen these inequalities by creating two tiers of humanity, those with tech and those without (Chace 2016). It is perhaps no coincidence that the majority of transhumanists are white, middle-class, high-tech men from the Global North, symbolized by Elon Musk.

Critical posthuman theories, such as new materialism and posthuman feminism (Braidotti 2022), start from a different, non-unitary image of the human, and from the lived experience of more marginalized kinds of humans. This approach challenges universalistic understandings of humanity and subjectivity, stressing the politics of locations or of immanence, the self-organizing 'force of living matter' and the ways in which 'nature-culture' has already been complicated by techno-scientific mediation. The critical line here is that, in seeking to re-centre ontology, epistemology is sometimes side-lined, producing a theory of matter that ultimately, thinks about matter alone (Braidotti 2019). For feminist critics, this neglect of epistemology results in an inadequate account of how new materialist perspectives and locations apply in a world where inequalities between humans remain (Alaimo 2016). This critique is also central to race theory, for instance, Zakiyyah Jackson (2015; 2020) warns that mere appeals to move 'beyond the human', if detached from the critiques of humanism made by Black and decolonial theorists, risk reinforcing racism and Eurocentric ideas of transcendentalism. All these critics raise the key question: *whose* conception of humanity are we supposed to move beyond? Who are 'we' in this critical practice?

The tendency to flatten out structural inequalities and systemic discrimination is manifest in moves towards the non-human that displace epistemology but avoid issues of power and social justice. Both transhumanism and object-orientated ontology (OOO) – which is sometimes classed as being part of the new materialist turn, sometimes not – exemplify such a stance, as scholars such as Sheldon (2015) and Braidotti (2019) have noted. Critical posthuman thought is the antidote to this spuriously neutral kind of posthumanism. Feminist new materialism, for example, works to situate understandings of matter as a naturecultural continuum, alongside and in relation to situated knowledge and intersectional feminist analyses of the differences between humans (Haraway 1991; 1997; 2016). This goes beyond a merely analytic displacement of epistemology and foregrounds instead the relational ways feminist new materialism, ecofeminism (Plumwood 1993), decolonial, race and Indigenous theory (Rose 2004) and posthuman feminism (Braidotti, 2022) tackle the problem of matter.

Critical posthuman theory, in bringing together critiques of both humanism and anthropocentrism, ensures that the question of matter's significance can be thought without risking the displacement of the important epistemological turns introduced by feminist, queer, critical race, postcolonial and crip theory, among others (Åsberg and Braidotti 2018). This move requires challenging the 'Universal (Hu)man' and its 'Eurocentric construction', this being a central tenant of the critical posthuman project (Lykke 2018). Thus, as Rosi Braidotti notes, while it 'may be difficult for people who have never been considered socially and politically fully human to adopt an affirmative relation to the posthuman predicament', including '[w]omen, LGBTQ+ people, the colonised, Indigenous peoples, people of colour and a multitude of non-Europeans who historically have had to right for the basic right to be considered and treated as human', this 'exclusionary notion of the human' is 'precisely what is challenged by' critical posthuman theory, including posthuman feminism (Braidotti 2022: 6).

Connection to other entries:
Convergences
The Distributed University
Emerging Ecologies

Rosi Braidotti and Emily Jones

D

DISMANTLING RISK

Risk analysis and the insurance mechanism were conceptualized as a colonial technology for the distribution of power and governance over human and non-human life. Though risk and the insurance principle have evolved into highly sensitive statistical and probabilistic financial systems, in their many guises, across a spectrum of fields, this remains their foundation.

Colonial merchants from North America were the first to convert the threats of sea travel into a commodity of its own, after observing the precarious nature of cargo in transit on turbulent seas, refashioning their collective insecurities into a new form of private property called 'risk' (Levy 2012). This cooperative process isolated risk as a separate commodity meaning risk itself could be shared, exchanged or sold, redistributing responsibility for the loss or damage that might affect cargo in transit. This perception of risk in relation to sea travel catalysed a series of violent actions that enabled the management and distribution of known and unknown threats in the future, and through this mechanism of transference, the principle of insurance was born (Rupprecht 2016). Insurance meant colonial merchants could purchase financial compensation in anticipation of their property being lost or damaged. The merchant insurer would provide the merchant owner with compensation for the lost value of his cargo, thus applying a profit-making logic as a collective strategy for economic security against the recognized risks of trading valuable resources across stormy seas (Hameed 2014; Baucom 2015).

The separation of risk as an autonomous commodity – distinct from the human or non-human subjects under threat – foregrounds a capitalist logic that provides the ability to trade and profit from decontextualized and de-physicalized resource commodities (Tsing 2015; Keenan 2019). This is as the maritime history of risk and insurance facilitated the inhumane colonial embrace of New World slavery, giving colonial merchants the right to own (and thus to risk) the black and brown bodies of slaves and the encountered other as they saw fit (Mbembe 2003). In this way, the colonial merchant could take on risk – by shipping human cargo (in the form of slaves) or non-human cargo (such as tobacco, sugar, etc.) – and profit from whatever situation that subject was placed in, regardless of whether the intended destination was reached safely or not (Harney and Moten 2013: 92). Colonial merchants were able to share the limit condition they had experienced from the risk of transporting valuable goods across treacherous seas, distributing this risk in order to give themselves power and license to impose a mode of governance on all encountered (Foucault [1979] 2008). It not only became a way of controlling the risks that confronted merchants at sea, but developed as a technology for conquering lands, resources, peoples and minds.

Introduced as part of a colonial duty to civilize, this process was imposed through a multitude of violent acts and registers, as a way to secure the future through a present governing action. This method of colonizing the future became a mobilizing feature of modernity (Ewald 1991; Beck 1992). Establishing an uneven global hierarchy of value in relation to human and non-human life, which is still in effect today (Hartman 2007: 6). This gave license to colonial merchants to place the lives of whoever or whatever they encountered (or decided to transport) in a position of heightened risk, whilst being insured against any danger, and so further profiting from this course of action (Venn 2009).

From its earliest conceptualization as a colonial project, risk and the principle of insurance were always unevenly distributed, favouring those valued or valuable enough to benefit from the use of its technology (De Sousa Santos 2015; Hartman 2007). Embedded therefore within the mechanisms of risk – even in their most evolved contemporary forms – is a system of profiteering that prioritizes some lives over others (Butler 2010: 138). The effects of this have unfolded in temporal and spatial terms, giving license to those in positions of power to place the lives of some (namely, the encountered and racialized other) in a greater position of risk. To emphasize the historic effects of the colonial conceptualization of risk, as both mechanism and technology of governance, is to establish risk as a financial and legal condition, produced through both conflict and capitalism (Khalili 2020). These violent processes, which decontextualize and de-

physicalize human and non-human subjects, aim to extract these entities into financial markets, which then rationalize their capital value (Keenan 2019). Through political and legal economies of resource extraction and distribution the speculative futures felt through risk – conjoined, constructed and present – are rooted in and affected by one another. This frames the argument for dismantling risk as part of an (insurgent) posthuman discourse (Papadopoulos 2018). The formation of risk and the insurance mechanism as defying binary analysis in regards to historic human and non-human relationships, forces a recognition that the human has and is always, in part, constituted by the non-human (Braidotti and Hlavajova 2018: 2). The colonial forces that distanced this relationship in the development of risk and insurance, engaged violent and inhumane approaches in breaking such ties, in order to allow the autonomous object of risk to become a separate exchangeable commodity (Harney and Moten 2013). This process described through 'capitalist transformations of the environment', goes beyond the production of a mere state of precarity, to produce life under known conditions of increasing threat (Tsing 2015). Risk mitigation argues for this state through the problematic concept of resilience building (Kazan 2020). Emphasizing that risk and the insurance mechanism developed in recognition of the dangers of transporting human and non-human subjects across treacherous seas, brings the undoing of this interconnectedness into sharp focus. At the heart of this technology of risk-taking, is human intervention, harnessing the forces of nature, to subject the human and non-human to the increasing degrees of threat. Another example of this process is observed in the use of widespread aerial bombardment, as forces of nature are co-opted and brandished for corrupt, extractive and violent gains (Kazan 2020).

In citing the history of violence perpetrated through colonial mechanisms of governance, an attempt is being made here to re-contextualize risk's operation – not as an autonomous object, but as a situated, uneven and context-specific condition, affecting people, land and resources, with multi-scalar human and non-human affect. Produced through conflict and capitalism, this condition is observed through transformations of the lived–built environment and the perceived restrictions of risk: spatial, material and psychological (Harvey 2006; Weizman 2008; Sadek 2016; Bhandar 2018, Bou Akar 2018; Kazan 2018). In these terms, as a limit condition, risk often builds as less visible accumulative processes of slow and structural violence, becoming visible in moments of rupture as spectacular violence (Nixon 2011). Therefore the project to dismantle risk: spatially, materially and psychologically, goes beyond the necessary acknowledgement of its colonial foundations, still in operation today. Attempts at a *methodological imagining* for dismantling this inherently asymmetric power structure may only be possible through sensitive readings and understandings of the complex, interconnected human and non-human histories and potential futures visible in its wake (Fisher 2009; Haraway 2016; Theresa Johnson and Lubin 2017; Yusoff 2018; Bhandar and Ziadah 2020; Bardawil 2020).

Connection to other entries:
Geontopower
Postcolonial Drone Scholarship

Helene Kazan

DEFAMILIARIZATION

Defamiliarization, or 'making-strange', is a shift in perception. It is an emancipatory gesture which we could define here in two ways: firstly as it was historically envisioned, as that which causes 'ordinary' things to be perceived as if for the first time, and secondly in posthuman terms, as that which seizes upon a state of enforced or uninvited estrangement and affirms it.

Coined by Russian formalist Viktor Shklovsky in his 1917 formalist manifesto 'Art as Technique' (or 'Art as Device', depending on the translation), the Russian word for defamiliarization *ostranenie* [остранение] was later quoted by Shklovsky as being spelt wrong. From *strannye* [странный] meaning 'strange' and therefore requiring a double *nn*, the word *ostranenie* was nevertheless repeated and disseminated throughout the world without the double *nn* which would link it to its root word, causing the term with its one amputated *n* to 'roam the world like a dog with an ear cut off' (Shklovsky quoted in Berlina 2017: 56). This was later corrected by Shklovsky, but the original spelling persists, which seems fitting for a term which is by its very nature a turn away from the norm. According to Shklovsky, it is the function of art to return sensation to perception, so that rather than perceiving things automatically with preconceived notions of what we are perceiving (which Shklovsky calls 'recognition'), we may perceive things anew (which Shklovsky calls 'seeing'). Recognition is the 'automatised' state; an absence of physical sensation. Hence the need for a reawakening, reorientation and reprioritization of the senses. To be anesthetized means to be estranged from sensory perception, but the movement of defamiliarization actually restores sensory perception in the Shklovskian model.

Defamiliarization therefore requires both proximity and distance; it restores sensations to things through a distancing that is also an approximation. Alternative English translations or synonyms of the term – 'estrangement' or 'alienation' (with the added complexities of their Marxist and Brechtian interpretations), 'making-strange', and even Benjamin Sher's neologistic 'enstrangement' – variously illuminate the dynamic gesture of the process, as an abstraction or moving-away from the correct path. Inspired by the explosion of the rules of representation that constituted the early Russian avant-garde, defamiliarization is all about doing it wrong, on purpose.

In the process of defamiliarization, subjects, objects, things and structures are liberated from the strictures of their preconceived referents and permitted multiple potential reorientations. Cinematically, the gesture has been linked to Dzviga Vertov's 'Kino-Eye' filming technique of the 1920s, one of which presents the scene of a Moscow street with the camera deliberately rotated sideways. The point of rotating, inverting or shifting the mode of perception causes the observer to see the object as if for the first time. The old forms are therefore not completely denatured, but are rather the perception of them is shifted; the forms themselves are revitalized.

To mobilize defamiliarization in this contemporary climate requires the second interpretation of the term – as an emancipatory gesture which seizes upon a moment of unwilled estrangement and affirms it. Defamiliarization for the posthuman age is polymathic, multifarious, transdisciplinary: it flies between articulations. As Rosi Braidotti writes in her book on the posthuman, it is simultaneously a critical and creative strategy of positioning oneself at a critical distance from the dominant vision of the subject. Braidotti discusses this using the figure of the Vitruvian man drawn by Leonardo da Vinci denoting Man as 'the measure of all things' (Braidotti 2013: 13) and how this might be repositioned.

To defamiliarize requires an entire spectrum of sensoria – human, non-human and/or posthuman – as well as our faculties of reason. Posthuman defamiliarization relies upon this connection of reason and feeling, which produces sensory experience immanent to thought. When we connect up reason and feeling we are able to feel as or with our fellow humans. We might use the term 'sympoiesis', from Donna Haraway, as a useful description of this relational and symbiotic process of embodied perception, a term for 'worlding-with, in company' (Haraway 2016: 58).

Taking one example of this manoeuvre, *queering* is one of many processes of defamiliarization that take a critical distance from the dominant vision of the subject. Queer defamiliarization is discussed at length in the monograph *Queer Defamiliarization* (Palmer 2020). Queering is an exemplary gesture of defamiliarization because it is also a shift in perception: queering, as the deliberate *un*straightening and *de*familiarization of bodies, desires and orientations. Just as defamiliarization seizes upon and affirms the negation of the 'estranged', queer seizes upon and affirms the negation of the term 'queer', lifting it out of its derogatory history and performing it in all its fabulousness.

Connection to other entries:
Convergences
Posthuman Critical Thought

Helen Palmer

DISAPPEARANCE

As Ackbar Abbas famously put it, the disappearance of the city of Hong Kong, and its possible reappearance, perhaps, marks the ever-so-restless life of this city. Located at the mouth of the Pearl River Delta, the islands of Hong Kong always served as a crossroad, spun between global empires and the whims of capital investments. It never had much to offer itself in terms of minerals, soil or other treasures at its territory. Hong Kong has never been the land of farmers, not even of fishermen actually; Hong Kong is the land always in a process of deterritorialization, where people live 'next to' nature, not working its territory but temporarily residing on the rocks. Once the islands were the home of pirate communities, who hid in their caves, today it is occupied by bankers hiding in air-conditioned concrete skyscrapers. Its current appearance is telling; one part of its territory is fully packed with skyscrapers (altogether twice as many as in New York) and home to its 7.5 million inhabitants, while the other part consists of national parks, untouched by humans.

Disappearance has been a central theme in the film industry, for which the city became so famous, since the 1970s and the 1980s. Do we recognize Hong Kong as the city of martial arts, of neon-lit backstreets, run by triads? Is it the city of penthouses where large sums of money and high tech solutions gather? At least the city seems the perfect getaway for so many blockbuster movies, far away from the gorgeously boring city-centres of Europe and the vibrant backstreets of the cities of the USA. Obviously the camera loves Hong Kong for its ability to play different roles in different stories. And especially in so called Hong Kong New Wave cinema,

this becomes all too clear, as Ackbar Abbas (1997: 26) notes:

> There is an important relation, then, between the new Hong Kong cinema and the *déjà disparu*: its main task is to find means of outflanking, or simply keeping pace with, a subject always on the point of disappearing ...

What, now, is believed to disappear? Abbas's reading of disappearing Hong Kong obviously recalls Italo Calvino's timely *Invisible Cities* who concluded:

> Cities, like dreams, are made of desires and fears, even if the thread of their discourse is secret, their rules are absurd, their perspectives deceitful, and everything conceals something else.

There is no city in the world that fits this definition better than Hong Kong. In Calvino's book the disappearance (or, the deterritorialization) of the city is relative, as all the fantastic stories by Marco Polo, the protagonist, in the end lead back to Venice, the city he lived in for so long. Hong Kong works differently, practicing a disappearance of the city which is absolute. This difference between relative and absolute is not simply about acceleration (more speed), and it also doesn't change overnight. The rocky islands of Hong Kong, long before the pirates arrived, embodied the disappearing city to come. In the prologue of his bestseller *Atlas, the Archeology of an Imaginary City*, Dung Kai-Cheung sums it up best; 'Hong Kong has been a work of fiction since its very beginning' (page xi). Hong Kong was never the beginning nor the end of any belt or road, it was always already the connection itself.

In our times, it becomes all too clear that a city like London increasingly detaches itself from the country that surrounds it (in general elections, in its relation to the European Union). Cities like New York and Tokyo seem to have done the same. Long ago, Saskia Sassen (2001) referred to them as Global Cities, suggesting that these cities replaced their local network for a global one. They 'outgrew' their environment, so to speak. But perhaps their relation to the land surrounding them did not really change; they simply grew into what 'the city' had always already been; not grounded, not 'cultured' in its meaning of organizing the land. Haven't concepts like identity and culture proven themselves to be dramatically reactionary in our days? Aren't all cities, by now, following the path that Hong Kong had outlined since its very start?

If there's one thing Hong Kongers today agree upon it is that Hong Kong has no future. For many different reasons many would also claim that it has no past. Hong Kong appears, and can only appear, in its disappearance. In her movie *In the mood for love* Hong Kong director Wong Kar-wai shows us exactly this impossibility of the city, this emphasis on dreams that cannot be realized. She speaks of 'a nostalgia for the future' (see Wasserstrom 2020: 19). Spun between the increasingly unstable global centres of power (political, economic, cultural), the city finds itself in a very fragile position, as it understands that all of the disturbances of its life lines, puts its very existence at stake. And as its very existence is its speed, then, in order to prosper it should not be slowed down, the city has to be restless and turbid, attract new energy, explore new dimensionalities and directionalities.

An important tool to slow down this city, both by its rulers from London and Beijing, has been to stress that Hong Kong was a place 'without culture', that the city lacks identity. This deeply humanist and relativist perspective, that values a location for what can be grown there (some 'particular' human knowledge, a 'particular' religious practice), is perhaps still valuable when we analyse a country, a land. But could we conclude from the above, from how its scholars and its cinematographers show us what Hong Kong is all about, that this perspective has nothing to do with the disappearing city that we refer to as Hong Kong? Perhaps, concepts like culture and identity also have less and less to say about cities like London, Beijing themselves. As well as Tokyo, New York and many more contemporary cities speeding up today . . .

Connection to other entries:
Collapse
Weird

Rick Dolphijn and Trixie Tsang

THE DISTRIBUTED UNIVERSITY

In thinking about the distributional regimes of the contemporary university, including its flight online in the midst of global pandemic, in this entry we will think through the concept of the distributed university. This concept draws on aspects of what Nuttall has called the redistributed university at the social, economic, political and cognitive levels (Nuttall 2020), while also building on Braidotti's work on planes of proliferation and encounter in the posthuman university. For Braidotti, this is about working in veins contrary to humanistic visions of subjectivity, including the ever elaborating vectors of technological mediation (Braidotti 2019). The distributed university intersects with aspects of posthuman critical theory in that it thinks with the shifting status of the human, bio-technically mediated bodies in the aftermath of the nature–culture divide and critical thought as both critical and creative. Critically, the concept is operationalized via cartographies of power relations and coupled to a mode of learning and thinking in relation to the possibility of assembling knowledge differently. It thereby draws on critical posthuman approaches and their productive intersection with the contemporary movements to decolonize the university (as outlined by Nuttall 2019), and calls for the need to restore Indigenous epistemologies (Viveiros de Castro 2015) and to develop socially just pedagogies (Braidotti, Bozalek, Shefer and Zembylas 2018).

Approaching the contemporary university in terms of its distributional vectors and regimes opens a focus on how the institution is operating in relation to multiple pressures and struggles. These include economic pressures, struggles for social justice and rapid technological change, not least in the era of the escalating epidemiological, economic and political crisis. It also enables a more adequate understanding of what it would take to build something like a university commons, in contradistinction to the neoliberal university of recent years, disputing its vocabularies and practices and building possible solidarities and conceptual vocabularies that restore us to the dual projects of care and critique (Donoghue 2008; Stimpson 2016).

Debates about how universities can make their walls more porous, about what constitutes their inside and their outside, about their publics, and about the figure of the activist-scholar who straddles the harsh boundaries of university and society, have been foregrounded in recent years.

Yet equally, knowledge production is being driven increasingly by extra-institutional formations, or is less circumscribed by institutions and disciplines. Knowledge itself has become less bounded in the distributional regimes of the past, less containable within the university itself – and more easily searchable, in an advancing technological age. The university is increasingly akin to a node in a network (Braidotti and Fuller 2019). Moreover, the rising power of algorithmic reason, in its avowedly posthuman modes of analysis and comprehension, challenges more traditional vectors of humanities scholarship, less versed in the abstractions of the algorithmic or in how to best interrupt algorithmic data and turn it towards the ends of social justice struggles in universities.

The post-pandemic university is increasingly run online and on screen or, sometimes, even via text: in poorer universities, some of them in the Global South, classes are run on WhatsApp due to data access inequality. This kind of university is both more open and more closed than ever before: dormant, yet captive to digitality – and the mediation of the University as such increasingly operated by – or even ceded to – technology corporations. In other words, the distribution of power circulates ever more widely and systematically through corporate techno-spheres. The latter in turn oversee access to data and digitality. While we may ask in one instance what happens, in this new terrain, to knowledge from the Global South and its compromised regimes of knowledge distribution and dissemination (Amaro 2022) we must equally ask about the non-human technological distribution regimes of the university now, and thus turn to a form of criticality alive to the inhuman, non-human and posthuman formations of which it increasingly speaks.

The distributed university of the present can be usefully articulated along two major vectors: first, the rise, with increasing visibility but varying degrees of fragility, of other or othered epistemologies, along decolonizing trajectories – and the unmaking of the colonial university (Tuhiwai Smith 2021). There is a proliferation of pluri-disciplinary spheres, places from which the multitudes of the 'missing people' of the academy can be drawn into its core, creating the conditions for a reciprocal community or commons (Braidotti 2022). Other epistemologies and modes of pluri-disciplinarity are made even more urgent in the era of climate change, which itself decentres the remnants of Enlightenment categories and modes of thought. Second, more-than-human technological mediation increasingly points to the need for a milieu-specific materialist analyses of media (Gabrys 2011; Parikka 2015; Jue 2020). This in turn speaks to the increasingly distributed nature of subjectivity itself (Alaimo 2010, 2016; Neimanis 2017). As our epistemic environments for thought fundamentally change due to digitality as medium, so does the situation of our knowledge production, the nature of our situated knowledges. Our distributed embodiment is one that must speak to the inhuman, the human yet to come (Wynter and McKittrick 2015) as well as to posthuman orders of distributed time, subjectivity and institutionality.

Connection to other entries:
Collaborative Politics
Convergences
Posthuman Critical Thought

Sarah Nuttall and Rosi Braidotti

E

ECOLAW

Until recently, legal theory has presupposed that law is entirely the creation of institutionally-defined human subjects acting as legislators and judges, and as the conduit for social conventions that inform legal change. As one of several related narratives that challenge the nature–culture distinction, posthuman theory helps to reimagine law as the product of ecologically-connected legal subjects and, in consequence, as continuous with the normative processes of living and non-living nature.

'We inhabit a *nomos* – a normative universe.' So wrote Robert Cover in his famous discussion of the interconnection of law with the multiple, complex, often conflicting meanings that characterize a society (1983: 4). Norms emerge from the thick textures of history, from the narratives that circulate between different lives and coalesce into *nomoi* or normative worlds – shared and inhabited in the way that myths and narratives are shared among members of communities. The image of dynamic plural normative worlds of meaning that intersect, conflict and hybridize, provides a strong critique of the image of a singular and self-defining state 'law' which remains, nonetheless, an emergent form – the normative 'world' that has, for the moment, achieved the power to impose itself (as sovereign, as ultimate decision-maker) on other normative worlds.

The anti-formalist traditions of socio-legal theory situate normative worlds in material social practices: in the everyday routines and relationships of social life (Ehrlich 1962; Ewick and Silbey 1998). To this extent, they open onto an ontological, in addition to an epistemic, pluralism – the fact that the different normative worlds humans inhabit are inextricable from existence, rather than overlaid as meaning that shapes or governs a substratum of physical matter. Once again, this socially created *nomos* does not exist as a structurally identifiable thing – it emerges from the iterative practices, the geopolitical attachments, and circulating narratives of shared lives and relationships.

Holistic knowledge based on the relationships of land, ecosystems and human communities is already held in different forms by multiple Indigenous peoples across the globe. Transitions in European-heritage knowledge traditions are currently underway that will hopefully permit a greater openness to Indigenous knowledges. In supplementing anthropocentric knowledge with a more complete understanding of the integration of human societies in ecological and physical localities, these transitions provide a further opportunity to deepen the image of normative plurality. More specifically, an opportunity exists at last to re-unite *nomos* with *phusis*, normative convention and physical matter. Recent theory across the humanities and social sciences, science and technology studies, as well as the many disciplinary philosophies of science, provide vast resources for theorizing the normativity of nature (see e.g. Canguilhem 1978; Mol 1998; Sagan and Margulis 2013). Classical legal and political theory has often taken *human* nature as the basis for developing normative worlds. But the human can no longer be understood as having an essential nature – first because such 'nature' has been imposed by the socio-political presumptions of a patriarchal and Eurocentric philosophy; second because nature (including human nature) is diverse, non-unified, and irreducible to any essence; and third, because human and non-human are natural beings in the sense that we are biological and physical as much as social and cultural (see eg, Lemm 2020). We are 'biocultural', 'biosocial', and 'biolegal' (see e.g. Frost 2016; de Leeuw and van Wichelen 2020). The normativity of nature has to be observed elsewhere than a human essence – in all of biological and physical nature.

Ecological thinking, in which all things are seen as connected in complex interacting systems, provides a launchpad for reconceptualizing law as *ecolaw* (Davies 2022). In theorizing law as ecolaw, it is possible to see plural normative systems as not exclusively human but crossing all of the limits conventionally used to define law: human–non-human; matter–meaning; is–ought; subject–object. After all, if matter and meaning are entangled (Barad 2010), then law and matter must also be entangled. The question is how to understand this entanglement given the dominance of ideas about law that confine it to a human and largely idealist sphere. There are many avenues into theorizing the ways in which law is enmeshed with

and how it emerges from material relationships. First, thinking ecologically involves placing the human law-maker as a complex embodied entity – a 'holobiont' (Gilbert et al. 2012) – into the biological and geological world. The iterations that make up the practices, pathways and customs that eventually become what we understand as law are not performed by humans in a separate human-only world, but always necessarily engagements with other complex interacting normativities. Second, looking more closely at the existences of non-human others, the processes by which life is generated and maintained can be understood as normative: Canguilhem for instance argued for a 'vital normativity' in which the constant emergence of new normalities is essential to life (Canguilhem 1978). Life can be seen as a series of endless iterative norming actions (i.e. actions that create norms). Third, taking 'nature' at large (that is broadly as understood by natural scientists) as an irreversible and purposive emergence of order from disorder (Prigogine and Stengers [1984] 2017; Sagan and Margulis 2013) provides resources for understanding the geobiological complex of Earth systems as normative rather than mechanical (see also Latour 2018). All of these and a multitude of other pathways combine in an image of eco-normative plurality – an image in which law can be understood as materially connected, not only to the human societies and meanings that give it form but also to place and time, land, ecology, non-human life and the emergent realities formed by relating.

In Western colonial thinking human law is frequently understood as an entirely separate human system which governs or at least constructs matter, plants, space, animals and relationships. But that is only one side of the many stories that connect law and 'nature'. Ecolaw is one way of conceptualizing the pluralities of normative connection across the human and the non-human.

Connection to other entries:
Collaborative Politics
Norms
Posthuman Agency
Posthuman International Law and Outer Space
Rights of Nature

Margaret Davies

EMERGENT ECOLOGIES

Theorists who imagined the human as an exceptional creature – outside of ecological entanglements – were shocked when a little-known virus suddenly disrupted the modern world system in 2020. Now it is easy to see that the posthuman condition has engendered novel kinds of wild life (Franklin 2003) – unruly agents that are circling back to transform the human with the looping effects of a feedback circuit (cf. Hacking 1999; Haraway 2008). New kinds of viruses, bacteria and weeds have emerged as a result of human enterprises (Tsing et al. 2021). We are *becoming beside ourselves* with glee and dissolution, to paraphrase Brian Rotman. Human nature is melting as we become multiple and parallel, in contingent articulations with our feral companion species (cf. Rotman 2008: 104). Nature and culture are being reconfigured by emergent ecological assemblages.

'Nature' has long been understood in relation to human enterprise, well before the idea of the idea of the ecosystem emerged or before scholars in the humanities began writing about the Anthropocene. In 1845 Marx and Engels recognized that unadulterated nature 'no longer exists anywhere (except perhaps on a few Australian coral islands of recent origin)' (2010: 40). The human became alienated from species-life, products of labour, the built environment, and the world of nature in social theory (cf. Vogel 1988: 370). At the same time, while biologists began establishing mechanistic theories of evolution, the field of natural history diverged from human history. The idea of ecology was introduced by Ernst Haeckel in 1866, with a two-volume treatise called *Generelle Morphologie der Organismen*, as he tried to understand the relationships that drive changes in organisms over evolutionary time:

> By 'ecology' we understand the comprehensive science of the relationships of the organism to its surrounding environment, where we can include, in a broader sense, all 'conditions of existence' ... We consider the entire relations of the organism to all other organisms with which it comes into contact, and of which most contribute either to its advantage or its harm ... [P]hysiology has largely neglected the relations of the organism to the environment, the place each organism takes in the household of nature, in the economy of all nature, and has abandoned the gathering of the relevant facts to an uncritical 'natural history,' without making an attempt to explain them mechanistically.
>
> **translated by Stauffer 1957**

In subsequent decades biologists began to explore basic ecological questions that still have relevance today: Do ecosystems have essential functional parts? If destroyed will ecological communities predictably emerge again in the same form?

A. G. Tansley, who coined the term 'ecosystem' in 1935, dispelled earlier ideas about ecological communities as 'superorganisms'. He described dynamic assemblages in constant flux: 'The systems we isolate mentally are not only included as parts of larger ones,' Tansley wrote, 'but they also overlap, interlock and interact with one another' (1935: 301). Ecologists in the late twentieth century took Tansley's idea of the ecosystem and made it unnecessarily concrete. Paul and Anne Ehrlich famously compared ecosystems to airplanes. They argued that it would be terrifying to ride on a partially disassembled flying machine. 'As you walk from the terminal toward your airliner, you notice a man on a ladder busily prying rivets out of its wing. Somewhat concerned, you saunter over to the rivet popper and ask him just what the hell he's doing' (1981: xi). Ehrlich and Ehrlich think that we should be terrified to live in ecosystems where essential parts, species, are being driven extinct – being popped out of finely tuned systems like rivets.

Popular metaphors are being questioned as a new generation of biologists describes the emergence of what they term 'novel ecosystems'. Joseph Mascaro, a plant biologist, rejects the airplane comparison, writing: 'Ecosystem function does not solely reflect species loss, as implied by the popping of rivets, it also reflects species additions' (Mascaro et al. 2013). Novel ecosystems 'are diverse but invaded, neglected but resilient, anthropogenic but wild,' in the words of Laurie Yung and colleagues (2013). Ecologists are now studying life in urban environments, considering possibilities for living with novel forms of wild life. Still, some biologists have expressed reservations about this conceptual shift: 'In today's predomin-

ant consumer culture there is a social value that ascribes worth to novelty,' writes Rachel Standish and colleagues. 'The concern, then, is that people will value novel ecosystems simply because they are new' (2013).

Emergent ecological communities are forming through chance encounters between lifeforms, historical accidents and parasitic invasions. The flight of capital, and the trajectories of diverse species across national borders and through fragmented landscapes, is engendering new multispecies assemblages. The idea of emergent ecologies is an invitation to rethink assumptions in conservation biology about the past as a legacy that should always be restored (Kirksey 2015: 3). Refocusing attention on the interaction of agential beings and powerful interests in contemporary ecological communities becomes an opportunity to reflect on future possibility. Regarding the posthuman as an organism living in emergent ecological communities also corrects errors in modernist ethical and ontological projects.

Evolutionary history, like human history, contains many surprises – accidents, small deviations, mutations or errors – that give rise to new forms of life and power (Foucault 1977b). The disruptive force of *entstehung*, or emergence, is clearly evident as a multitude of parasitic agents invade our schemes and interrupt our dreams (cf. Serres 2007). As we navigate new symbiotic possibilities – while living in situations not entirely of our choosing – the key questions become: How do plants, animals and fungi move among worlds, navigate shifting circumstances, and find emergent opportunities? As unruly forms of life run wild, is the modern human capable of intervention? Can the posthumanities generate new proposals for disrupting, derailing and rearticulating the looping effects of emergent ecological systems?

Connection to other entries:
Convergences
Critical Posthuman Theory
Parasitology
Syndemic
Transcorporeality II
Viral

Eben Kirksey

EMPATHY BEYOND THE HUMAN

Traceable to Edward Titchener's 1909 coinage from the German *Einfühlung*, literally 'in-feeling,' empathy has become a catch-all for a range of experiences involving cognitive, affective or imaginative engagement with another's perspective or experience (Coplan 2011). Its appeal – evidenced by its endorsement across academic disciplines, in the popular media, and in corporate discourses – derives from the widely-held perception that it is intrinsic to being human, grounding intersubjective relations and underpinning ethics, serving, even, as 'the bedrock of morality, the glue of society' (Hoffman 2014: 96). Scientific scholarship has focused on the 'biological roots of empathy' (Dolby 2019: 404), drawing on the discovery of mirror neurons to reframe it as a kind of 'embodied simulation' (Gallese 2007) employed across species. However, the implications of research into mirror neurons are contested (Leys 2012), and humanities scholars continue to distinguish between the range of experiences classified as empathy, from emotional contagion to imaginative perspective-taking (Oxley 2011: 16; see also Andrews and Gruen 2014: 195), and their ramifications for conceptions of subjectivity and ethical responsibility. Some of these conversations are restricted by individualist notions of the human and humanist conceptions of value; on the contrary, posthumanist approaches to these issues interrogate assumptions about selfhood and value, gesturing towards a post-anthropocentric notion of empathy.

The increasing interest in empathy coincided with a shift in focus in Animal Studies from 'rights to lives' (Pick 2011: 11). Research grounded in the rights-based tradition foregrounded animal cognition and other capabilities to argue that some animals (usually higher mammals) merited political rights (Singer 1976; Regan 1983). These approaches neglected embodied experience, disavowed emotional connections between species, and reinforced anthropocentric conceptions of ethical value. The displacement of rights as the sole account of value corresponded with a supplanting of 'bounded individualism' (Haraway 2016: 5) by intersubjectivity, relationality, and more dynamic models of selfhood (Aaltola 2018). Such accounts reject hierarchical models of cross-species interaction and ethical value, focusing instead on shared experiences of embodiment and vulnerability (Pick 2011; Hird 2013; Alaimo 2016) and expanded notions of care (Bellacasa 2017). Many endorse affective approaches to cross-species relations, suggesting, for example, that in providing a social adhesive, affect underpins progressive ecologies (Davidson, Park and Shields 2011), or that in disrupting the 'self-contained interiority of the individual', it reveals new connections and configurations

(Vermeulen 2015: 8). Empathy, in particular the embodied experience of empathy within and across species (Mensch 2011), holds a specific place within this broader turn to emotion and affect, both in popular ethology (de Waal 2010) and in the humanities (Weil 2018). The latter is exemplified by Lori Gruen's notion of 'entangled empathy', which builds on the cross-species potential of care ethics to describe an 'experiential process involving a blend of emotion and cognition in which we recognize we are in relationships with others and are called upon to be responsive and responsible in these relationships' (Gruen 2015: 3).

An increasing body of scholarship investigates the limitations of empathy, revealing the audacity of its bolder endorsements. Neither a secure source of insight into others' experiences (Koehn 1998), nor a necessary generator of sympathy or altruism (Coplan 2004), empathy is poor at motivating change (Prinz 2011), and hence, 'not intrinsically moral' (Oxley 2011: 4). Paul Bloom's provocatively-titled *Against Empathy* goes further: narrowly focused and dependent on proximity, subject to manipulation, and facilitating a parochialism which fosters existing relationships rather than forging new ones, empathy is a poor moral guide (Bloom 2017). The smooth integration of empathy into corporate jargon is troubling; empathy foregrounds individual relations to the neglect of problematic structures; it 'follows the trajectories of capital' (Whitehead 2017: 157), usually under the guise of ethical judgement. The role of identification in empathy is disputed. The conflation of the two risks 'narcissistic identification' (Hartman 1997: 4), where one obscures the other by taking on their suffering and making it one's own. For Hartman, reflecting on the hidden forms of racial domination informing the ongoing legacies of slavery, this 'too-easy intimacy' (Hartman 1997: 20) perpetuates undisclosed power relations. Empathy has the disturbing capacity to harbour or even nurture 'repression, usurpation, theft, vampirism, or ventriloquism' (Veprinska 2020: 20).

If empathy proceeds from a comprehensible resemblance between the two parties, cross-species empathy risks species-parochialism – favouring the familiar, the mammalian or the cute – and the reinforcement of anthropomorphic anthropocentrism (Sands 2019b). Explicitly limited by sentience (Gruen 2015), the ethical potential of empathy is restricted by the pressing environmental need to think ethically about beings, such as insects, at the 'edges of sentience' (Loo and Sellbach 2015: 80) and beyond. In the search for a non-anthropocentric 'vegetal ethics' (Marder 2012: 262), the structural difference between humans and plants (where the latter denaturalizes the model of interiority that empathy presupposes) both exposes the inescapable narcissism of the empathetic process, and gestures towards a disruptive, as yet unrealized, 'ontological empathy' (Marder 2012: 268).

Indiscriminate endorsements or dismissals of empathy disregard its complexity, which emerges from its implication in unresolved questions of selfhood, value and power. The intellectual value of empathy is found not in instances where it succeeds – which presuppose proximity or commonality – but in moments of 'empathetic dissonance' (Veprinska 2020: 3) which expose our imaginative failures and tendency to project, and at its peripheries, where it begins to destabilize our conceptions of the human (Sands 2019b).

Connection to other entries:
Posthuman Agency
Posthuman Care
Posthuman Nursing
Rights of Nature

Danielle Sands

ENDOMATERIALITIES

'Endomaterialities' are formations of human and other-than-human bodies and lives as hormonal. The word 'hormone' was coined in 1905, the same year Sigmund Freud published his *Three Essays on Sexuality*. Both events reframed sex as a scientific problem; something to know and manage. Across the twentieth century, diverse apparatuses of power/knowledge set out to address these aims: the scientific fields of sex endocrinology and psycho-analysis; vast networks of clinics and professional organizations devoted to training professionals and treating clients; and substantial literatures exploring the complexities of the psyche and the actions of hormones at increasingly micro scales. Endomaterialities derive from the intense scientific elaboration of the human consti-tuting the emergence of the posthuman that exploded reproduction and sexuality into a plethora of assemblages.

Unlike psychoanalysis, endocrinology was as much interested in other-than-human animals and plants as humans. As Adele Clarke (1998) has shown, endo-crinologists reframed animal and plant reproduction as a set of intervenable biolo-gical processes. From the outset, biomed-ical endocrinology also brought humans and other-than-human animals into new relations: in the late 1800s, renegade 'founding father' Charles-Édouard Brown-Séquard, injected himself with the crushed testicles of dogs and guinea pigs to reju-venate his sexual drive; later in the twenti-eth century, a hugely profitable industry supplied hormones from pregnant horses to menopausal women for similar reasons. In-Vitro Fertilization (IVF) techniques moved from farms to clinics and back again, while late twentieth century concerns about endocrine disruption, sex and reproduction range across frogs, seagulls, alligators and humans.

Endomaterialities are deeply inter-twined with political and cultural change: 1905 was also the year that Britain's Women's Social and Political Union began a new phase of militant activism; meno-pause was reframed as medical problem during second wave feminism; and IVF is core to contemporary changes to sexual and social life. Endomaterialities are often contested. Take, for example, current debate about the availability of 'puberty blockers', a treatment delivering human-made hormone analogues to interfere with the endogenous hormonal flows associ-ated with pubertal development. Widely approved for use in early developing chil-dren, Gonadotropin-Releasing Hormone analogues (GnRHa) are also used to treat children and young people who identify as trans. In recent years, demand for GnRHa has soared alongside both supportive and critical media portrayals of young trans people, their families and gender identity development services.

In the UK, GnRHa are offered to trans young people only through the NHS Gender Identity Development Service (GIDS) provided by the Tavistock and Portman NHS Foundation Trust or by private clinics. In December 2020, the High Court controversially ruled that access should be even more tightly controlled, with clinics told to seek the Court's permission to prescribe on a case-by-case basis. Refraining from passing direct judgement on the medication's effects, the Court argued that patients under sixteen could not understand the social and psychological significance or potential long-term consequences of this treatment, even though GnRHa only temporarily suspend puberty (which may have long-term, potentially irreversible, effects on bone mineralization and on fertility) (Giovanardi 2017). This decision gave little credit to the GIDS' careful screening practices, instead fuelling public debates about biomedical and socio-cultural determinism. Fortunately, in September 2021, this judgement was quashed by the Court of Appeal who noted that there was no legal precedent for the Divisional Court to have made such a decision, noting that the guidance provided by the Court had been 'inappropriate' (Bell v Tavistock [2021] EWCA Civ 1363, para 89).

Puberty blockers are also used to postpone breast and pubic hair growth and menstruation in early developing children. Although GnRHa may lead to loss of adult height, some parents describe the treatment as socially desirable, even necessary (Roberts 2019). Other parents and clinicians prefer to provide psycho-social support to early developers, arguing that early onset puberty has few long-term consequences. Public discourse around puberty blockers for early developers is notably muted in the UK – clinicians, parents and young people make decisions about using hormones to shape puberty in peace. The similarities and differences between these two endomaterialities are instructive. For young trans people, future transition is framed as a worrying outcome; for early developers, 'on time' puberty is understood as an inherent good.

The British debate around GnRHa is reminiscent of several other moments in the history of endomaterialities: the mid-century use of sex hormones to 'treat' homosexual men and women (Terry 1999); feminist criticisms of early IVF practices (Franklin 2013); and the 'designer baby' controversy of the early 2000s (Franklin and Roberts 2005). At such moments, clinicians' capacity to intervene in reproductive/sexual bodies – although gradually won – comes to public notice and is presented by interested actors as scandalous, even dangerous. At these junctures, the capacity to hormonally shape sex/gender and reproduction is figured as too much control: 'an unacceptable enactment of medical or patriarchal power'; 'playing God'; 'harming vulnerable children'. In many cases, however, patients and health activists have intervened, winning the right to refuse or to access treatments and reframing public perceptions of specific endomaterialities. As noted above, parents, activists, clinicians and young people are currently undertaking this work in relation to puberty blockers. Public and legal debate around GnRHa shows the struggle inherent in transition points between human and posthuman articulations of sexual and reproductive life, clearly demonstrating that endomaterialities are embodied politics.

Connection to other entries:
Surrogacy
Toxic Embodiment
Transcorporeality II

Celia Roberts

EXISTENTIAL POSTHUMANISM: A MANIFESTO

Posthumanism is the philosophy of our time, a way of coping with the urgency for an integral redefinition of the notion of the human in the twenty-first century. This is a unique opportunity for generative exchanges that are forging, not only public opinion, but also the lives of the people involved, as well as the evolution of society, the future of humanity, the dignity of non-human entities, and the health of planet Earth. The issues at stake are very high. And still, often theory and practice do not go hand in hand: theorists write about posthumanism, but posthumanism is not necessarily changing the way we live and behave. This is why existential posthumanism develops the posthuman turn not just as a theoretical approach, but as a practical and applied way of existing. In short, we do not have to wait apocalyptic hyper-technological futures to be posthuman, but we can actually become posthuman right now: for instance, in the ways we – the human species as a whole – live; in the ways we, as individuals, behave; in the ways we, as organisms, (inter-)act. This existential take engages posthumanism at all levels: from the personal to the social, the biological, the planetary, the ontological and beyond. Such a message is urgently needed by the humans of the twenty-first century, who are re-addressing and re-envisioning themselves in the era of the Anthropocene, of global pandemics and of the rise of artificial intelligence. It is also of vital importance to all the non-human agents of the planet.

What is existential posthumanism?

Existential posthumanism is a path of self-enquiry and self-discovery: by daring to fully embark on this journey, we humans can comprehend the extension of the resonances, impacts, affects and effects of our being in the world. Existential posthumanism refers to full existential awareness; in this sense, it is not simply an academic trend, but a much deeper realization. This journey of self-knowledge starts by understanding the inter-being of the self: as individuals, societies, species, planet, cosmos and so on. Existential posthumanism, as a philosophy of life, approaches humans (in all of their diversities), non-human animals, technological entities and ecological systems relationally, investigating the human condition as a cosmic co-emergence. Existential posthumanism implies full existential commitment at the individual, social and planetary levels, bringing forth multispecies coexistence and existential dignity that embraces all beings. As such, it deconstructs any discrimination based on human-indexed differences, species-related categories or other types of constructions where difference is defined as pejoration and negativity: ultimately, diversification is approached as the spark of existence, at the core of the dynamics of biological, and technological, evolutions. By extension, existence is not approached in competitive, nor in hierarchical ways, but in open terms of affinities and co-emergences. For instance, existential posthumanism embraces radical ecology and far-reaching technology: one does not have to thrive at the expenses of others. In a post-Darwinian approach to evolution, existential posthumanism does not recognize the survival of the fittest as a natural law, but for instance, underlines the foundational relevance of cross-species symbiotic collaborations. The cyborg turn, as well as the urgent climate crisis of the Anthropocene, show that long-lasting survival has all to do with planetary balance.

How to enact existential posthumanism?

Existential posthumanism is an existential approach which changes ways of existing, allowing us to ask not only ontological macro-questions, but also practical micro-questions related to our daily routines. Both dimensions are relevant in the constitution of our existential expressions and manifestations. It is currently a field in full expansion, which has to do with integral ethics, that is, ethical conduct based on post-humanistic, post-anthropocentric and post-dualistic praxis. What about the food we eat? What about the thoughts we have? What about the social intentions that inform our technologies, and our individual intra-actions through technologies? What about our material stewardship of the Earth and the land(s) we are the fruit of? It's time to pause and be real. There are no absolute answers, each situation must be approached pluralistically and with originality. More clearly, we do not have to repeat the canons set by past narratives dominated by anthropocentric and human-centric assumptions. Such ideologies are outdated, because they do not recognize the (post)human condition in the twenty-first century, nor the human as an integral part of the planet. They merely reinstate the privilege of *some* humans over other beings; and thus, even though they are still reiterated in some human societies, we no longer have to accept them, nor follow them. We don't even need a revolution: the evolution of the Earth speaks for itself. The ice-melting poles are crystal-clear: climate change is not a notion, but something we experience every day. Everything is changing, and we – the inhabitants of this planet – can change right now, manifesting different ways of existing, enacting our own cosmic game. Existential posthumanism can be expanded through the realm of posthuman spirituality, but the two fields are not synonyms.

What is the difference between posthuman spirituality and existential posthumanism?

While spirituality transcends the ordinary experience, eventually leading the spiritual posthuman to the mystical experience, existential posthumanism is a praxis that can work within the constituted categories of social and political archetypes, in order to deconstruct and transform them. In such an endeavour, existential posthumanism does not need to let go of the primacy of the intellect (an overcoming that is a *sine qua non* in the path of the posthuman spiritual seeker). And still, existential posthumanism can be seen as a reference point to those people who have realized that words by themselves are only seeding, and do not necessarily flourish. Enactment requires another level of existential commitment. This is a breath of fresh air for those committed posthumanists, who have invested in the intellectual capital of society as a radical source for deep social and individual transformations, for those cyborg posthuman activists who are aware of the fact that there is no original beginning to re-constitute, therefore, there is no original sin to purify. We are constant beginnings, and constant ends. This brings to the table unlimited power at the species level, the power of the collective (un)conscious and its ability to inform the intra-changes of the community at large, as informed by individual realizations. 'Posthuman' in this existential sense, means being brave enough to know that the human condition is neither our destiny nor our nature, but a spatio-temporal manifestation of unlimited material and poietic possibilities.

Connection to other entries:
Convergences
Critical Posthuman Theory
Empathy Beyond the Human
Posthuman Care

Francesca Ferrando

EX-COLONIALISM

A contraction of the phrase 'exit-from-colonization', the neologism ex-colonialism signals a socially transformative process of historical discontinuity that breaks resolutely with settler-colonial formations, such as those characterizing Australia, Aotearoa-New Zealand, Canada and the Americas. As a movement of discontinuity, ex-colonialism provides a framework for disrupting and healing the ongoing social traumas inflicted through settler-colonization (Bignall 2014). However, ex-colonialism differs from reconciliation processes that rely upon an assimilationist politics of unification and expects Indigenous peoples to 'reconcile' themselves to a continuing set of settler-colonial norms. Ex-colonialism is instead conceived in posthumanist terms as an exit or a break from a problematic present, in complementary alliance with a 'politics of refusal' accompanying Indigenous nation resurgence, such as that described by Leanne Simpson (2017) as a 'radical and complete overturning' of the settler-colonial nation-state.

While acknowledging the political and ethical significance of specific Indigenous standpoints as drivers of decolonization, ex-colonialism nonetheless posits a collaborative pathway for a more hopeful politics of interaction, also crucial for future social and environmental sustainability. The collaborative politics of ex-colonialism is potentially available to Indigenous and non-Indigenous agents alike, who believe global histories of geographical entanglement have committed all of humanity to a conjoined future, and who are consequently seeking to work together in a transcultural movement of 'co-resistance' to settler-colonialism. Often motivated, in part, by a shared concern for the damaging effects globalized capitalist imperialism has inflicted upon environments that previously flourished under Indigenous stewardship, the allied politics of ex-colonialism breaks with longstanding colonial habits of engagement and governance. It renews a permanent social potential for forming transversal styles of relationship amongst more-than-human agencies, appropriately supported by bicultural, transcultural or intercultural legal, political, economic, social and environmental institutions.

As a 'way out' of contemporary systems of racialized oppression and environmental destruction that have their origins in modern Western ideologies and settler-colonial projects of domination, ex-colonialism creates conceptual alliances between posthumanist and Indigenous philosophies of relationality. These similarly insist upon the complex interdependence of nature-cultures, and both convey an affirmative ethics of relational sovereignty predicated on concepts of interconnected subjectivity, ontological generosity and shared empowerment. Accordingly, whereas settler-colonialism proceeds through the dehumanization of a subjected Indigenous class and the institutionalization of a regime of inhumane political technologies of segregation and racist assimilation, ex-colonialism depends upon resistive processes through which diverse peoples share in 'becoming-human' through processes of ethical engagement. However, as a 'becoming-human', ex-colonialism does not seek to reinstate the version of humanist 'progress' connected with anthropocentric European modernism and associated imperialist programmes of global 'civilisation'. Rather, ex-colonialism is an intercultural framework that brings Indigenous philosophical perspectives of 'more-than-human' existence and ontological plenitude, together with the frameworks of affective subjectivity conceived in Continental posthumanism. That is, ex-colonialism is an intercultural ethical perspective for guiding positive transformations in complex affective orders that are fundamentally open and dynamic, formed through expansive relations and environmental agencies that both constitute and bind subjects in shifting structures of mutual interdependency, subjectivity and sociability.

Ex-colonialism does not describe an end state that can be realized conclusively and for all time; rather, it sets a perpetual task for postcolonial humankind, which must respond to the ever-present danger that historical attitudes of white superiority and colonial structures of domination will continue to inflect contemporary relations of power. Ex-colonial perspectives acknowledge that political society does not only take its ideological character from the

'macropolitical' control exerted through the structures of government, law and policy as the institutions of sovereignty in which power is concentrated. In fact, power invests the entire social field through dense networks of mobile and productive relations of struggle and subjectivation that Michel Foucault describes as 'micropolitical' and feminists define as 'personalpolitical'. Accordingly, a governing body does not simply impose colonial rule crudely upon a population. Rather, colonialism is an affective disposition that threatens power relations wherever they appear, and whatever their scale. Furthermore, because it is an affective disposition, colonialism emerges initially as a mode of desire that is then instantiated and given substance in actual practices – in power relations – which in turn become sedimented and institutionalized as the overall set of political arrangements defining a colonial-type society. Ex-colonial resistance to colonialism therefore necessarily involves reflexive and critical analysis of the desires that shape subjects and their intimate relations – and ultimately invest the social field – coupled by conscientious reinforcement of alternative relations of desire and power that materialize nonimperial modes of existence.

Ex-colonialism is therefore an attitude of affective practice that is ontologically, politically and ethically opposite to humanist imperialism and settlercolonialism. It involves the kind of interaction that Gilles Deleuze (2004) describes as 'the resonance of disparates', when diverse entities seek to combine productively and respectfully through complex processes of shared composition. Ex-colonial relations can accommodate both agreement and disagreement simultaneously, because ex-colonial agents understand each other as complex, mobile and multidimensional collectives; they interlace 'bit by bit' in 'piecemeal insertions' and selective encounters, and not in their respective entireties (Bignall 2014; Deleuze 1990: 237–43; Deleuze and Guattari 1987: 504). Over time, cohabiting powers can learn to appreciate and affirm those aspects of their coexistence that bring mutual benefit (even if these are overall or by comparison very few or minor in nature), and to avoid or minimize interactions where disagreement is trenchant and irresolvable. From selective engagements that bring positive affections and shared enhancement, further benefits might actively form over time. An approach to political identity as open, complex and shifting – and to social relations as partial, selective and piecemeal – gradually enables the incremental transformation of widespread hostility born from colonial control towards more amicable forms of sociability built from alternative dispositions and forces of constitution. Ex-colonial partners will join carefully in piecemeal and selective encounters that aim for mutual enhancement at recognized sites of shared agreement, while respecting resilient differences that define the specificity or uniqueness of each party and should not be denied, erased or coerced into submissive sameness. These ex-colonial styles of engagement rely upon an affirmative ethics for the enrichment of all life, such as we find in the posthumanist philosophy of Rosi Braidotti or in the Indigenous gift paradigm described by Rauna Kuokkanen (2019). Careful conduct and respectful practices of intercultural intimacy potentially then become institutionalized over time and with common determination, as the sanctioned structures of an ex-colonial public culture and a more-than-human society-to-come.

Ex-colonialism proposes to break with the past for the sake of the future; but it does not claim to surpass the past that remains with us today as the basis on which our present action takes place. Furthermore, colonial legacies of systemic injustice have entrenched vastly uneven playing fields that influence the dynamics and potentialities of contemporary political struggles. If Indigenous authorities today are willing to partner in treaty with settler society and will tolerate a continuing settler presence on the ancestral lands that colonizing forebears have seized and degraded, the best we can do towards our recovery of a shared humanity is to create our futures on the basis of a different set of power relations. These may advance when an alternative spirit of engagement and comportment enables new forces of association that strive for reciprocity and parity in processes of social construction. Micropolitical relations joining culturally diverse citizens in piecemeal civil engagements propel this kind of shift, which over time can incrementally consolidate a macropolitical order as the institutionalized habits of an ex-colonial society. Ex-colonial social transformation is a challenge we have scarcely begun, but for all that it is not a utopian or ideal endeavour. Ex-colonialism exists already as a minor or counter-actualizing force within every settler-colonial society, dispersed through social networks, exercised intimately through positive intercultural relations and mutually productive encounters. Colonial racism is a longstanding weapon of choice both for the imperial modern humanism of progressive Enlightenment, and for the dehumanizing biopolitics of postmodern control. By contrast, ex-colonialism is a transformative tool of critique, which diverse citizens of the settler postcolony may wield collaboratively to advance a potential for posthuman liberation.

Connection to other entries:
Acting as Country
Collaborative Politics
EcoLaw
Posthuman Agency
Relational Sovereignty

Simone Bignall

F

FEMINISM AND OCEANS

Western feminisms arrived in waves (Helmreich 2017: 30). Underneath the waves, lie 'myriad silences and ruptures in time, space, history, ethics, research, and method' (Sharpe 2016: 11): wet ontologies that emerge in feminist posthumanisms and find their sister–brother–sibling unbreathing, ungendered, underwater, deep in the oceans. There are traces of these racialized histories in feminist storytelling, welts, just as there is a long re-telling of subjectivity, who is subject, that propels feminisms into stark contrast with the propertied men who wrote landed histories of knowledge in Europe, and the colonies, and now discourses of intervention. This entry engages the ocean as a mechanism for drawing together feminist posthumanism with feminist accounts that complicate gender through exposing racialized histories of subjectivities, while drawing in intersectionality and challenging the persistence of colonial forms.

Feminist accounts of the ocean traverse the Atlantic and the Pacific with histories of slavery, colonialism, militarism and capital. This is an intervention into the waves of Western feminism and into Western subject formations. So that the 'ungendered' (Spillers 1987) oceanic flesh, bodies-not, bear witness to understanding that '[t]he visual and historical evidence betrays the dominant discourse on the matter as incomplete' (Spillers 1987: 73). Feminisms must visualize, listen to, and understand their incompleteness just as feminism theorizes the incompleteness of theories of property, histories of conquest and acquisition. The oceans, like feminisms, are simultaneously sites of power and unruly commons. The tentacles of under-sea cables mirror the trade routes of empire, joining state capital to state capital, while ignoring the ungendered flesh left to take residence in the ocean (Sharpe 2016:18). Feminism arrived at the sovereign state and knocked on the doors of the state in waves, but the waves were carried by the bodies unbreathing in the waters underneath the journeys of colonialism and slavery.

Neimanis questions white feminism, asking 'What happens if we go deeper?' (Neimanis 2019: 491). Sharpe writes of all in the Middle Passage as those 'who passed through the doors of no return [and] did not survive the holding and the sea, they, like us are alive in hydrogen, oxygen; in carbon, in phosphorus and iron, in sodium and chlorine. This is what we know about those Africans thrown, jumped, dumped overboard in the Middle Passage, they are with us still, in the time of the wake, known as residence time' (Sharpe 2016: 18). For feminist posthumanist Neimanis, the subjectivity that feminisms have interrogated, shaped through Western human and Western state, must also be re-remembered in the body of the ocean, which holds the histories of abjection, the trade routes of empire and the emphatic arrogance of European explorers (Neimanis 2019). Feminisms and the oceans are intertwined – visually, affectively and embodied – in non-human, interspecies, and the technologies of the High Seas as a global commons (for the enjoyment of all humankind and legally designated a common heritage) that reside with the afterlives of ocean crossings, while pregnant with the legacy of nuclear radiations, in the salty expanses. For Federici (2010) 'the language of the commons has been appropriated . . . put at the service of privatization'. A feminist posthuman account of the ocean needs an alternative account of watery possibilities.

In the Marshall Islands feminist protest interweaves with histories of nuclear explosions in the oceans (DeLoughrey 2013) that not-so-accidentally collide the story of the Anthropocene with the military greed that displaced and diseased indigenous populations, infusing reproductive health with the history of the ocean. Women on Waves (Hodson 2019), are in the waves and the waves are inside them. The ocean, de-territorialized space, fluid, feminized, mastered yet protected, is more than metaphor in feminist thinking: simultaneously gendered; 'motherly amnion, fluid matrix, seductive siren, and unruly tide' (Helmreich 2017: 29), and means to escape from gendered selves; '[s]wimming, then, is an opportunity to have a sense of identity detached from others, but the fact that this has to be purposefully sought speaks volumes about the gendered constraints on identity formation' (Throsby 2013).

Queer feminism/s describe an oceanography of dislocation,

> submerged and intersecting diasporas
>
> that reimagine the routes to understanding.
>
> Tinsley 2008

In Europe, today and yesterday, right now, there are migrant bodies that float and sink in the Mediterranean, the ships, also gendered 'she', that refuse to rescue or to recognize humanity (Perera 2013). Posthuman feminisms seek to undo the landed histories of Enlightenment and undo their own pernicious centring of humans as origin to search out her unremembered, ungendered ways of doing, ways of seeing, telling differently, hearing for writing, spilling out of categories, dissolving containment, distrusting contentment. Probyn interrogates oceanic consumptions (Probyn 2016). Swimming and crossing Other oceans, indigenous feminisms tell of saltwater swimmers (Stronach et al. 2019) and a recognition of the need for how '[r]estoration of ancestral knowledges continues to be an important part of enacting alternatives to settler colonial, capitalist enclosures' (Goodyear-Ka'Poa 2017: 186). These enclosures are intimately connected to stories of territorial enclosure that presuppose land as starting and end point of human relations/human encounters, while non-human encounters and lore are displaced and rendered primitive, before man, all for not seeing the border between land and sea so effectively conjured by the Captains on the ships.

Federici concludes 'if commoning has any meaning, it must be the production of ourselves as a common subject' (Federici 2010: 7), for Kahaleole Hall 'the ocean becomes the space that connects the people', while Haraway's Chthulucene dribbles its tentacles into a consciousness that drifts differently. This is not the global commons that the oceans of popular imagination infiltrates, Federici's commoning, Neimanis's weathering, Sharpe's residence time, Spillers ungendered flesh, Tinsley's transoceanic dislocations, Haraway's tentacular thinking, are feminisms oceans.

Connection to other entries:
Composting
Hydrofeminism
Low Trophic Theory
Transcorporeality II

Gina Heathcote

FERMENTATION

Living with kefir is difficult. I start with a few grains. There are not enough for the quantity of milk in the jar, and the kefir is watery. The grains keep growing. Now, the kefir is good. The grains keep growing. Only a day later, the kefir they make is too sour. There are too many grains in the jar. What to do with extra grains? The grains keep growing. I get a second jar. There is now too much kefir. I become irritated. The grains keep growing. They demand attention. They make me feel guilty. I can't throw living things down the toilet. Guilt makes me angry. I am now angry at bacteria that take care of me.

Making kefir, sauerkraut, miso, beer, wine and kombucha are practices of fermentation, i.e. working with bacteria and yeasts (fungus) to achieve a transformation in food or beverage, whether at home or on industrial scale. Fermentation has a range of meanings: from a wider use in food-making which covers any micro-bial process, with or without oxygen, to a narrower definition in biochemistry that refers to the use of carbohydrates to produce energy anaerobically. With oxygen, the generation of energy starts with glycolysis, where glucose is converted into pyruvic acid that is used to generate adenosine triphosphate (ATP), which delivers energy to cells. Without oxygen, lactic acid is produced, which also leads to ATP. Fermentation, thus, is anaerobic respiration. Microbes and individual cells have the ability to switch between two different modes of respiration: the fermentation mechanism is present in cells in 'higher' organisms. We feel the results of fermentation in our muscles when they ache from lactic acid produced during intense exercise.

Fermentation was the main method of energy-production before the presence of oxygen in Earth's atmosphere. It is the oldest 'metabolic pathway' that unites eukaryotes (cells with nucleus enclosed within a nuclear envelope) and prokaryotes (bacteria without the nuclear envelope): 'When stressed, our bodies ... "remember" the times before the atmosphere became suffused with oxygen. Such physiological flashbacks re-present past environmental conditions and the bodies that evolved to live in them' (Margulis and Sagan 1995, 66).

This capacity shared between prokaryotes and eukaryotes makes fermentation not only a process that occurs in the human gut, which should be attended to for healthy living, but also a lens for the form of attention that gave birth to hypothesis of symbiogenesis. Lynn Margulis's work on the origin of eukaryotic cells that led to symbiogenesis changed contemporary biology and had a huge resonance in cultural theory

(Margulis and Sagan 2002). Emphasizing the importance of cooperation and non-linearity in evolution and undermining essentialist ideas of individuality, endosymbiosis ('living together on the inside') inspired affect theory (Clough 2008), work on gender and reproduction (Parisi 2004), body theory and the cultural analysis of chimerism (Shildrick 2015). The conceptual effervescence of contemporary biology in its focus on bacteria continues being a great resource for critical thinkers. The genomics revolution allowed biologists to see that humans are literally made of microbes: at least 50 per cent of cells in a human body are bacteria. They are key for body development, metabolism and the building of our immune systems. Bacteria, thus, not only sustain life but also create an understanding of being that is profoundly porous, symbiotic, relational, cooperative and incomplete.

Work on bacteria, fungi and viruses is not only the preserve of biologists and critical theorists. Understanding the importance of bacterial and mycorrhizal fungi webs in topsoil (Puig de la Bellacasa 2017) is foundational to indigenous and traditional knowledge and to movements such as permaculture (Mollison and Holmgren 1978) and the use of growing techniques such as agroforestry (forest gardening), urban permaculture, Hügelkultur (burying wood in growing beds) and many other practices of living well with microbes.

During my Soviet childhood in the 1980s, the time of various deficits, including of food, I ate large amounts of sauerkraut, gherkins and fermented tomatoes. In the autumn, my parents would ferment cabbage in 30 kg batches. It would last us through winter and spring, when vegetables and fruit were scarce. Growing food and preserving it by fermentation was a key element in sustenance across the territory of the Soviet Union. Love for some of fermented food is still strong. However, as the great popularizer of fermentation Sandor Ellix Katz reminds us, the barrier that separates fermentation from rotting is cultural (Katz 2016, 2020). Practices of fermenting marine mammal products in Chukotka were almost annihilated during the Soviet times when the smell and taste of such food appeared undesirable (Yamin-Pasternak et al. 2014).

While fermentation is a knot that ties together privilege and resources for taking care of one's health and *savoire vivre* with traditional practices of healthy survival under threat from intensive farming and fast food, there is no denying that fermentation is key to the art of living and eating. Fermentation preserves nutrients, but also breaks them into a more digestible form (Mollison 1993; Katz 2016). It can reduce or eliminate toxic compounds found in roots, grains and legumes, which is especially important for equatorial Africa and Asia relying on cassava that can contain toxins. The whole world is undergoing 'the nutrition transition' (Popkin et al. 2012), feeding on a global standard diet (Khoury et al. 2014), and becoming fat and living fast (Popkin 2009, Wilson 2019). Linking to the food justice and social inequality concerns of food and fat studies, fermentation maintains heterogeneity – in bodies, cultures, environments – reorganizing the ontologically-weighted distribution of the luck of being born in a certain place, being of a certain ethnicity, gender and class.

Heterogeneity also includes ambivalence. Apart from producing nutrients, vitamins and enzymes, fermentation also generates carbon dioxide and methane. The methane produced in cattle's rumen is a substantial contributor to global warming. The politics of food, animal rights, ecological activism and the business of laboratory-grown protein are also brought together by fermentation.

A chemical process that unites the cells of my muscles with the making of vodka, fermentation seems to be in the middle of everything. Personal, political, biochemical, cultural, conceptual, activist, everyday, abstract, lively and deadly, – it is a perfect subject of the posthumanities.

Connection to other entries:
Agrarian (Post-)Humanities
Composting
Emergent Ecologies

Olga Goriunova

G

GEOENGINEERING

Geoengineering is typically defined as interventions to moderate global warming that are (1) deliberate, and (2) large-scale. Thus, burning fuels, while planetary-scale in its effects, wouldn't be defined as geoengineering; neither would local weather modification. Geoengineering has been criticized for centering the human as the agent who would make the climate; discussions of 'how we could modify the climate' tend to evoke what Braidotti has called 'an abstract idea of a 'new' pan-humanity, bonded in shared vulnerability or anxiety about survival and extinction' (2016: 23) Yet a critical posthuman approach to geoengineering can qualify this 'we', as Braidotti calls for, 'through grounded analyses of power relations and structural inequalities in the past and present' (ibid). As I argue in my book *After Geoengineering* (2019), there is a need to think more deeply about geoengineering, including the multiple forms it may take, and to think about 'our' shared responsibility to tackle climate change in the context of a lack of action thus far. Further, as, for example, the xenofeminists have argued (Laboria Cuboniks 2018), there is a need to challenge unquestioned technophobic standpoints and, instead, to think in more complex ways about the role science and technology can play in the fostering a better planetary future for all.

Geoengineering may have been first mentioned by Italian physicist Cesare Marchetti in 1977, in a paper called 'On geoengineering and the CO_2 problem', which suggested disposing of CO_2 in the deep ocean near the strait of Gibraltar in a scheme christened the Gigamixer. The idea of intervening in the climate to stop global warming emerged here and there throughout the subsequent years; a 1992 report by the US National Academies of Sciences appraised geoengineering techniques. But it didn't receive much more widespread or sustained attention until 2006, when atmospheric chemist Paul Crutzen published an editorial essay in the journal *Climatic Change* entitled 'Albedo enhancement by stratospheric sulfur injections: A contribution to resolve a policy dilemma?' The essay noted that the preferred way to resolve the policy dilemma of climate change is to lower greenhouse gases, but efforts to do so have been unsuccessful; thus it called for active research into geoengineering while cautioning about the need to estimate side effects. This paper provoked discussion, in part because of Paul Crutzen's stature in the field – the chemist, who also popularized the term 'Anthropocene', earned a Nobel prize for his work on the atmospheric ozone hole and also contributed to research on nuclear winter. But it could also be that some parts of the scientific community were ready to consider more urgent measures to confront climate change.

In 2009, the UK's Royal Society published an influential report, *Geoengineering the climate: Science, governance and uncertainty*. The organization and framing report set up two 'classes' of geoengineering techniques, which persisted throughout the next decade: carbon dioxide removal and solar radiation management. Carbon dioxide removal refers to techniques that can remove carbon from the atmosphere; this report focused on land-based methods and ocean ecosystem methods, though many taxonomies today focus on biological vs engineered removals. Solar radiation management describes techniques for reflecting a fraction of incoming sunlight back into space to cool the earth. This might involve putting aerosols into the stratosphere, where they would circulate around the globe for a year or so, or using salt spray to create clouds at sea, which would be reflective.

However, in the 2020s, these umbrella concepts of geoengineering or climate engineering have somewhat fallen out of favour. If Google Trends is to be believed, interest was highest around 2014–2017. Carbon dioxide removal has become a field of its own right, in part because the Intergovernmental Panel on Climate Change indicated in a special report in 2018 that hundreds of billions of tons would need to be removed from the atmosphere to curb warming to 1.5°C. Net-zero climate goals, which have cropped up around the globe, rely upon the capacity to generate some amount of negative emissions to compensate for residual positive emissions. Carbon dioxide removal has matured, and to do so, it had to become unmoored from the idea of geoengineering, and the hubris and disreputability it connotes.

Solar geoengineering and solar radiation management are still talked about.

But there is a host of new terminology, some of which studiously avoids the word geoengineering. The National Academies of Sciences talks about 'climate intervention' and 'albedo modification' (National Research Council 2015). More fringe groups and think tanks focus on 'climate restoration', with solar geoengineering wrapped up in the idea of 'Arctic restoration', and removing enough carbon to drop greenhouse gas concentrations in the atmosphere akin to restoring a preindustrial climate. This isn't an unproblematic framing – some climate change impacts can't be restored (like extinction); others can't be restored on timescales relevant to humans (like sea level rise). Moreover, 'restoration' inevitably brings up the question of baselines, and whether the baseline is set to an optimum for humans, or for non-human forms of life. The explosion of new terminology and new frames reflects how geoengineering was both a contentious and inaccurate signifier. The question remains if an umbrella term is truly needed, and what other phrase for intervening in the climate system would be true to what's actually possible and not just a form of climate grift in an era of climate despair.

Connection to other entries:
Geontopower
Internet of Trees
Posthuman International Law and Outer Space
Rights of Nature

Holly Jean Buck

GEONTOPOWER

Geontopower refers to the governance of human and more-than-human existence through the divisions and hierarchies of Life and Nonlife and to the toxicity of existence this division has left in its wake. It operates through a set of discourses, affects and tactics used in late liberalism to maintain or shape the coming relationship of the distinction between Life and Nonlife. Geontopower is the axial rotation that transfigures without homogenizing Western epistemologies and ontologies such as the distinctions between geology and biology and the natural sciences and critical philosophies. In biology geontopower appears in the difference between Life (Life{birth, growth, reproduction} Death) and Nonlife. In philosophies it lurks in the differences between those things that have an inward unfolding potentiality and those that come into existence inert; between Dasein (event, *conatus/affectus* and finitude) and *entelecheia*. Geontopower depends on the drama of the carbon imaginary – a propositional hinge that joins the natural and critical sciences and creates the dramas of three figures – the Desert, the Animist and the Virus.

Geontopower is also a concept meant to indicate and intensify the contrasting components of nonlife (geos) and being (ontology) currently in play in the late liberal governance of difference and markets. The concept of geontology was first introduced in 2012 at the Australian National University as part of the Annual Meeting of the Consortium of Humanities Centers and Institute's 'Anthropocene Humanities' Symposium. The invitation to participate was my initiation into the concept of the Anthropocene. My previous book, *Economies of Abandonment,* has examined the dove into the critical literature on biopower – Arendt and her Greeks; Foucault and his figures; Agamben and two modes of potentiality; Mbembe and

the spectacles of postcolonial necropower; Esposito and his positive and negative biopolitics – in order to focus on a certain moment, or condition, in the life of alternative social projects; those moments, or those conditions in which a social project is neither something, nor nothing, but rather violent oscillation in the torrents of late liberal power. When I was invited to present a talk at the Anthropocene symposium, I was struggling, in the wake of *Economies of Abandonment,* to articulate a space of governance that didn't preclude, even as it subsumed, biopolitics. How could one celebrate an otherwise that is located within landscapes where the 'wavering of death' defines a space and yet does not worry how existence can endure such, let alone the sustain the dynamics wherein an immanent otherwise might thicken to a something—i.e. become something that act self-referentially—such that it can deepen and extend itself before the weight of late liberalism crushes it? What was needed was a sociology of the otherwise rather than a philosophy.

Geontopower emerged to speak to this critical blindness within the scholarship on biopower. However, geontopower is not a power that is just now emerging to replace biopolitics; biopower (the governance through life and death) has long depended on a subtending geontopower (the difference between the lively and the inert). It is a critical language to account for the moment in which a form of power long operating in the open in settler late liberalism was now becoming visible globally under the name of Anthropocene and Climate Change. We might say that like necropolitics is to biopolitics, so geontopower is to both. The supposed inability of various colonized peoples to differentiate the things that have agency, subjectivity

MORE POSTHUMAN GLOSSARY

and intentionality of the sort that emerges with life has been the grounds of casting them into a premodern mentality and a post-recognition difference.

Geontopower seeks to make this form of governance visible as well as disrupt it, rather than to establish a new ontology of existence. Its primary goal is to illuminate the cramped space in which Indigenous worlds are forced to manoeuvre as they attempt to keep relevant their critical analytics and practices of existence. And to provide a fuller account of the shape of a set of critical discourses and figural images coming into view as the presuppositional nature of *geontopower* cracks, more importantly how critical thought recapitulates a form of colonial reason even though it seeks to confront and unravel it.

Connection to other entries:
Agrarian (Post-)Humanities
Collaborative Politics
Ex-Colonialism
Posthuman Agency
Relational Sovereignty

Elizabeth Povinelli

H

HUMUS ECONOMICUS

Humus economicus is simultaneously an invitation, a proposal and a practice of becoming with soil. As a feminist figuration (Braidotti 1994), humus economicus could be seen as both a creature of 'imagined possibility' and of 'fierce and ordinary reality' (Haraway 2008: 4), since it turns our attention to radically altered human–soil relations. The creature invites us to sense and make sense of soils otherwise. It proposes that neither *homo economicus* nor finance are at the heart of economy, but living soils. Humus economicus therefore offers itself as a reframing tool that reclaims economy as an ethical, relational and intragenerational (Fredengren and Åsberg 2020) material-discursive practice, which in turn re-embeds societies in soils and lands (Krzywoszynska and Marchesi 2020).

Industrialized urban societies suffer from severe soil blindness (Holmstedt 2020), in that they are ignorant of the importance and connection with soil-as-living (Puig de la Bellacasa 2013), hence soil, commonly thought of as dirt, is a matter much taken for granted. Soil blindness leads, just as plant blindness (Wandersee and Schussler 2001), to a lack of understanding for ecological relations and biological diversity. Could we, through thinking with soils and the figuration humus economicus, turn anthropocentric notions not merely on their heads, but outside in? To do this, the creature of imagined possibilities proposes, we, the soil blind and ignorant, need to imagine humans not as surface dwellers on planet Earth, but rather as critters cohabiting its very belly.

Working with soil as medium and as an urgent matter of care (Puig de la Bellacasa 2020) throws us into tangled posthuman borderlands of what gets to count as nature and culture. After all, even the very concept of culture originates from the handling of soil and agricultural practices (Williams 1976). Soils are living multispecies heritages. At the same time, rights to land and soil are bound up with imperialist practices, gender regimes and global territorialism, excluding those traditionally regarded as less-than-human, indigenous to the land, racialized and in/appropriate/d others (Minh-ha 1989). Soils tie together political ecologies into conflict zones where nature and culture, human and non-human cannot easily be discerned and held apart. The matter of soil thus urges us to stay with these troubles, with these fierce and ordinary realities where, at the same time, imagined possibilities reside. Far from being dead substrates waiting to be fertilized by humans, as monocultural and agro-industrial practices might have one think, healthy soils are teeming with life and constitute a next to unknown universe beneath our very feet. They compose the living skin of planet Earth. This pedosphere (from Ancient Greek *pédon,* 'soil', or 'the ground') regulates and facilitates fluxes and exchanges between atmosphere, hydrosphere, biosphere and lithosphere. The multifarious, dynamic and porous soil bodies of the pedosphere thus act as transformative membranes, biogeomembranes. To think of the pedosphere as a skin though, regardless of how powerful this image is, positions humans on the surface of things. Plants have taught me otherwise, they are the teachers of the economy of soil, as well as of sustainable economic behaviour and exchange. 'See the roots,' they urge, 'see the work of the radicals in the multispecies body of soil.' It turns out that the root zone, the rhizosphere, is just as porous as the pedosphere, this too is a dynamic community of microorganisms regulating and facilitating exchanges. From a plant perspective, soil is not a skin, it is their digestive system. This is the belly we are in. The human home (*oikos*) is in the stomach of the Earth. The skin folds into a sack and a metabolic continuous feast celebrating life and death, the processual ecologies of the non/living (Radomska 2020). 'The earth and its heat serv[es] them in the place of a stomach,' Aristotle pondered while observing metabolic plant–soil relations, animals on the other hand that move from place to place have 'an earth inside them' (quoted in Sprague 1991: 222) The 'heat' of the earth that Aristotle mentions, I gather, is the heat of the compost that we today might refer to as microbial kin. Humus economicus invites us to listen to and think as part of this gut, the earth outside and within. It inspires soil-centred and situated ways of weaving lived and not-yet existing practices, knowledges, spheres and publics together into a multitude of different regenerative place-based patterns, capable of regulating and facilitating exchanges for mutual benefit.

Home, *oikos* in Ancient Greek, stands as metaphor and etymological root to both economy and ecology, though today they have become incommensurable sciences. The Latin word *homō,* denoting a human being, is similarly related to *humus,* meaning 'ground', 'earth', 'soil'. Humus economicus proposes a shift in perspective from the supposedly rational considerations and activities of *homo economicus,* to an economy of soil in the Ancient Greek sense of the word *oikonomíā,* i.e. household management, or the caring of resources as part of an extended family and home, *oikos,* which in turn is intertwined with ethics and the art of living. Here settler cultures humbly could learn from many Indigenous teachings and practices where the family always have been of a more-than-human kind (Kimmerer 2013; Yunkaporta 2020; to mention but a few recent voices). We can also learn how to make peace with earth (Vandana 2013; Tamm and Wägner 1940) from the women that feed the world as smallholders – more than 50 per cent of the food produced globally are produced by women (FAO 1996) – and many other soil publics (Krzywoszynska and Marchesi 2020) that have shown the numerous ways in which humus economics is a practice that needs to be practiced in order to make, and demand, time for care (Puig de la Bellacasa 2015).

Soil is not a charismatic other (Lorimer 2007) that manage to mobilize empathy and action, it does not exude sympathy like whales or ice bears might. Soil is rather uncharismatic and constitutes a wider form of bio-agency. The living biogeomembrane is too large to be seen. Humus economicus proposes that we need to account for wider forms of bio-agency, integrate more-than-human approaches, and decentre the anthropocentric perspectives prevalent in most environmental and urban studies (Ernstson and Sörlin 2019: 366). It invites us to call forth embodied knowledge of, and empathy with, an environment that to a large extent is invisible, difficult to grasp, un-charismatic, and which is being altered in anthropogenic ways. It challenges us to perceive other worlds and very different spatio-temporal scales without succumbing to well-meaning anthropomorphism. What we, as soil blind, might do then, is to turn to soil for advice on economic and organizational behaviour, where gifting as excess, as opposed to a closed economy of exchange (Hird 2007), is played out in unfathomable complexity. Here, in the gut-logic and humus economicus practice of hyperdiversity, resides biocultural hope (Kirksey 2018). Ecce humus.

Connection to other entries:
Agrarian (Post-)Humanities
Composting
Empathy Beyond the Human
Geontopower
Intragenerational Justice and Care
Low Trophic Theory
Posthuman Care
Vibrant Death

Janna Holmstedt

HYDROFEMINISM

We are all bodies of water, leaking, sponging, sloshing, dripping, sipping (Neimanis 2017). As watery, we experience ourselves less as isolated entities, and more as oceanic eddies: situated, temporary, relational.

soak up
relinquish
precipitate

Hydrofeminism (Neimanis 2012) is an action concept that flows from this embodied material imaginary. Following Adrienne Rich, hydrofeminism begins 'with the geography closest in – the body' (1986: 212). Understanding our own human bodies as bodies of water invites us into a different kind of relation to other bodies of water, and a feminism of relation. Hydrofeminism asks: if we are all bodies of water, what does this connect us to? What can we give, and what do we owe?

pour
pool
circulate

A hydrofeminist hydrological cycle insists that we relinquish any lingering illusion of separation, as we decant ourselves into one another as an inevitable matter of physics. We are disbursed through both space and time. As Charles Darwin once quipped: 'Our ancestor was an animal which breathed water, had a swim bladder, a great swimming tail, an imperfect skull, and was undoubtedly a hermaphrodite!' (cited in Zimmer 1998: n.p.) These fishy beginnings connect us to all life that came from the sea, figuring own watery bodies as evolutionary 'carrier bags', to use Ursula K. Le Guin's term (1989). Our bodies hold things, and hold things in relation. Hydrofeminism asks: what do our own sloshy sacks of matter carry in trust for other bodies, still to come?

puddle-jump
time-travel

Hydrofeminism thus confirms that we humans have always been (and always will be) more than our species. Just as Angela

Davis confirms that feminism 'involves so much more than gender' (2016), hydrofeminism reminds us that feminism involves so much more than humans, too: it is planetary, elemental, multispecies, multibeing. As the oceans warm and struggle to breathe, as rivers no longer make it to the sea, as drinking water is commodified, as the seabed is mined, as all of the multitudes of life forms that depend on these waters are made increasingly precarious, caring better for other bodies of water is a hydrofeminist imperative.

care
carry

Learning from the generations of feminisms that it has ingested, hydrofeminism is also obligated to continually critique the trickles of white supremacy, colonialism, classism and body normativities that circulate within projects that call themselves feminist. Even as waters hold us together as hydrocommons, aqueous connection is neither assimilation nor universal confluence. Water does not ask us to confirm either the irreducibility of alterity or material connection. Water flows between, as both: a new hydro-logic. Hydrofeminism acknowledges that the unknowability of the other nonetheless courses through me – just as I do through her. In political terms, this also recognizes the need for tributaries and sovereign waters, for shifting sites of confluence.

differentiate
channel

This uncontainable gestational impulse is moreover held in wondrous tension with water's insistent perpetuity: to understand the 'always time' of water, even in its circulations of difference and repetition, is also to consider that water remembers. Water is retentive, writes Janine MacLeod: 'All of the moments of the past have this same water as their witness' (2013: 48). Toni Morrison parses this a bit differently: 'Everything is now. It is all now' (1987: 198).

hold
hold on

Water, an archive of matter and feeling, thus reminds us that there is no such thing as 'away'. Sinking to the seafloor, we discover all manner of our dumped desires: SPAM cans, car tyres, chemical traces, carbon takeovers. Indeed, our evolutionary carrier-bag ontology has literalized itself: nonbiodegradable white petroleum hauntings, masquerading as sad two-handled jellyfish, floating on a gyre of deep futures later to be pulled in the form of hundreds of kilos of plastic bag guts from the belly of a whale washed up on a beach. The gifts of our bodies to other bodies of water are not necessarily welcome gestures.

repeat,
but differently

Moreover, water's archive holds traces of all the differences that water has made. Christina Sharpe draws our attention to the oceanic archive of the Middle Passage, still animated by the antiblackness that persists in its wake. She writes: 'Because nutrients cycle through the ocean, … the atoms of the [enslaved] people who were thrown overboard are out there in the ocean even today' (2016: 40). Hydrofeminism must also attend to the different manners in which our bodies have been carried, or not. We do not all thirst, or flow, equally. We are not all gestating the same futures.

suspend
harbour

Put otherwise, for hydrofeminism care as and for waters is never 'only' environmental. Any calls for sustainable futures must consider how issues of pollution, extinction and meteorological change are also questions of social injustice and infrastructures of inequality. Environmental catastrophe must be understood as a symptom – the proper trickle-down – of deformed human relations that flow across the planet.

We are all bodies of water, but as watery, we are not all the same.

And, if we are all bodies of water, then are we all, in some way, already at sea?

untether

In the English language, 'to be at sea' is an idiom to suggest discombobulation or confusion. To lose one's bearings. To be alive as bodies of water, in these catastrophic times, might also be to feel tetherless, and at sea.

As a transfer point of queer time, hydrofeminism is also a praxis of speculation – not only for the futures, but for the many presents that we are already imagining otherwise. For hydrofeminism, then, tetherless can be another way of saying: get free.

step up
speak out
say no

let go
lift up
step back

For hydrofeminism, tetherless can mean refusing the false compass points, and learning new tricks of planetary navigation. Following Alexis Pauline Gumbs, hydrofeminism invites us, 'we who would be whales' and 'immersed in a substance we could not breathe' (2020:17), to follow other watery beings who have long been swimming, floating, submerging, growing different kinds of worlds.

dive,
deeper

Hydrofeminism helps foster practices of fugitivity and care, not primarily for the sovereign self, but for the hydrocommons of wondrous difference that finds us in this time, and this place, at sea.

dissolve

Connection to other entries:
Feminism and Oceans
The Meltionary
Posthuman Agency
Posthuman Care
Transcorporeality II

*** Astrida Neimanis***

INTERNET OF TREES

Forests in locations ranging from Honduras to Wales and Italy are sending messages over the internet. These messages contain information about the inner workings of forest environments, including data on temperature, humidity, moisture and light levels. They communicate details about the location, movements and expansion of individual trees. The presence of smoke, fire and airborne chemicals can trigger alerts to indicate when a wildfire might be occurring. Microcomputers and sensors now populate forest environments to undertake this ongoing monitoring and detection. The data that these devices collect is sent across local Wi-Fi networks or uploaded to a low-orbital satellite service to ping across networks, servers and clouds; and then to be included in displays and visualizations on data dashboards.

This technological infrastructure, otherwise known as the Internet of Trees, provides a way to manage forest areas through more remote and automated measures, whether for maintaining carbon sinks or determining when to harvest trees. On one level, it seems the Internet of Things (IoT) has simply popped up in a forest environment. Yet on another level, the Internet of Trees raises the question of how environments and technologies mutually constitute and inform each other, and to what consequence (Gabrys 2016).

The Internet of Trees performs a computational remaking of forest environments. In this way, forests include multiple different types of 'sensors'. Plants such as trees could be described in computational terms: They are sensors that process environmental inputs and transform them into environmental outputs. They also actuate as much as sense their environments by taking decisions about stimuli, signalling phase states, mitigating environmental conditions and transforming environmental surroundings. Plants complete computational, albeit analogue, operations. Indeed, there is a longer history of environmental analogue computing unfolding through pebbles, ponds and many other media (Blohm et al. 1987).

In this sense, there is another version of the Internet of Trees that relies less on electronics and more on fungi and root systems to transmit messages. The 'Wood Wide Web' is a term used to describe how trees within forests signal to each other across extensive root systems, aided by mycorrhizal relations and the dense organismal registers of soil (Simard 2021, 165–166). Internet of Trees and Wood Wide Web are phrases that are sometimes used interchangeably, despite the Internet of Trees also being used in a different way to indicate IoT developments (Fleming 2014). The Wood Wide Web is a phrase that indicates how plants are operating as more than computers in their digital designation. But in so doing, they also rework the scope of what computation is and how it could operate in and on the world. The networks, signals and relations that trees and other organisms cultivate underground are characterized by reciprocity, mutualism and collectivity. *This* Internet of Trees makes up a forest. In the process, it forms a somewhat grander project than the dashboards and alerts that materialize from that other version of the Internet of Trees mentioned in the introduction to this text.

In drawing together these two instances of plant-computational operations – the Internet of Trees that is a version of the IoT, and the Internet of Trees that is the Wood Wide Web – we can see clear divergences in what these networks connect and create. Yet they also converge in other ways. The Internet of Trees/Things becomes a way to 'network a network' by sensing plants to detect environmental changes, and attempting to manage and even mitigate potentially catastrophic events. Proposals within this area include schemes such as the Internet of Nature, which emphasizes the intersection of ecological and digital forms of communication across ecosystems and IoT infrastructure. As this scheme identifies, 'nature' has its own ways of communicating, which IoT can tap into, amplify and further coordinate. Technologies ranging from remote sensing and sensors, data loggers and cloud computing, 5G and machine learning, are seen to be able to contribute to the functioning of ecologies by enhancing and providing new forms of 'self-organisation, self-regulation and automation' (Galle et al. 2019).

Here, technologies seemingly would not just connect up and improve the flow of cities as ecosystems, but also would enhance the perceived mitigating, purifying and balancing functions of vegetation to solve the unwieldy problem of environmental change. These projects involve realizing 'ecosystem intelligence' through connections with smart technologies, whereby the communicative processes of plants would fold into the circuits of digital technologies. In this co-constitution of plants (among many other organisms) and digital technologies, urban environments are meant to become more intelligent, resilient and adaptable. The intelligence of plants and digital circuits would then mutually augment and inform each other so as to better address environmental change and climate crisis.

And yet, these technologies are not simply joining up with organisms, trees and forests to address the challenge of environmental change. Instead, they are delineating which organisms and environments are considered to be most intelligent and observable, which actors are best placed to harness this information for urban ecosystem development and governance, which urban-environmental collectives might be activated and sustained, and which forms of social-political action are most relevant and suitable for participating in these digitally augmented worlds. Computing is a way of counting, processing and accounting for worlds and how they matter. While these different variations on the Internet of Trees could bring into view some exchanges across organisms, they also can organize different ways of engaging with wildfires and drought, climate change and resource scarcity, forest inhabitations and environmental citizenship. At the same time, the digital version of the Internet of Trees has the potential to require billions of digital devices that require mined elements, resources and energy to manufacture and power, as well as hazardous waste facilities to treat, dismantle and otherwise dispose of these toxic technologies once obsolete. Plants may have always been computers. But computers have yet to become plants.

Connection to other entries:
Algorithmic Governmentality
New Materialist Informatics

Jennifer Gabrys

INTRAGENERATIONAL JUSTICE AND CARE

The thinking tool of *intra-generational* justice and care can be used to start the discussion on how materiality, human and more-than-human generations are entangled in each other over longer stretches of time. It has implications for how to address heritage and sustainability in more productive ways, and for work with rights, in/justices and care. Rosi Braidotti (2013, 113) has urged us to turn grieving of the loss of nature into political and social action for sustainability and to take responsibility for future generations. The term *intra-generational* is a figurative innovation that responds to this. It has implications for re-thinking the messy links between heritage/legacies and more-than-human future making.

The Brundtland commission states that sustainable development cares for the 'needs of the present without compromising the ability of future generations to meet their own needs' (UN 1987, 41, UN 1972). This principle is addressed in several international treaties and in the Sustainable Development Goals. When our futures are territorialized by climate change, toxic deposits and species depletion, it is important to ask questions of who is included in those future generations eligible for care? This question also blazes through current movements of climate activism where charges are pressed against polluters and governments on the basis of the harm they bring to future generations (UNEP 2018; McIntyre 2020).

There are a number of studies that deals with justice between generations, such as Brown Weiss (1992), Rawls (1971), Parfit (1984), de-Shalit (1997) and Gosseries (2008). Some of these philosophies have landed in almost unsolvable paradoxes when dealing with the moral justification for saving the world for future generations. One of these – the non-identity problem (Parfit 1984) – claims, that one cannot have a responsibility towards someone that does not yet exist, such as an individual of the future. Questions around *intergenerational* justice run into trouble due to their want of existing future individuals that are separated from each other in body, space and time, and that can be mirrored in legislation. If there are no such bodies to have claim of justice on the past/present, no one to represent and nothing to represent with, it is hard to argue that actions break the rights of future generations.

Many social and legal theories also build on ideas where 'the world is composed of individuals – presumed to exist before the law, or the discovery of the law – awaiting or inviting representation' (Barad 2007, 46). However, also notions of 'future generations' hides neoliberal imaginaries of a unitary self. Such perceptions are critiqued by gender theorists such as Naffine (1997, 84-85) who writes that law not only represents, but often produces and privileges certain male bodies as wholes, while female bodies are produced as 'pierced' and not as firmly bounded and hence oppressed by law.

These imaginaries can be further challenged by posthuman feminist theories of subjectivity, that highlights the relational nature of existence (see Braidotti 2006). With relationality as a base for understanding bodies and by taking on the Baradian 'intra-' (Barad 2010) as a measure to focus on the entanglement, co-becoming and livelihood across generational and individual splits, it is possible to formulate a novel approach with the *intra-generational* as an evolving vista for ethics and care. This can be compared to the notion *inter-generational* justice that keeps generations analytically apart. Both sustainability arguments and actions find another footing if *intra-generational* contacts were approached as productive meetings across more-than-human generations, in ways that observe liveability, carefulness and fairness in the build-up of long-term relationalities.

Our thinking tool acknowledges bodies that interlink *transcorporeally* (Alaimo 2010) and also in time and space, as it focuses on processes that works *transtemporeally*. Thinking through the *intra-generational* lens challenges assumptions that subjectivities are firmed up in time during the physical bounds of a body's life. Instead this figuration highlights how subjectivities are dispersed in time through relations, actions and material reconfigurations. One can move from a perception of people as stable, physical entities bound in body and time, to an understanding of them as situated and trans-temporally interwoven, more-than-human phenomena. If so, this means that the foundation for discussing relationships between generations turn out different.

As discussed in Fredengren (2018) and Fredengren and Åsberg (2020) it is urgent to move beyond a 'human-only' sustainability to include the multispecies entanglements of future generations. The notion of *intra-generational* justice and care (ibid.) might be a fruitful way of fostering more-than-human trans-temporal, non-linear, post-representational ethics. This means to explore how to come together and form companionships across generations, through acknowledging how generations are entangled with each other in intricate, material-discursive and situated ways. On the one hand, it can be argued that present more-than-humans are already braided into future generations and hence, care and justice with them, is also care for a future diffracted life/subjectivity/self, but the argument does not stop here.

Traditionally *sustainable actions are those that leave freedom of choice for coming generations.* In the climate crisis such freedom is limited. CO_2 emissions produce climate change as a heritage that entangle with more-than-human generations for far futures. Species depletion and the loss of nurturing environmental niches might, in places, be irreparable. Such interventions braid the past/present into various situated futures. As neither present or future generations are firmly stabilized in time, nor in body, it might be more productive (and less negative than to ask if future generations have rights) to map how subjectivities in the past-present are woven into and facilitates future lifeworlds. Then this implies questions of how to do this in the best possible ways and to ask what heritage is needed to get on in a drastically changing world. Just as the past interlace with the present, it is unavoidable to pass on inheritance to the future. Due to this it is important to expose various non-linear territorialities of the future, such as the deep time interventions of garbage disposal or nuclear storage (Fredengren 2018), and to both critically and affirmatively engage with the politicization of the long-term, that both the handling of heritage and the sustainability paradigm plays into.

Connection to other entries
Humus Economicus
Relational Sovereignty
Rights of Nature

Christina Fredengren

L

LINGUISTIC INCOMPOSSIBILITY

One of the core tasks of literary studies in the posthuman convergence is to create new ways of thinking about language that adequately reckon with linguistic difference. This is now linguistic difference in the widest sense: there are different degrees of difference between multiple naturalcultural languages, from human multilingualism to biosemiotics. The languages of artificial intelligence, the child and the deep-sea squid all exist alongside each other, with no claim to a common tongue. They are contradictory and yet coexistent, part of different worlds and yet part of one world – our world. These different languages are incompossible.

The ontological concept of incompossibility is used to describe different worlds which, taken on their own, are possible worlds. However, taken together, these worlds are incompatible or inconsistent. Neither fully possible nor impossible, they are caught in a tangle whereby they each contradict the others and yet their existence is constituted by their multiple relations with each other. Incompossibility is thus a way of figuring the affirmatory possibilities of divergence, disjunction and difference across a series, a way of considering a world made up of multiple co-existing yet contradictory beings, becomings and relations.

Linguistic incompossibility conceptualizes the simultaneous yet divergent quality of linguistic difference, thus opening new ways of conceiving of language itself in the posthuman convergence. The 2016 US science fiction film *Arrival* presents an interesting case of linguistic incompossibility. Two life forms – human and extra-terrestrial – attempt to communicate using their respective languages. However, the languages are incompossible: the language of the humans cannot exist in the world or even the temporal scale of the aliens, and vice versa. Eventually, a human linguist learns the alien language and finds herself caught between worlds. Through her traversal of two different worlds, the temporal linearity of her life becomes rewritten incompossibly: her new timeline contradicts human temporality and yet is part of it. If we focus on the incompossibility of languages – the languages, for example, of the human and the alien life form – the incompossibility of these languages allows us to position them as productive and communicative without asserting the scientism of the master, the claim to know, and the subject/object division. This is precisely because the languages are an affirmatory contradiction. In this way, linguistic incompossibility is productive untranslatability; it is found in the different incompossible worlds of different languages which cannot be subsumed via a logic of equivalence. This is a posthuman empiricism which foregrounds the incompossible multiplicity of the contradictory series: the *and ... and ...* of multiple becoming rather than the static and limited *is* of being (Deleuze 2001: 38). This difference is all the more productive for its incompossibility. The posthuman notion of linguistic incompossibility is expansive: the language of the child, the artificial intelligence, the deep-sea squid, are all incompossible. They present worlds which cannot exist together in the same place at the same time, but yet because of this are communicative. This is the positive affirmation of incompossibility established by Deleuze in *The Logic of Sense*, in which 'divergence is no longer a principle of exclusion, and disjunction no longer a means of separation. Incompossibility is now a means of communication' (Deleuze 1990: 173–174).

Much twenty-first-century literary theory focuses on the potentiality of language to open up worlds. Within critical posthumanism, however, an analysis of linguistic *incompossibility* rather than compossibility allows for a deviation from humanist mechanisms of capture of forces that are non-human, molecular, posthuman. Likewise, conceiving the worlds of literary language as incompossible rather than compossible is a way of avoiding notions that the limit of language is concurrently the limit of the salient, the imaginable, the referential. Linguistic incompossibility is a way of making space for difference, the linguistic divide, non-human subjects whose languages we cannot learn to speak fluently but must meet halfway in gesture and behaviour and translation. It is the beginning of thinking language 'disathropocentrically' (Cohen 2013: xxiv). An analysis of linguistic incompossibility gives a theory of literature which is attuned to in/difference (Weinstein 2016), 'an ethics of relationality without recognition, one figured around

[Deleuzian] difference rather equality, one that begins from imperceptibility' (jagodzinski 2019: 105). This indifference and imperceptibility become affirmative within the incompossible languages of literature. Within the singularity of literature – or the literary machine – strangeness and alienation become an advantage and language becomes a material process rather than an end-point of anthropocentric rationalized comprehension. The incompossibility of linguistic worlds suddenly becomes revealed as productive and favourable, especially in the way that this reveals the contingency and incompossibility of the world of the reader (Clemens 2022). Importantly, linguistic incompossibility is not a critical 'problem of language'; language is not positioned as a problem to be solved. Rather, the productive incompossibility of language is a way of drawing an accountable cartography of language in the posthuman conjunction. This offers an expansive conception of language which positions difference and conjunction as affirmative incompossibility.

The concept of incompossible language can be situated among broader conceptions of language in posthumanist thought. In the *Posthuman Glossary*, Iris van der Tuin rebuffs the interpretation that new-materialism is 'a dismissal of everything linguistic' (Braidotti and Hlavajova 2018: 278). She notes that a core imperative of posthuman and new-materialist criticism is to account for the matter of language itself. The field of biosemiotics has already begun to build important links between the disciplines of biology, philosophy, linguistics and communication studies. Material ecocriticism asks readers to become-with the ecological via the interaction of interpreting (Iovino and Oppermann 2014). Meanings and matterings emerge in different material-semiotic nodes (Haraway 1988: 575), which together form a 'pluriverse' (Bennett 2010: 122). The different differences can be read diffractively 'through one another in ways that help illuminate differences as they emerge' (Barad 2007: 30). Kalevi Kull and Peeter Torop (2003) propose 'biotranslation' as a way of investigating the mutual translatability (or productivity) of untranslatable (or incompossible) Umwelts. The nomadic mode of becoming is found in 'moving between languages, speaking several and mastering none, living in constant simultaneous translation' (Braidotti 2002: 94). This idea of linguistic incompossibility has an adventitious root in literature: the potentiality of literary language to enable us to imagine otherwise, to think incompossibly.

Connection to other entries:
Convergences
Cosmic Artisan
Posthuman Feminist Aesthetics
Weird

Ruth Alison Clemens

LOW TROPHIC THEORY

Grounded in transdisciplinary work at the crossroads of feminist posthumanities, environmental humanities (with a special focus on the oceanic), field philosophy and arts of sustainability, the concept of 'low-trophic theory' (Åsberg and Radomska 2021; Radomska and Åsberg 2021) refers to the situated naturalcultural research on the entanglements of consumption, violence, more-than-human care and coexistential multispecies ethics of environmental adaptability.

The term 'trophic' originates from the Greek word trophē, standing for 'nourishment, food' (Harper n.d.). In the context of ecology, the notion of 'trophic level' signifies the group of organisms occupying the same level in a food chain, that is, positioned at the same distance from the primary energy source. What this ecological categorization highlights is the very question of nourishment and consumption, which all living organisms depend on. It is the matter of consumption that permeates both 'slow' and 'spectacular' cases of anthropogenic violence unfolding on a planetary scale: the consumption of other creatures, of biomass, of space and potential futures.

However, in the context of human cultures, consumption – in both its narrow sense of food intake and the broader understanding of consuming every aspect of the world – is not only about nourishment and material survival. It also amplifies and is amplified by one's identity, belonging, culture, belief and habit, among others. Moreover, none of these factors remains fixed, immutable, independent from its surroundings, or innocent. We do not live in a vacuum. Traditions, rituals or habits, even if cultivated, cherished and preserved, are always performed and entangled in the social, cultural, economic and ethico-political conditions of a given time and place. Some of these factors are challenged every day in a world where, as consumers, by way of making choice, we also choose to remain complicit, or to resist the structures of environmental violence and injustice. Those choices are not only about the food we eat, its cost in terms of both the carbon footprint and the suffering it may have caused, but also every product or service we decide to buy, out of need or habit, as well as knowledges and stories we prefer to recognize, nourish ourselves with, digest and consume. There is no 'outside' or 'elsewhere': we are all differentially situated and differentially responsible inhabitants of this planet. The question therefore is rather 'how can we imagine this world (from within) otherwise?' Inside, and with no exit from 'field work' ever possible, how can we inhabit our earthly companionship with less of that slow violence hinged on human ignorance and supremacy?

In the context of mariculture, the cultivation of low-trophic LEVEL species is perceived as beneficial to sea ecologies as it circumvents many disadvantages of land-based food and biomass production such as the need for fertilizers, chemicals and irrigation (Nixon 2011). Sustainable sea farming as supported by the cultivation of low-trophic level species counteracts coastal eutrophication, stimulates biodiversity and acts as an important carbon sink. Coastal villages may gain value by a (re)development of maritime enterprise, and participants learn how to eat well as human-induced climate change unfolds. What is needed is also a cultivation of the sense of wonder and ecological belonging and a deeper understanding of how the development of sustainable low-trophic mariculture may influence our common future and interaction with society.

Looking at the low-trophic practices of local coastal communities, like careful seaweed foraging attuned with the processes and capacities of the ecosystems they are embedded in, we turn to the theoretical and ethical implications of the 'low-trophic'. This concept may allow us to theorize in ways cognisant of our own patterns of consumption, potential violence, complexity and the ecologies in which we as subjects, living beings, educators, creators and knowledge producers are

implicated. Furthermore, it may help us – in our practices as thinkers, scholars, educators, activists, artists but also, plainly, humans – to account both for the relations we enter and the connections we cultivate, but also for the exclusions that we implement (Giraud 2019).

Cultural studies taught us to pay attention to the mundane matters of life, to look at them with curiosity, and see everyday life, popular culture and consumption patterns not as unworthy lowly concerns, but as the very essence of how we become who we are. If we now see multispecies studies as a form of cultural studies in the non-human turn, we may also consider low-trophic mariculture as a sustainable practice of eating and socializing. It also fosters modes of thinking better together, through an ethics of cohabitation and mutual flourishing. Low-trophic mariculture thus defined, points beyond the 'twin spectres of sacralizing and cannibalizing' (Bryld and Lykke 2000:203) nature and its resources. It relocates consumption to the sustainable conceptual registers of multispecies flourishing. In an accountable response to environmental change, it also explores ways to adapt to climatic seasons and cycles of pollution in land and oceans.

Sustained these relations, mindful of and accountable for the violence it may be potentially complicit with, and freed of any illusion of innocence, low-trophic theory strives to find comfort in the immanence of here and now. It is a dynamic response to the present as well as to potential futures. Low-trophic theory is thus a practice of thinking and theorizing that requires creativity and imagination and takes more-than-human hospitality and responsibility seriously. It is aware of and accountable for the patterns of consumption it depends on, both materially and epistemologically.

Last, but not least, it is accountable for the complexities, entanglements and exclusions in which it is implicated. Although low-trophic theory cannot undo the ongoing abuse or slaughter of the 'natural' worlds, especially those that are 'out of sight' like polluted marine ecosystems, it nonetheless enhances understanding of our situatedness as both individuals and communities inscribed in various institutions and systems (of power and oppression). It points to the complicity and complexities of our interaction with the world in which we are implicated, and to the inextricable links between set patterns of consuming the world, and the longings of a radical ethical imagination.

Connection to other entries:
Feminism and Oceans
Humus economicus
Hydrofeminism
Toxic Embodiment
Undead

Cecilia Åsberg and Marietta Radomska

M

MANUS ISLAND AND MANUS PRISON THEORY

An evolving ecosystem of philosophical and artistic visions and lived realities, Manus Prison Theory emerged out of seven years of work between Behrouz Boochani and myself. The theory is represented by a growing body of artistic outputs and diverse forms of knowledge production; our encounters within particular socio-cultural processes and through political actions; and the dynamics of creative and intellectual collaborations. We conceived Manus Prison Theory during Boochani's six years of indefinite detention in Manus Prison, a term he introduced to rename Australia's offshore immigration detention facility in Manus Island, Papua New Guinea (Boochani was incarcerated from 2013 to 2019 when he managed to escape to Aotearoa New Zealand and was granted a permanent visa). Our philosophical and artistic activities constitute a coherent intellectual, creative and abolitionist project and are examples of the shared philosophical activity I first referred to in my translator's note for Boochani's multi-award winning autobiographical novel, *No Friend but the Mountains: Writing from Manus Prison* (Picador 2018).

As a long-term project Manus Prison Theory involves collaboration, consultation and sharing between the two of us, and also with other supporters and confidants. A detention regime that aims to isolate, hide and distort the existence, suffering and resistance of people seeking asylum has transformed into unique and radical networks of scholarship, art and collective action. After the release of *No Friend but the Mountains* and winning the 2019 Victorian Prize for Literature – which was followed by many other prestigious awards – academics, artists and writers have been engaging with Manus Prison Theory and the conditions that gave rise to it; the multifarious dimensions of our critical analysis and action have opened up new spaces, discussions and approaches pertaining to border politics in Australia and around the world. In this entry I outline some of the central tenets of Manus Prison Theory and describe how Australia's border-industrial complex has connections with other forms of violence and domination in Australian settler-colonial society, culture and history. Boochani and I also argue that this border-industrial complex is global and we explore the different ways Manus Prison Theory pertains to border violence and intersectional discrimination, exploitation and subjugation on a global scale. Our work also places special emphasis on how systems of oppression are interconnected, mutually reinforcing and self-replicating. Manus Prison Theory draws on decolonial and intersectional approaches from different marginalized and stigmatized groups and philosophies of resistance, and analyses contemporary border violence using concepts such as kyriarchy and what I refer to as 'horrific surrealism'. In addition, we expose how border violence in Australia is rooted in the nation state's colonial imaginary and has a symmetrical relationship with its socio-political structures and institutions.

Papua New Guinea is a former colony of Australia who has used Manus Island as an offshore prison since the 1960s when West Papuan people seeking asylum were held there. Australia first banished people seeking asylum by boat to Manus Island and the Republic of Nauru (Manus for men travelling alone and Nauru for women, unaccompanied minors and families) in 2001 as part of its 'Pacific Solution' which was introduced under the extreme right-wing government of John Howard. The Labour government under Kevin Rudd officially closed the prisons in Manus Island and Nauru in 2008 but they were reopened in 2012 by Labour under Julia Gillard – soon after she was replaced by Kevin Rudd as prime minister who introduced a new policy on 19 July 2013 stating anyone arriving by boat after that date would never enter Australia. When the Liberal Party were voted into power in the months after the new laws, then immigration minister Scott Morrison (who later became prime minister) and subsequent immigration minister Peter Dutton further militarized Australia's border control policies by introducing and reinforcing Operation Sovereign Borders.

The exile and indefinite detention of refugees by Australia is exceptional, but it is also unexceptional when we consider the history of what was once a penal colony – a paradox which we discuss through Manus Prison Theory. The image of exiled refugees in Manus incarcerated by a liberal democracy without charge and with no end date is surreal. This quality manifested in Boochani's work and in our collaborations; Boochani was writing and trying to create new spaces and opportunities for resistance and disruption, together we were trying to create new ruptures and imagine new philosophies and abolitionist practices. The surreal circumstances and occurrences during our collaborations were remarkable and extraordinary, they were horrific and surreal.

As a schema for interpretation, a generative notion and heuristic device, horrific surrealism captures the absurd and tragic qualities of the phenomenon of indefinite mandatory detention in Australia, both onshore and offshore. It is pivotal to the introduction and development of Manus Prison Theory, its meaning and application illuminates fundamental aspects of the whole picture pertaining to the border-industrial complex and its historical antecedents. We argue that horrific surrealism characterizes the contemporary political landscape in Australian and its relationship with other border regimes; the positionality of the incarcerated refugees and their relationships with those with citizen privilege; the structure and content of work produced in these spaces, their mode of production and their reception; and the dynamic and perverse exchanges and inseparable ties between the border and settler-colonial society. So many aspects of these dimensions and the networks of people and institutions can be discussed in terms of features such as fragmentation, disruption, disjointedness, shattered experiences and interpretations, paradox and incongruous juxtapositions, and free flow of the subconscious, especially through dream visions. The connection with dreams is especially poignant particularly in the context of the narratives, ideas and images in *No Friend but the Mountains*. Also, horrific surrealism accounts for the way the built environment and natural environment are used in creative ways or assemblages within acts of resistance and survival, but also in strategies and techniques of violence and submission by authorities. These elements help interpret the lived experience, endurance and fight of people like Boochani and also the perverse political situation in Australia; but they also reflect the way, for instance, we interact with each other and the way he interacts with others outside the prison.

Consider the fact that he received awards and prize money from the same political institutions that were torturing him, with me often accepting awards on his behalf while he was imprisoned – I usually had to facilitate his address to the audience using WhatsApp. Similarly, Boochani was appearing in prestigious events in Australia through WhatsApp or video link while incarcerated. He has never been to Australia and will never be allowed to enter the country but his presence has always been palpable – he continues to travel across Australia through his work and resistance. Boochani and the rest of the imprisoned or recently released refugees are, in fact, part of Australia and its history; a fact that can never be ignored and which drives and informs many elements of Manus Prison Theory.

When I came across Boochani's writing I could already see there was a very well trained and astute journalist behind this work and also someone with deep philosophical insight. As I began to collaborate and translate, and after reading drafts of his book I noticed how he was incorporating philosophical reflections, psychoanalytical examination, anti-colonial political commentary in addition to new forms of storytelling, poetry, myth, epic and folklore. He was also drawing on his Indigenous Kurdish heritage including the history of Kurdish resistance, creativity and intellectual life. I felt he was the perfect person for me to collaborate with on multiple levels because of my own training in philosophy and related fields, my own experience of displacement and exile, my research into Australian settler-colonialism and border politics, and my community advocacy and scholar activist work. In addition to the themes and features explained above, Manus Prison Theory critically examines externalization of borders and the symmetrical relationships between what occurs on the border and what occurs within the nation; the weaponization of time; the role of multinational companies within the border-industrial complex; a rejection of white saviour tropes and illumination of refugee agency, resistance and self-empowerment; transnational and ecological dimensions to survival and struggle from inside the prison camps; radically new imagining of displaced and exiled peoples and dismantling common patronizing and damaging tropes; the significance of the radical feminist concept of kyriarchy and its role in our construction of the term 'kyriarchal system'; the place of a colonial logic when examining border violence; the importance of experimentation and creativity for dismantling border regimes; hope, joy, celebration, pride and love as political acts; and the political and epistemic significance of radical acts of naming. Boochani and I argue that as Manus Prison Theory grows it will open up new spaces for people with lived experience of displacement and exile; it will empower them to contribute to various discourses and political organizing, and it will also transform the way a lot of academic work is produced.

Connection to other entries:
Ex-Colonialism
Nauru Imprisoned Exiles Collective
Posthuman Agency

Omid Tofighian (with Behrouz Boochani)

THE MELTIONARY

'The Meltionary' is a growing experimental directory that investigates different materials, metaphors and modes of melting. It consists of Meltries which are playful instructions to unnerve definitions, videos and photo series of melting processes, reports on failure (Halberstam 2008), experimental instructions for initiating chemical reactions, circuits for DIY measuring devices and theoretical-poetic texts – all of which unhinge stability and experiment with melting. In our arts-design practice, we boil up insights from chemistry, crip technoscience (Hamraie and Fritsch 2019) and trans*feminism to study and set in motion transformative material processes. Working with the material processes of melting, as well as trans* and crip survival practices in the midst of climate chaos, our arts-design research traces how melting flows towards changing political and epistemological modes. Melting is a shapeshifting figuration that changes what it touches and drips, spills, oozes, boils, expands, permeates, leaks. In this entry, we trace discursive, topological and temporal dimensions of melting and discuss crip and trans* strategies of survival.

The physical process of melting leads to a phase transition from a solid to a liquid state. In the case of ice caps, glaciers and other frozen portions of the Earth, this is resulting in rising sea levels globally. Melting is one of the key effects that fall under the umbrella of the term climate change. Within Western climate change discourse, melting is tied to meeting certain 'deadlines' in order to mitigate the harms of climate change (BBC News 2019). Some news agencies proclaim that it is already 'too late' (Letzter 2020) to slow down those effects of our warming world that are more heavily experienced by Indigenous people and people in the Global South. As Sheila Watt-Cloutier reflects on climate change and language, for Inuit people living near melting glaciers 'the metaphors have already become a literal reality.' (2015: xviii).

Colonial extraction and the burning of fossil fuels has accelerated melting as a force of climate change, dissolving the polar ice caps; impacts of this melting unequally effect human and non-human life on Earth (Pellow and Park 2002: 59). Melting also causes vast environmental damage, for example, the melting of the grounds on which Inuit people move (Watt-Cloutier 2015), furthering the rising of sea levels that both lead to the disappearance of islands (Tsosie 2007) as well as changes in the pH levels of the oceans, contributing to the dwindling numbers of some animals, such as salmon along North American shorelines (Whyte 2017: 2). Melting is a terraforming (Haraway 2013) process because it changes the topology of sea- and landscapes across the globe.

Melting as a posthuman phenomenon challenges Western anthropocentric assumptions of Universal human time. Denise Ferreira Da Silva describes heat as displacing Universal human time: instead of figuring change in terms of temporal progression, she considers change through material transformations, moving 'towards a non-anthropocentric account of what exists or what happens' (Da Silva 2018). If heat displaces Universal time, this happens particularly through melting, which changes land- and timescapes. Though met with an abundance of measuring technologies, melting exceeds the logic of human time: the Yellowstone Caldera's magma floor, which erupted approximately 640,000 years ago, is still moving today (Andrews 2020), and the effects of today's melting glaciers on the global climate can be roughly estimated, but not surely determined. Susan Schuppli gives insight into the ways in which 'glacial ice sheets have been registering and thus recording the slow accretion of carbon' (2020: 284) – as the glaciers melt, they release artefacts and traces from a time long past, thus playing back time (ibid.) while disappearing.

Yet critical posthuman theory has never only been about the material world alone, about re-thinking anthropocentric tropes, it also seeks to challenge humanism and hierarchies upheld between human subjects (Braidotti 2013). Becoming with these ongoing transformations, melting resonates with crip and trans* temporalities that unsettle notions of stability (Pritchard et. al. 2020). As Patty Berne explains, creative problem-solving has been a strategy of queer and trans* disabled people of colour that have long survived in the midst of structural and environmental oppressions. Building on their knowledge, she finds that 'diversity is the best defense against the threats of climate change' (Berne and Raditz 2020: 232). In trans* and crip scholarship, chrononormative norms, which describe a 'social patterning

of experiences of time' (Amin 2014: 220) are often challenged. Ellen Samuels notes how crip time allows 'time travel. Disability and illness have the power to extract us from linear, progressive time with its normative life stages' (2017). On trans* time, Reese Simpkins writes that a trans* 'tangibility of material embodiment operat(es) according to a non-linear framework where past, present and future comingle and evade chrononormative time' (2016). Similarly to Ferreira Da Silva's refusal of Universal human time, crip and trans* scholars, albeit from a different perspective, refuse Universal time. This is because Universal time brings with it the mandate for cures with the aim of eliminating disabled people from the future (Kafer 2013), or the imposition of heteronormative timelines on trans* people (Chen and cárdenas 2019). While heat and melting displace Universal anthropocentric time, trans* and crip experiences already inhabit non-linear and non-normative timelines and shape potentials for survival within climate change. Our work seeks to figure how these posthumanist and post-anthropocentric realities of melting can be fused to re-think, re-fuse and re-shape our worlds.

'The Meltionary' studies melting to figure political ways of undoing temporal and material normativities. In solidarity with those effected by ongoing environmental damage, we research what melting as a material and metaphorical phenomenon literally *does*. For example, through our arts-design experiments we have studied how an ice cube in our hands seems rigid at first, but over time dissolves into liquidity. This experiment helped us to think through the undoing of seemingly rigid socio-technical and material-discursive matter(s). Unstable material matters forge imaginaries for disability justice (Sins Invalid 2016) and trans*feminist (Stone 1992, Cárdenas 2016) social justice movements. Studying material transformations therefore evidences that the toppling over of rigid (material-social, socio-technical, political) structures is always possible.

Connection to other entries:
Crip Theory
Fermentation
Feminism and Oceans
Posthuman Agency
Posthuman Care

MELT (Ren Loren Britton
and Isabel Paehr)

N

NAURU IMPRISONED EXILES COLLECTIVE

I introduce the term Nauru Imprisoned Exiles Collective to reflect the body of work and resistance of incarcerated refugees in Australia's offshore refugee prison in the Republic of Nauru, and also the work of those within academia and civil society who actively oppose Australia's disastrous border regime. I draw upon this body of work in this contribution with the aim of encouraging more profound combinations of political action and scholarly engagement about Australia's offshore prison in Nauru; an approach which can be extended to examine and challenge similar carceral sites in Papua New Guinea, Christmas Island and onshore. My contribution to the Nauru Imprisoned Exiles Collective includes my one terabyte archive of photos and videos which I gathered during my six years of detention in Nauru, and my related artworks and critical analysis of Australia's offshore refugee prisons and the border-industrial complex that runs them. The other exiles in this collective have contributed impactful and seminal works, and as the collective grows, so does its drive to end Australia's illegal and inhumane imprisonment of people seeking asylum. This entry will focus on the offshore prison in the Republic of Nauru, which was for women, unaccompanied minors and families who arrived in Australia by boat asking for protection, but it is important to understand this phenomenon in conjunction with the prison in Manus Island, Papua New Guinea, which was for men. However, given the unique social dynamics and history of Nauru, and the diverse group of exiles who were or still are incarcerated there, it deserves dedicated examination to inform the development of abolitionist strategies that can be successfully applied in the Nauruan context.

The exiles imprisoned in Nauru had fled from countries where they were impacted by war, life-threatening oppression and systemic discrimination. To support my critique of Australia's border violence it is necessary to compare the experiences of these imprisoned exiles in Nauru with the situations they were forced to flee. My own reasons for fleeing Iran relate to the well documented official discrimination against women following the 1979 Iranian Revolution.

After experiencing various forms of oppression and being threatened by state actors, life in Iran became unliveable under the Islamic Republic and I had no choice but to seek asylum overseas. I arrived in Indonesia in 2013 and boarded a small wooden boat from Java headed for Christmas Island, a territory of Australia, arriving after 38 hours. It was August 2013 when we were moved to the Christmas Island detention centre. We thought we would be kept there for two weeks before being transferred to another centre in mainland Australia where we could apply for refugee status. I was still unaware that reaching Christmas Island was just the beginning of my oppression and imprisonment, not my salvation from it.

All of us held on Christmas Island could not believe the Australian Government was transferring women, unaccompanied minors and families to a detention centre in a tiny remote island called the Republic of Nauru, a former protectorate of Australia, or that they had purpose-built a place there for torturing us. I was exiled to Nauru at the beginning of 2014. Like many other women, children and men I had been exiled twice – first fleeing Iran and then sent to Nauru to be locked up. I had been totally wrong about my understanding of Australia's commitment to human rights, my experience from that point on would reveal the cold realities about unequal power relations and intersectional discrimination in our globalized, modern world. In time we saw how consecutive Australian governments used us to reach their political goals, and how many companies made huge profits from the suffering of innocent and vulnerable people. Their plan worked, winning election after election by spreading xenophobia and hatred by falsely smearing refugees as potential terrorists and criminals, and successfully terrifying the Australian people. The leaders of this Western democratic country have been cynically violating international law for their own domestic political purposes. I had been forced to leave Iran and was then faced with another form of violence from Australia.

I always think of these six years of imprisonment in Nauru as painful years involving harsh realizations; years of being physically and mentally humiliated and tortured by the people whom I had asked for help. I realized that democracy and freedom do not really exist in the way I had imagined them, or in the way that it was portrayed in the mass media.

During my time in that desolate prison camp, I witnessed the Australian regime's treatment of vulnerable women, children and families; some of the children were even born there in that prison. There were over 2,000 sexual assault allegations which were all denied by the Australian Government. Men and women in Canberra have been making decisions for women's bodies in Nauru by preventing them access to abortions, and in some cases pressuring women to terminate their pregnancies early with drugs by giving them fake obstetrician reports stating that their foetuses were deformed. I witnessed that. I witnessed the failure of humanity. The concealed borders, where violence, discrimination and modern slavery are used to grease the wheels of a brutal border-industrial complex. During these years I observed how ruthless human beings could become, and how nothing would stop this system as long as it continued to provide the rich and powerful with more money and power.

The border-industrial complex was extracting blood money from us refugees, except it was our blood and their money, it was us who were being bled for their profits. There was a common saying among the refugees incarcerated in Nauru when describing the people who worked for this 'border-industrial complex' – we would say they are 'dipping their bread into our blood', playing off the common analogy of financial corruption as the 'eating' of ill-gotten money, and thus our blood was a mere condiment to be enjoyed by these unscrupulous contractors.

It was a system that spared no woman, man or child, all brown or black people. This violence is intensified when one's religion is deemed to be 'wrong', the bad religion. This place was especially difficult for the hundreds of women and girls of all ages, from newborn babies to frail old grand-mothers nearing their eighties, who were all sent there without regard for their individual situations. Those selected were sent to a place with no legal protection for women, no services for women, a country already suffering from rampant sexual assault, rape and domestic violence, and no authorities or even media to turn to when it happened; it was a place where the victim was always blamed for the crime and called a liar and troublemaker. All such incidents were always referred to the Nauruan Police Force, a highly corrupt and deliberately ineffective institution in Nauru, trained and closely monitored by the Australian authorities. Consequently, it was a place where women and children could be assaulted with near total impunity, and it made the perfect local-ity for conducting the cruel experiments of the border-industrial complex.

The border-industrial complex is a tool of fascism; it is a huge two billion dollar a year programme that currently achieves, on paper, little more than holding around 300 refugees hostage on tiny islands far away from Australian society. Australia's border-industrial complex has managed to manipulate the Australian people and quietly syphon away their tax dollars to fund destructive and illegal machinations out of sight of the Australian public. Despite the unequivocal human, fiscal and moral disaster that is Australia's 'offshore solution', the border-industrial complex nonetheless continues to promote it as a model for other rich countries to emulate, and many companies can now offer their expertise in this emerging sector having gained lucrative experience in Nauru, Manus Island and Christmas Island. It is therefore essential that grassroots political action in support of refugee rights, is combined with scholarly engagement and research, to confront this emerging global threat to human rights before it entrenches itself deeper within international political discourse and further influences national refugee policies.

Connection to other entries:
Manus Island and Manus Prison Theory
Posthuman Agency

Elahe Zivardar, also known as Ellie Shakiba (with Mehran Ghadiri)

NEW MATERIALIST INFORMATICS

New materialist informatics is an emer-ging transdisciplinary research field that brings together new materialist scholar-ship and informatics/computer science as well as information technology design and development. Foregrounding new materi-alist principles of troubling categorical distinctions, espousing relational ontology, highlighting material agency, and focusing on onto-ethico-epistemological premises of knowledge and artefact production, new materialist informatics destabilizes the normative humanism that is prevalent in computer science and seeks to open space for embodied, embedded, enactive and accountable ways of doing computing and technology design.

Computing as a technological practice is embedded within contradictory imagin-aries of material hardware and immaterial, abstract software and computational processes. However, as numerous media, feminist and science and technology studies scholars have noted (e.g. Kittler 1992, Hayles 1999, Suchman 2006, to name just a few), this contradiction is questionable both on practical and conceptual levels. Computational processes rely on electrical current and its abstraction through hardware (Blanchette 2011), conceptually enabling signs and signals to interface and be manipulated at higher levels of abstraction (Nake 1994). Furthermore, as one of the core technologies behind the fourth industrial revolution, computing has material socio-economic and political effects. Nonetheless, the perceived 'immateriality' of computing technologies, often reinforced by metaphors such as 'cloud computing', structures the imaginary of computation as disconnected from socio-political processes and environmental conditions (Taffel 2019).

New materialist informatics (NMI), relying on new materialist understandings of matter as relational and agentive, and phenomena as always already material-semiotic (Coole and Frost 2010; van der Tuin and Dolphijn 2012), traces, highlights and investigates material dimensions of computing and grounds material-semiotic perspectives as the basis for design of computing technologies. Historically, NMI can be tied back to Donna Haraway's work (Haraway 1991) and her interview with Lisa Nakamura on the need for 'materialist informatics' (Nakamura and Haraway 2003), as well as the work of Felicity Colman and other new materialist and posthumanist media scholars (Colman 2015, Colman et al. 2018, Hayles 1992, 1999). However, it also extends and builds on cyberfeminist tradition of materialist feminist critique of digital technologies

(Featherstone 1995; Plant 1997; Stone 1991, Munster 1999; VNS Matrix 1991) and its contemporary reconfigurations through dialogues with race-critical, decolonial, postcolonial and ecofeminists (Fernandez et al. 2003; Gajjala 2003; Nakamura 2008; Sollfrank 2018). NMI also can be approached from within materialist media theories (e.g. Parikka 2011; Parikka and Feigelfeld 2015, among others) and it further resonates with some Indigenous and decolonial approaches to informatics (Ali 2016; Laiti 2016, 2021; Mills and Chakravartty 2018) and the calls for intersectional computing (Kumar and Karusala 2019; Schlesinger et al. 2017) as well as critical algorithm studies (Kitchin 2017).

NMI scholarship can be tentatively grouped into four overlapping directions (Klumbytė and Draude 2022). First, it investigates the material premises of computing, computational infrastructures and their effects. Here research ranges from investigating material agencies of computational matter and computing as material practice (e.g. Dourish 2017, Fuller 2007), to environmental impact of computing (e.g. Lorenz-Meyer et al. 2019). The second direction explores matter as computational, including the dis/continuum between biological and computational matter and the agentive and political processes of computational mattering (e.g. Fitsch and Friedrich 2018; de Freitas 2016; Papenburg et al. 2018; Treusch 2017; Schmitz 2021). The third direction consists of materially-grounded political critique that inquires into socio-cultural-political consequences and the racialized, sexualized and naturalized materializations of power within informatics (for instance, Apprich et al. 2019; Noble 2018). Last but not least, the fourth direction centres around new materialist approaches to information systems design, experimental and artistic research on NMI and design of computational artefacts (Britton et al. 2019; Draude 2017; Klumbytė et al. 2020; Treusch 2020, among others).

As an emerging field, NMI does not have clear boundaries or institutional demarcations. It spans the humanities and social sciences, as well as human–computer interaction, robotics and AI research, with feminist new materialist and posthumanist perspectives being taken up in technology design and development (Forlano 2017a) and more-than-human design (e.g. Akama et al. 2020; Coulton and Lindley 2019; Nicenboim et al. 2020). Furthermore, as this wide web of inter-connections with existing interdisciplinary areas of study shows, quite a few materially-grounded research and design traditions resonate and converge with NMI approaches without necessarily using the new materialist terminology. This is particularly noticeable in perspectives grounded in artistic research and technology design that acknowledge and work with agencies and capacities of digital and analogue matter in technology. Nonetheless, NMI can be said to distinctly centre agentive capacities of computational matter and material-semiotic intra-actions within computing and technology design.

Through more-than-human approaches to design, NMI also highlights the inhuman, non-human and posthuman aspects of computing, without losing sensitivity to power differentials. Furthermore, it re-envisions the subject (or in computing terms: 'the user' and 'the designer') as multiple, relational and not exclusively human, troubling the normatively humanist premises of computational practices. NMI centres the creation of space for practical design and technological experiment-

ation within research and therefore encourages to investigate what would a new materialist computational practice and relational digital ethics look like.

Connection to other entries:
Convergences
Internet of Trees
Pattern Discrimination
Postcolonial and Decolonial Computing
Posthuman Data
Posthumanism and Design
Surface Orientations

Goda Klumbytė and Claude Draude

NORMS

To gloss posthuman norms, one could start either with the normative architecture of the human or with the phenomenon of norms. Beginning with the human entails tackling questions such as: which norms have secured the human and how; and what becomes of those norms as the human is shown to be dispersed, networked, unduly privileged and routinely entangled with the non-human? All sorts of significant normalizing work may be seen to revolve around, and be sustained by, objects and subjects other than humans. Proceeding from norms, on the other hand, involves foregrounding how standard-setting patterns may operate without regard to, or in spite of, human action or intent. Norms are, of course, typically understood as the outcomes of human deliberation or acculturation. Once instantiated, they often depend on humans, and on ideas of the human, to realize their prescriptive force. Nonetheless, norms have always manifested between and beyond the human, and implicated non-humans. Calling anthropocentrism and androcentrism into question – as posthumanist writing and creative work has sought to do – helps illuminate an array of 'minor', historically marginalized and meta-legalities and normative complexes, including those of First Nations peoples (Deleuze and Guattari 1983; Johns 2013; Ruru 2018).

Let us tackle the term 'posthuman norms' from each end, starting with the (post)human. Becoming recognizably human is an effect of norms and normalization (Foucault 1977a: 184). Those norms involved include legal, social and political norms, among them norms of subjectivity. Once hybridized, networked and put in motion by posthumanism, however, the human is no longer a natural focus, stable tether or necessary culmination of much normative endeavour. Rather, humans are one among many 'connection-making entit[ies]' or normative nodes (Braidotti 2006: 200). The potential range of normative embodiments and actants expands accordingly. For instance, the question of what could and could not come within the ambit of legal personhood is enlivened afresh: trees, robots, and animals may all be so endowed (Braverman 2018; Grear 2013; Stone 1972; Teubner 2006).

At the same time, the human turns out to depend on many normative mechanisms and types of infrastructure only contingently responsive to human cognisance or control. Norms do not just embrace more-than-humans. They bypass and interpolate humans as well. Some norms are executable more or less without recourse or reference to humans – mechanisms of ordering embedded in computer code, for example (Galloway 2004). Intracellular forces (biological and synthetic) and insect swarms prove to be doing significant normative work in their

conditioning and modelling of human possibilities (de Leeuw and van Wichelen 2020; Arvidsson 2020). Work on so-called 'smart contracts' – routing contractual norms and other legal relations through blockchain and other forms of distributed ledger technology – raises anew the spectre of norms' self-enforcement without the 'inefficiency' of human tethers (Verstraete 2019). Yet the last of these examples is but one, recent instance of a long-fraught effort to grapple with the apparent automaticity or systemic force of norms, legal and otherwise, especially (for some) the normative force of capitalism (e.g. Althusser 1970; Kennedy 1986; Lopez 2009; Zumbansen 2007).

Posthuman norms are, then, norms oriented towards forces, flows and figments that are multiple. Their points of embarkation and destination include inanimate entities and multispecies aggregates. Thinking norms post-humanely directs attention towards normatively generative sites, mechanisms of normative transmission, and processes of (or obstacles to) normative change that are only partially answerable to human direction, if at all, or afford human experiences relatively little concern. Investigations of posthuman norms cast humans into relation with non-human and hybrid associates and antagonists, including some long obscured or subordinated by humanist reflexes.

Connection to other entries:
Algorithmic Governmentality
Critical Posthuman Theory
Geontopower
Posthuman Agency
Relational Sovereignty
Rights of Nature

Fleur Johns

0

ONTOLOGIZED PLASTICITY

I argue that when one examines the history of science, law and philosophy, black(ened) female flesh persistently functions as the limit case of 'the human' and is its matrix-figure, due to the central role reproduction plays in determining species demarcation and the racialization of that function. Given that the limit of the human has and continues to be determined by how the means and scene of birth are interpreted coupled with globalizing histories that cast humanity in blackness as debatable or contingent, the black(ened) female figure was, and I argue remains, the fulcrum of categorical distinction writ large. To render one's humanity provisional and circumscribed by abjection, where the spectre of nullification looms large, is precisely the work that racism does. Thus, ontological integrity cannot always be assumed and not all humans are idealized and exceptionalized *via their humanity*. In my book, *Becoming Human* (Jackson 2020), I investigate blackness's relation to animality rather than presuppose black(ened) people's relative power and privilege *as human*, vis-à-vis non-human animals. Thus, my work focuses on humans whose humanity is a subject of controversy, debate and dissension in order to reveal the broader political stakes of 'the animal' as a problem for contemplation. For posthumanists to do accurate, fully theor-ized and principled work, they must show how the question of the animal bears on the question of hierarchies of humanity.

While scholars of race have investig-ated and critiqued the conflation of black(ened) humans with animals found in Enlightenment discourses, ontologized plasticization reframes the confluence of race and animality (Chen 2012; Lundblad 2013; Seshadri 2012; Wolfe 2003; Kim 2015; see also Jackson 2013 and Jackson 2015). I reinterpret Enlightenment thought not as black 'exclusion' or 'denied human-ity' but rather as the violent imposition and appropriation – inclusion and recognition – of black(ened) humanity in the interest of plasticizing that very humanity, whereby 'the animal' is one among many possible forms blackness is thought to encompass.

Ontologized plasticization is not inter-changeability, replaceability or exchange-ability. It is not the conceptualization of how a good or asset is understood as being of equal value to another. If we consider the history of antiblackness, for instance, we might recall how a slave was commod-itized alongside, and made exchangeable with, a cow or a horse. This familiar image is related to fungibility, our thinking on which is indebted to Saidiya Hartman's indispensable *Scenes of Subjection* (1997), but ultimately 'fungibility' is not synonym-ous with ontologized plasticization. As a concept engaged with the new material-isms, ontologized plasticization concerns what is called hylomorphism or the form-matter distinction. Ontologized plasticization is a conceptualization of form itself rather than a conceptualization of how a form is taken up within the logics of law, economic markets or political economies. In other words, it is not a conception of the commodity and its uses. It is a conceptualization of property – but of the properties of form.

'Plasticity', as concept and thematic, has been differentially articulated and inflected by thinkers as diverse as Hegel ([1807] 2018), Lévi-Strauss ([1958] 1963), Darwin ([1859] 2009), and most recently the French philosopher Catherine Malabou (2009). Ontologized plasticization is not defined as the unnatural ordering of man and beast. It is a mode of transmogrification whereby the fleshy being of blackness is experimented with as if it were infinitely malleable lexical and biological matter – a form where form shall not hold – such that blackness is produced as human, subhuman and suprahuman at once. The 'at once' here is important: it denotes immediacy and simultaneity. Blackness, in this case, functions not simply as negative relation but as a plastic fleshy being that stabilizes and gives form to 'human' and 'animal' as categories – precisely via blackness's inability to access conceptual and material stability other than that of functioning *as* ontological instability for the reigning order. To put it another way, the concept of ontologized plasticity maintains that black(ened) people are not so much dehumanized, cast as non-humans or as liminal humans, nor are black(ened) people framed as animal-like or machine-like or simply exchangeable with these non-human forms; rather, black(ened) people are cast as sub, supra and human *simultaneously* and in a manner that puts being in

peril because the operations of simultaneously being any-thing and no-thing for a given order constructs black(ened) humanity as the *privation and exorbitance* of form. The demand for willed privation and exorbitance that I describe does not take the structure of serialized demands for serialized states but demands that black(ened) humanity be all forms and no form simultaneously; human, animal, machine, object . . . (Moten 2003). In other words, plasticization, here, is a mode of ontologizing not at all deterred by the self-regulation of matter or its limits, nor by what Malabou has described as 'the fragile and finite mutability' of the form we call black (2009: 81). Black studies scholars have often interpreted the predicament of black(ened) being in relation to either liminality (movement from one state to another state) or interstice (being in-between states) or partial states (Spillers 1984; Wynter 2003; Weheliye 2014). What the concept of ontologized plasticization suggests is that these appearances are undergirded by a demand that tends towards the fluidification of state or ontology. This demand for statelessness collapses a distinction between the virtual and the actual, abstract potential and situated possibility, whereby the abstraction of blackness is enfleshed via an ongoing process of wresting form from matter such that antiblackness's materialization is that of a de-materializing virtuality. We must think critically about the enthusiasm for ontological slippage in much recent posthumanist, ecocritical, and speculative-realist critical theory when that very imagination has been conditioned by anti-black extractivism and its racialized phantasy of bound(ary)lessness that recognizes the protean capacities of the flesh only to boundlessly exploit it. What is at stake is the definitive character of form, its determinacy or resistance, which is potentially fluidified by a willed excess of polymorphism and the violent estrangement of form from matter.

This approach also departs from how plasticity has been talked about in the sciences, and in popular science in particular. Plasticity in those contexts is usually framed in terms of a kind of ableist promise of the optimization of life – a cure for autism, for instance. I maintain that this ableist and eugenic imaginary is underwritten by a shadow history of experiments with blackness: a praxis that seeks to define the essence of a black(ened) thing as infinitely mutable, in antiblack, often paradoxical, sexuating terms as a means of hierarchically delineating sex/gender, reproduction and states of being more generally.

Connection to other entries:
Ex-colonialism
Racializing Assemblages
Toxic Embodiment
Transjectivity

Zakiyyah Iman Jackson

ORGANOIDS

Recent advances in stem cell technology enable the creation in a dish of human tissues called organoids. Organoids ('mini-organs'), are three-dimensional and recapitulate at least some of the basic architecture and function of real-life human organs, although currently only a couple of millimetres in size (Bredenoord, Clevers and Knoblich 2017). They are cultivated from human stem or progenitor cells and are capable of self-organization and self-renewal, which implies that a small amount of human cells can be used to grow a virtually endless amount of organoids. Researchers are able to make mini-intestines, mini-livers and even mini-brains that have a close genetic and functional link to the tissue provider. This breakthrough in stem cell research opens avenues for science and personalized and regenerative medicine (Bredenoord, Clevers and Knoblich 2017). For patients with Cystic Fibrosis (CF), for instance, their intestinal organoids can be used to predict their responsiveness to novel, expensive treatments (Chakradhar 2017).

Organoid technology research focuses on parallel lines of scientific and technological but also ethical enquiry (Boers 2019). Embedded in a clinical environment where the technology is developed for medicine and care, organoid research is carried out in collaboration with scientists, physicians and patient organizations. Considering the extent to which the complex tissue products involved in organoids research touch upon corporeality, personhood and identity, these technologies also interrogate the boundaries between and the implications of human–posthuman relations.

In my PhD research on the ethics of organoid technology, I employed an interdisciplinary methodology that als involves art practice (see entry: 'Arts and Bioethics'). I conducted qualitative interviews with patients with CF for whom intestinal organoids are tools for personalized medicine. By integrating insights from different theoretical disciplines, the arts and empirical practice, I was able to conceptualize the moral value of organoids and propose ethical recommendations for their global exchange. This methodology implies the recognition of organoids as hybrids, that is to say entities that precede categorizations and are neither human nor non-human (Latour 1994). Organoids are such ontological hybrids. The technological transformation of human bodily tissues into new entities entails novel intrinsic values and relational as well as instrumental and commercial worth (Boers 2019; Boers, van Delden and Bredenoord 2019; Boers 2018). To acknowledge their hybridity while accepting their exchange value and commercial worth, the creators and users of organoids develop binding ethical obligations towards the human tissue providers, the patients and society in general. Ideally, these obligations are given shape via a 'consent for governance' model. This means that after the initial consent procedure an appropriate governance model allows for the multiple parties involved to shape and optimiate the value of organoid technology for research and care, while negotiating and aligning their different interests and perspectives.

The hybridity of organoid technology and its inter-connection with other biotechnologies is what makes it especially relevant for posthuman thought. The convergence in organoid technology includes synthetic biology, tissue engineering, stem cell research, genomics and 'genetic engineering'. What these converging domains have in common is that they enable the transformation of 'ordinary human tissue' into increasingly complex human tissue products (Boers 2019). This process is complex in a biotechnological sense, because staggering new creations can be made, such as cerebral organoids ('brain organoids') that recapitulate some functions of the human brain, and that may come to supersede normal human bodily function (Farahany et al. 2018). But

it is also complex from a moral point of view, because the human tissue products associate with multiple, potentially conflicting, value regimes. The conflictual aspects reside in the fact that organoids challenge a classical subject–object distinction, that still underlies dominant ethical debate and regulation over the retrieval and use of human tissue. The creation of cerebral organoids, for example, raises questions of *intrinsic moral value*: do these entities have value in themselves and therefore are they worthy of protection? Other types of organoids have *relational moral value*: value in relation to tissue provider, as they relate to autonomy, privacy, well-being and bodily integrity. Intrinsic and relational moral values are traditionally associated with subjects. Simultaneously, organoids have values associated with objects: technological, instrumental and commercial values. They serve as instruments for science, care and for drug development. Novel drug candidates can effortlessly be tested on large batches of organoids in Petri dishes, without any physical inconveniences for either animals or humans, making them of interest to the pharmaceutical and biotech industry (Boers, van Delden and Bredenoord 2019; Boers 2019).

Their moral complexity is reinforced through the exchange networks in which organoids acquire further meanings and values. Organoids can, for instance, be created out of patient-derived material in a public hospital for personalized care purposes and subsequently be stored in a biobank: a repository of tissue (products) coupled with data for future use. Biobanks enable worldwide and endless distribution of organoids. The emerging technologies facilitate ongoing and unforeseen transformation and re-utilization of these tissue products. When exchanged globally, organoids move through the realms of research, care, and both non-profit and for-profit spheres. This means that multiple parties are involved whose interests can potentially conflict. Autonomy rights or well-being interests of patients, for instance, do not necessarily align with organoids being an anonymous commercial product.

The resulting ethical challenges include, but also go beyond, those traditionally seen in bioethical debates regarding the use of human tissues. These have focused mainly on the appropriate type of informed consent, privacy protection, and ethical oversight (Chalmers et al. 2015). The complex exchange of novel human tissue products raises questions about their moral value and the optimal ethical shape of their design – for instance, what are the boundaries to the complexity of cerebral organoids? They also question the governance of their exchange, so as to safeguard the interests of individual patients, researchers, care-givers, (for-profit) companies, institutions and societies (Boers and Bredenoord 2018). In essence, organoid technologies strike to the core of the fast-changing relations between human and posthuman components of contemporary subjects of knowledge and ethics.

The academic discipline of bioethics raises and struggles with these questions. Bioethics has become an eclectic field in which the disciplines of theology, philosophy and the social sciences coexist. There are growing calls to combine these disciplines in order to tackle the internally contradictory problems raised by the organoids and other emerging biotechnologies in their proposal for 'ethics parallel research' (van der Burg 2009; Jongsma and Bredenoord 2020). In ethics parallel research ethicists evaluate and co-shape novel technologies by addressing together human and non-human parties involved in their development and use. That includes researchers, companies, patients, citizens, etc. This requires a shift from just thinking *about* to thinking *with* a diverse range of practices.

Connection to other entries:
Art and Bioethics
Empathy Beyond the Human
Posthuman Care

Sarah N. Boers

P

PARASITOLOGY

Parasitology, in our times, is often narrowed to a discipline within biology. There, it differs significantly from other disciplines in the broader life sciences because its scope is neither determined by the organism nor by the environment in which life takes place. It is also not interested in particular diseases. Parasitology rather addresses 'a way of life', it studies a very particular relationship. It might be attributed to particular 'species' (as it happens within biology departments), but in the end that is not what defines the relation between the parasite and the host. Parasitology has a lot more to say about what can be seen as a posthuman politics that somehow marks the ways of life of many. Especially in art theory, authors like Anna Watkins Fisher (2020) are showing us that parasitology offers us a way of studying resistance beyond the limits of humanism.

In *The Parasite* (1980, 2007), Michel Serres coined parasitology as an overall political theory. Christopher Watkin (2020) summarizes Serres' approach, stressing first of all that parasitology is universal in the sense that it happens all around us, always. Or better even; parasitology has always already happened/started happening everywhere. In line with this, Watkin adds that parasitology necessarily happens before group processes, before all contact and before the law. In fact, all groups actually follow from 'an original parasitism', since the communality necessary for any group, follows from the recognition of the parasite; from the recognition of the noise that pollutes the relationship before. After the parasite is eliminated, after the noise is killed, the (group) relationship comes into existence.

In terms of the social this means that rather than emphasizing the (class) struggles that supposedly determine inter-human relationships, and map a Capitalist, phallogocentric, postcolonial and gender-based status quo, parasitology is much more the study of radical metamorphosis, of speculation and of everything that comes-to-be. And although Serres himself only makes few references to Marx and his followers (see Wolfe, note 21, xxvii, in Serres [1980] 2007), it is obvious that he questions its emphasis on exchange (the equilibrium which always occurs when supply hits demand) and the ideas of optimalization that contemporary Marxist thinkers are so fond of. They practice a humanism that encourages us to forget the earth. And thus, somehow, Marxism itself, has become part of the metabolic rift that Marx himself analyses so well in his Grundrisse: just like the capitalist (dualist) system, contemporary Marxism, all too often causes an alienation of the earth (we, humans, estrange ourselves from the metabolisms of life in which we function).

Our misreading of Marx, Japanese philosopher and Marxist Kojin Karatani (2014, 2020) claims, has much to do with our misreading of the state. The state, Karatani claims, always conquers or occupies pre-state societies. It does so by interrupting its organization, interrupting and disturbing the ways its higher-level and lower-level groupings relate. The state, though hardly noticed when it starts, quickly finds a way to overtake its host society in two ways. On the one hand, as Max Weber already put it, the state aims to establish a complete monopoly on violence such that even harming oneself (e.g. suicide) is quickly to be considered illegal, in the state. On the other hand, the state, like the proper victor, also 'plunders' its citizens. Yet it doesn't do this by simply taking all the money they can get their hands on. Similarly, to how the state claims the ownership to violence for an infinite period of time, and erects the institutions necessary to realize this, the state also searches for ways for the pillaging to continue. And again, the state realizes a monopoly here; no one else is allowed to ask for taxes or forced labour.

Karatani concludes 'the state is established through the transformation of plunder and violent compulsion into a mode of exchange' (2014: 68). The state is already happening everywhere, it disturbs and creates communities (peoples) everywhere, it created what we commonly refer to as human cultures and identities, while blurring the way these humans related to the great outside (non-human life, the earth). The state gave form to the hierarchies, placing the (male) warriors on top (from nobility to venture capitalists), and the masses at the bottom. Happening before the law, it created the law, the system which made sure the host (= the people), despite the fact that they form a much larger body than the state apparatus which controls it, continues to give, blind to its own fate.

Moving away from modernist dualism and working instead with a Marxism focused on parasitology, will open our eyes for a posthuman politics. Of course, this has been done before, and not just by Karatani. When Deleuze explains us the affects of the tick, the 3-fold desires through which this very simple creature has been awfully successful for so long, he proposes a parasitology. When Susanne Langer (1955), long before Watkins, tells us that art occupies a virtual space that is always already intervening into our systems of thought, disturbing our realities and rearranging them at the same time, she practices a parasitology. The support Serres in his claim that parasitology often concerns an invisible revolution a much more common revolution than the one realized through class struggle, Serres (2007: 185) was right: 'The theory of being, ontology, brings us to atoms. The theory of relations beings us to the parasite.'

Connection to other entries:
Emergent ecologies
Syndemic
Transcorporeality II
Viral

Rick Dolphijn

PATTERN DISCRIMINATION

Pattern discrimination characterizes the imposition of identity on input data, in order to filter, that is to discriminate information from it (Apprich et al. 2019, Chun 2021). As such it is a highly political issue, not least because it challenges the anthropocentric idea of the human subject as an autonomous being. With information-processing machines, such as recommender systems and search engines, the subject gets chopped up into discrete data points and is reassembled according to predefined categories (Cheney-Lippold 2019). Yet pattern discrimination has always been an essential part of human, but also non-human cognition: in order to filter signals from noise, we rely on certain socially defined patterns. In this sense, algorithmic cultures are not so different from ancient Greece, when the voices of children, women and slaves were excluded from public discourse; they may have been quantitatively significant but were qualitatively irrelevant (Steyerl 2019: 2f.). The problem of pattern discrimination, therefore, points beyond current discussions that ask for better data, policies or regulations. Its main concern is not simply to show that filter algorithms contain human bias, a fact every machine-learning practitioner already knows about, but rather that algorithmic filtering poses an intrinsic problem to the solution itself: you cannot not discriminate when making use of algorithmic systems.

Instead of providing a more 'objective' basis for decision making, the delineation and application of algorithmic patterns are deeply problematic. The criteria to decide what to include and what to exclude are more and more hidden behind automated and self-learning machines (Alpaydin 2016, Amoore 2020, Crawford 2021). As a consequence, systems of knowledge, perception and affect unfold beyond what can be directly observed, even though, paradoxically, the tools to critically reflect on and engage with them are more available than ever before. In light of these developments, we have to ask how can we come up with new forms of critique vis-à-vis pattern discrimination by thinking about and working with these technologies? What is it that algorithmic filtering brings to the world? And how is the world shaped by it? Astonishingly enough, most of today's recommendation systems, which automatically filter information for us, are built on the same premise, namely that of the homophilic 'nature' of connectivity (Kurgan et al. 2019). In algorithmic cultures, we are constantly being lumped together, compared to others who are supposedly like us. To better understand these segregating and discriminatory effects, we need to address the troubling problem of algorithmic filtering.

Imagine the following scenario: a supercomputer, based on the newest quantum technology, runs a simulation with an artificial population of 'identity units' who live as human (or other) beings, albeit unaware that their world is just a simulation. One day the technical director of the programme gets informed by one of the units that the world she lives in is yet another simulation. This is not only the plot of Fassbinder's sci-fi film *World on a Wire* (1973), but also the rationale of so-called simulation theory, which has become very popular over the last years (see Bostrom 2003). Now the gist of the story is not only that these kinds of simulation theories reflect a – predominantly white – fear of losing control over the 'real' world, but also that in a completely simulated environment machines will still have to discriminate on some basis to form identity units. Even in the most artificial of all worlds, identity categories will be used to set individuals apart. In the words of Danielle Sands: 'The most pressing concern for the (post)humanities is not that the human will change, but rather, that even in a world rendered materially unrecognizable by technology, political and social hierarchies will remain exactly the same' (Sands 2019a: 182). The challenge algorithmic filtering thus poses to (post-) humanism lies in the fact that pattern discrimination is no longer an aesthetic problem alone, but has become a political one. We are faced with the almost impossible task to think of an 'art of discrimination' (Draxler 2019) capable of coding and, at the same time, decoding our lives.

So what is there to be done then? I think – and here I am, of course, not the only one – that critical (post-)humanities (e.g. decolonial theory, gender studies, critical race theory, algorithmic and critical code studies) have a wide range of instruments at their disposal with which problems such as data discrimination can be tackled (Braidotti 2019). This critical knowledge will be necessary to think against new essentialisms in digital cultures, precisely because certain categories are again set as 'natural' and 'given'. What we teach these algorithms ultimately reflects back on us, and it is, therefore, no wonder when filter algorithms start to discriminate on the basis of race, class, and gender (Benjamin 2019, Eubanks 2018, Noble 2018, O'Neil 2016). By the same token, gender, class, race are not just alibi terms, but analytical tools to get under the shiny surface of algorithmic cultures, to – and that would be the next step – also come up with other algorithms and filters in which difference instead of similarity, openness instead of predetermination set the tone. What we need is a level of knowledge that is able to combine artistic, scientific and theoretical disciplines to better understand algorithmic filtering processes (Rieder 2020; Brunton 2018; Fox

2013). Ultimately, a knowledge to face the impossible, but nonetheless crucial question: how can we discriminate – that is information from data – without being discriminatory?

Connection to other entries:
Algorithmic Governmentality
New Materialist Informatics
Posthuman Data
Racializing Assemblages
Surface Orientations

Clemens Apprich

PETROCULTURE

Patricia Yager has argued literature can be classified according to its relations with resources from wood, whale oil, gasoline and atomic power (Yager 2011). Energy resources can shape narrative structures, providing the fuel to transport characters to distant climes or create the pathways to pivotal events. Rather than organizing culture according to human 'progress' and history, how might ecology and non-human lifeforms shape our understandings of the cultural sphere? Petrocultures invites such a project involving a cross-species and environmental focus to perceive how our worlds are shaped by non-human processes, the biological residue which we classify as natural resources and commodities.

Amitav Ghosh's 1992 article, 'Petrofiction: The Oil Encounter and the Novel', declares that there is a certain muteness and silence within the literary imaginary when it comes to crude oil. Though the oil industry has shaped global modernity, effecting everything from our infrastructure to our interpersonal lives, for Ghosh 'the history of oil is a matter of embarrassment verging on the unspeakable' (Ghosh 1992). Ghosh regards Abdul Rahman Munif's *Cities of Salt* ([1984] 1989) as one of the sole works to grasp the enormity of the influence of our oil-based economies in culture, leading him to lament the absence of the Great American Oil Novel. In recent years since Ghosh's declaration on this apparent silence, scholars from the humanities have responded with a plethora of research which explores the ways petroleum is imbricated and immersed within our cultural and artistic practices. Graeme Macdonald suggests that although aspects of Ghosh's argument remain salient, the growth of Petrocultures as a field challenges the supposed absence of oil in the cultural and social sphere. As Macdonald argues, Ghosh may have been unfamiliar with the pivotal work of Upton Sinclair's *Oil!* (1926) or did not deem it worthy of the adjective 'Great' (Macdonald 2012). Situating crude oil as both a natural and cultural phenomenon leads us to a form of ecological thinking, taking us beyond the domain of the human.

Petrocultures fosters a crucial intervention within the Environmental Humanities of uncovering the ways in which crude oil has shaped the social and cultural imaginary of the twenty-first century. Imre Szeman and Sheena Wilson, co-directors of the research collective Petrocultures in the University of Alberta, contend that an energy transition from our fossil fuel intensive lifestyles requires not just an economic and structural shift, but a cultural and social one. As Ross Barrett and Daniel Worden suggest in their collection on *Oil Culture*, the field addresses crude oil not simply as a business but an aesthetic, a natural resource and a trope (Barrett and Worden 2014). Contending with the ways crude oil is often 'hidden in plain sight' (Szeman et al. 2017), is the task petro-critics have undertaken exploring the implications of what Stephanie LeMenager terms as the 'aesthetics of petroleum' (2013). The fantasies of unlimited energy are underpinned by a culture which propagates a world of speed, fast energy and unimpeded consumption of fossil fuels.

But how and in what ways can we begin to critique this aesthetics and culture of petroleum to imagine ourselves as different types of being untethered from destructive and extractive energies? Sheena Wilson has focused on the petrosexual relations of Western feminisms. For Wilson, the complex relation between the oil industry and the rise of Western feminisms is rife with ironies: the advancement of feminism, as well as 'reinforcement of longstanding patriarchal conceptualizations of woman as object and as property' (Wilson 2014). Unpacking the relation between crude oil and feminism, is essential for environmental justice and a transition away from fossil fuel dependency. Jennifer Wenzel has similarly made a crucial intervention within the field focusing primarily on fictions from the Niger Delta, highlighting how legacies of imperialism underpin extractive economies and petroculture (Wenzel 2014).

While these scholars have contended with the multiple dimensions of petroculture, Melissa Haynes proposes a vital question of 'why are animals absent from so many histories of energy development?' (Haynes 2017). Haynes question invites further inquiry into what the implications of petroculture are on our more-than-human world and ecologies. As Melanie Doherty asks, how might we advance a non-anthropocentric imagining of crude oil (2014)? If we return to petroleum's origins, a strange amalgam, millions of years of photosynthesis formed from plankton and animal bones, we soon discover its planetary beginnings. In Heather L. Sullivan's words, we need to begin to think of petroleum's vegetal origins (Sullivan 2019). Fantasies of petroleum render it both a resource curse and a prize, an aesthetics and a culture, which perhaps obscures its planetary form that is 'derived from long and varied forms of botanical output that grows, dies, rots underground, and then re-emerges in new and fiery forms' (Sullivan 2019). Contending with this multifaceted understanding of crude oil as something posthuman and simultaneously socially and culturally constructed advances the ways crude oil has shaped human and non-human worlds. Emerging from Petrocultures Research Group, the research collective, *After Oil* note 'the energy question is, at its core, a human question, a social question that concerns accounting for the quality of human experience under the fossil economy, reckoning with the increasing precarity of life under fossil fuels' (Petrocultures Research Group 2016). However, the energy question is not simply 'at its core, a human question' (Petrocultures Research Group 2016) but rather a question that engages all creatures from animal to plant life. The question of energy transition from the fossil fuel economy is therefore one that engages us within our own and different cultures and beyond to more-than-human life-worlds.

Connection to other entries:
Convergences
Geontopower
Humus Economicus

Josephine Taylor

POSTCOLONIAL AND DECOLONIAL COMPUTING

The history and politics of computing have been relative latecomers to postcolonial and decolonial analyses, despite the centrality of information and communications technologies to the foundations of global capitalism and imperialism (Adas 2015). Although postcolonial and decolonial approaches to computing differ in their geographic and temporal focus, both challenge the prevailing Eurocentric humanist rhetorics of universalism and development. Postcolonial and decolonial critiques allow us to trace the lineages of today's global information economy to the 500-year long history of European and American colonialism rooted in dehumanization, violence and extraction.

Psychiatrist and political philosopher Franz Fanon argues: 'In the colonies the economic infrastructure is also the superstructure. The cause is effect. You are rich because you are white and you are white because you are rich. This is why a Marxist analysis should always be a little stretched when it comes to addressing the colonial issue' (Fanon 1963: 40). Applying this argument to information technology, we need to 'stretch' our existing analyses of computing to account for the ways in which the history of colonialism renders capitalist infrastructure as superstructure. As the underbelly of the 'information economy' and misinformation have captured public attention, today there is growing scholarly interest in addressing the historical absence of analysis of settler colonialism, chattel slavery and imperialism in relation to computing, past and present (e.g. Alhassan and Chakravarty 2011; Arough 2012; Kuntsman and Stein 2015; Parks and Kaplan 2017).

Political Economists have documented the late-nineteenth-century inter-imperial rivalries between European colonial powers and the rising economic and military power of the US as they competed over underwater cable companies, telecom companies and news agency cartels and internationalized communications infrastructure (Hills 2010; Winseck and Pike 2007). This work holds that imperial expansion is explained by cooperation and collusion amongst private firms to expand networks across Africa, Asia and Latin America, but sidesteps Fanon's insight that we must stretch the analysis to account for the legacies of what Cedric Robinson calls 'racial capitalism' (2020). In contrast, Black feminist scholars like Simone Browne (2015) and Ruha Benjamin (2019) have effectively traced the continuities between racialized commercial information infrastructure, for example from the Brooks slave ship, to the design, operation and implementation of biometric identification or proprietary algorithms of policing and detention. Business historians such as Caitlin Rosenthal have argued that modern accounting, 'quantitative management', and other information technologies arose in the context of plantation slavery prior to that of the industrial factory (Rosenthal 2018). Similarly, Indigenous studies scholars have challenged the race neutral or 'anti racialism' that obfuscates the racial and colonial hierarchies that shape contemporary struggles waged by Indigenous communities over their own data and intellectual property (Reardon and Tallbear 2012).

Writing in the 2010 landscape of digital and mobile media, Lilly Irani, Janet Vertesi, Paul Dourish, Kavita Philip, and Rebecca Grinter (2010) launched a broad scholarly conversation about postcolonial computing with their publication of 'Postcolonial Computing: A Lens on Design and Development'. Addressed to the human–computer interaction (HCI) community, this article urged a shift from 'development' thinking to a design sensibility founded on postcolonial theory, by which they meant attention to colonial legacies in all aspects of computing. Mineral, labour and knowledge extraction from former colonies; colonial rhetorics of 'assistance' and 'development' that accrue capital for old centres of power in new processes of technology transfer; longstanding biases concretized in high tech design – these are the typical practices of computing in the postcolonial period, which postcolonial theory critiques and revises.

Philip, Irani and Dourish followed up with a 2012 article on 'Postcolonial Computing: A Tactical Survey', published in *Science, Technology, & Human Values* and aimed at a more interdisciplinary audience. A critical Postcolonial Computing, they argued, frames objects of computing in terms of political economy; foregrounds tech work and other forms of labour in narratives of technology; looks for 'alternative practices' of design and technical diffusion (without romanticizing them); and understands innovation in capacious terms not defined by market logics. In the last ten years, scholars have amassed a robust set of case studies regarding the colonial politics embedded in computing artefacts, from anglophone linguistic imperialism in operating systems to software based on white prototypes and datasets. Others trace colonial patterns in all aspects of computer supply chains and disposal, from idea theft to pollution from e-waste. In another vein, still other scholars emphasize maintenance and repair over 'innovation', and document the complexities of use and non-use (from personalization and piracy to forced use to exclusion and resistance).

More recently, scholars of computing have taken up decolonial theory, formulated by critical and Indigenous scholars tracing the long history of Spanish and Portuguese, in addition to British and French, settler colonialism across the Americas, Australia and the Asia Pacific islands. Decolonial computing refers not only to sovereignty and self-reliance over land, labour and resources but to the 'decentring' of Western humanist epistemologies and ontologies to consider non-capitalist, non-extractivist, Indigenous and other subaltern worldviews and practices.

As Anita Say Chan (2018) explains, a decolonial approach to computing has 'potential not only in recognizing the diverse vibrancy of existing challenges to 'digital universalist' models that problematically elevate narrow versions of Western and elite digital practice and innovation as the only relevant pathway to the future, but in cultivating knowledge practices that indeed foster a decentring of the self as a generative asset towards the creative co-production of alternative futures.' We have asked whether computing technology – the embodiment of rational calculation and a driver of post-industrial global capitalism – can indeed be stretched, even overhauled or appropriated for decolonial ends (Chakravartty 2018). Chan (2018) looks to Indigenous language software and collaborative computing practices in Latin America as examples. Indigenous activists and decolonial scholars have launched numerous projects around the world to 'decolonize data', from asserting control over healthcare data collection to reframing the datasets that train and drive AI (artificial intelligence) to visualizing 'cartographic sovereignty' (Bonilla and Hantel

2016). Other scholars, such as Mustafa Ali (2021), Miriyam Arough (2012) and Aouragh et al. (2020) and Nick Couldry and Ulijes Meijas (2019), emphasize the decolonial critique of extractive computing and big tech giants, specifically the colonial military and racial capitalist logics at work at every level from algorithms to contact tracing to internet governance. The vertiginous scale of Big Tech is exactly what new projects for postcolonial and decolonial computing face.

Connection to other entries:
New Materialist Informatics
Pattern Discrimination
Posthuman Data
Posthumanism and Design
Racializing Assemblages
Surface Orientations

Paula Chakravartty and Mara Mills

POSTCOLONIAL DRONE SCHOLARSHIP

Traditionally, the human subject has been deemed the central subject of the humanities. The posthuman turn has, however, challenged this idea, calling for the humanities to consider more thoroughly the more-than-human (Braidotti 2013, 2019). However, a question remains around how one can foster the post-humanities when many are yet to be recognized as fully human within the vast swathe of the humanities (Sundberg 2014). While some scholars of the posthuman turn have worked to ensure that inequalities between humans remain a central focus of posthuman scholarship, with those drawing on postcolonial and feminist traditions being the most prominent voices here (e.g. Braidotti 2022; Amaro 2018; Bignall and Rigney 2019; Alaimo 2010; Jones 2018b), others have, in their turn to the non-human, side-lined those that have never achieved full access to so-called humanity (e.g. see Choat 2017). This question of focus is extremely poignant when considering posthuman scholarship on drone warfare, especially given that the necropolitical impact of drone warfare is felt in the Global South yet often theorized in the Global North. While posthuman approaches to technology have sought to challenge hierarchical relationships between the human and the technological (though not always to render them the same), this approach, without first recognizing 'monohumanism' (Wynter 2003), or the differences between humans (Steyn and Mpofu 2021) risks manifesting as a one-way subjugation process on the subaltern body who has already been pre-excluded from the so-called universalism of 'humanity' (Monirul 2016).

The existing literature on technological warfare spans a myriad of disciplines and sub-fields, making mapping the literature a difficult task. Broadly, however, a few common themes emerge. One core theme is that this literature often centres US foreign policy in its analysis and is primarily concerned with the strategic implications of warfare on geopolitics and foreign policy (Boyle 2015; Zegart 2018). Other works ponder the compatibility of drone warfare with Western democratic governance (Sauer and Schörnig 2012) while evaluating the morality of drone operators (Enemark 2020). It is clear that most of the literature on drone warfare, in line with US foreign policy rhetoric, is oblivious to the orientalist assumptions (Espinoza 2018) that inform the US drone

programme, and which label the loss of human lives as 'casualties' and 'collateral damage' (Crawford 2013).

In contrast, critical work on drone warfare shows how the 'out of sight, out of mind' approach (Saha 2019) and its minimization of 'boots on the ground' (Buchanan and Koehane 2015) result in the construction of drone warfare as a more 'humane' method of warfare (Nair 2017). Likewise, the portrayal of drone strikes as 'clean' and 'precise' in US media outlets (Sheets et al. 2015) has led to the conflation of the efficacy of drone warfare with ethicality (Zehfuss 2011). On the other hand, another stream of scholarship can be seen within those works that focus on the drone operator and on drone warfare's 'radical asymmetry' (Renic 2018), asking whether remote killing disengages drone personnel from the killing itself (Holmqvist 2013). Likewise, several works ponder drone operators' (dis)identification with ground troops and the (de)humanization of victims (Gregory 2012; Wilcox 2015). Drone warfare's emotional toll on drone operators and the latter's susceptibility to developing PTSD are largely explored themes here (Chapelle et al. 2014; Bayard de Volo 2016; Bentley 2018; Hijazee et al. 2019). On this note, Alex Edney-Browne (2017: 29) ponders the ethical implications of addressing drone personnel's mental health and reminds us of the 'leakiness of human-technology interaction, including the possibility for counter-hegemonic resistance within hegemonic technological apparatuses'. As far as this literature goes, and although critical on the surface, it still centres the drone operator/perpetrator in its analysis. This centring, when juxtaposed with the discourse of drone operators' mental well-being and their empathy with the bodies they kill, stirs a rightful anger and prompts Gregoire Chamayou (2015: 108) to question military psychologists' insistence on adding a 'layer of humanity to an instrument of mechanized homicide'.

Conversely, several important works, many of which draw greatly on posthuman theory, emphasize the biopolitics and (dis) embodied long-term implications of surveillance technology (Shaw 2013; Wilcox 2015). Similarly, critical feminists engage posthuman paradigms to move the conversation on technological warfare away from limited and limiting realist interpretations of warfare by showing how objects, subjects, nature and technology interact relationally. They successfully challenge the myth of the drone's 'God-trick' (Haraway 1988: 586) of an all-seeing eye by uncovering the skewed (gendered, racialized, sexed) algorithmic calculations of drone operators (Wilcox 2017a). They also successfully challenge the myth of technology's refinement by exposing the reiteration of existing unequal gender dynamics, notably the masculine/feminine binary, in drone warfare (Bayard de Volo 2016; Manjikian 2014) and in Robotics industries (Roff 2016), and the recreation of the battlefield's masculinist standards through the use of assistive technologies for returning soldiers (Heathcote 2018). By rendering visible the futuristic workings of intimate systems of power, these authors successfully caution us against the possibility of equally racialized, sexed and gendered futures. Such works are unquestionably motivated by and geared towards uncovering the seemingly innocent alienation that novel technologies produce – a task they largely succeed in. Nevertheless, much of this scholarship continues to privilege a particular human–non-human assemblage above all others; namely, the drone operator cyborg and the ontological security of the liberal subject at the expense of the postcolonial subject (Agius 2017).

In permanently occupied territories, from Gaza and Syria to Iraq, the nature/culture divide – one of the main pillars of drone warfare scholarship – never took hold to begin with. In these geographies, the human, the animal, the natural, and buildings and ruins constitute a singular matter, that of the terrorist, the brown, the other. The geographical border entraps them, besieges them, and fuses them into one singular mass. There is no place to hide. The inside is terrorist. The outside is terrorist. The in-between space is terrorist.

To think the self as 'reassembled and disassembled' in line with Haraway's (1988) cyborg, is to acknowledge the workings of human–non-human assemblages as constantly reaffirming and undoing the oftentimes machine-backed regulatory functions of meta-narratives, state institutions, geopolitics and everyday parlance alike. In a world that relies on estimated natural reserves, automated service economies, speculative financial markets and precarious trusting relations in the realms of diplomacy or political representation for instance, it is imperative that we return to the human, the quintessential analytical unit in the Humanities. Otherwise, we risk losing ourselves in conversations about sexual innuendos (Daggett 2015), overly stated dystopic futures (Allinson 2015), insectoid becomings of drones (Wilcox 2017b) and robots gone rampant (Kroker 2014). The drone is, indeed, 'unbearably human' (Shaw and Akhter 2011) and thus the challenge for posthuman theory remains: how can we adequately theorize the non-human in a world where so many have yet to be recognized as human?

Connection to other entries:
Critical Posthuman Theory
Ontologized Plasticity
Post-humanitarian Law
Swarm Warfare

Sabiha Allouche

POSTHUMAN AGENCY

Anthropocene conditions often seem to call for a misanthropic politics that marginalizes human presence and impact upon the natural world. Yet, humankind is not always humanist and humanity is not an inevitably damaging force. Humanism is a culturally particular philosophical perspective; it aligns with cultures that reify the superiority of human organization as a rational process of separation from natural or animal life, which becomes a mere instrument for human use and development. In fact, the interconnected quality of existence across nature-culture continuums implies that human society has always shaped the natural world, and has itself always been subject to natural powers. The character of this influence depends significantly upon the cultural quality of the connection a human society practices in its environmental codes of conduct and its attitudes to non-human entities. For example, many Indigenous arts of cultivation have for aeons aligned with a science of prudent governance and a conceptualization of legal personhood extending to all life forms, which together safeguard a trade economy of sustainable productivity for flourishing ecologies (Pascoe 2014; Berkes 2012).

Non-humanist conceptualizations of agency and influence have also always been present as submerged strains within Western philosophy and are finding new vitality in contemporary Continental philosophies of posthumanism. For example, Gilles Deleuze (2004, 178) considers agency is not an individual or intentional phenomenon specific to human being; rather, 'the true subject is the structure itself'. As a new kind of 'structuralism', posthumanism 'is not at all a form of thought that suppresses the subject, but one that breaks it up and distributes it systematically, that contests the identity of the subject, that dissipates it and makes it shift from place to place, an always nomad subject' (Deleuze 2004, 190; see also Braidotti 1994). Crucially, this decentred and dispersed subjectivity is not devoid of agency or coherency, and in fact counters the dehumanizing tendencies of neoliberal desubjectivation, 'dividualization' and the radical splintering of collective life that Deleuze (1992) elsewhere identifies as a key feature of a fragmenting and debilitating politics of control. As individuals and as collectives, posthuman subjects are formative processes resulting in dynamic structures, affectively embedded within wider complex systems comprising intercultural, multispecies nature-culture continuums. Humanism defines human being by a set of *properties* essential to Man – his natural autonomy, rationality, competitiveness, possessive individualism and so forth. By contrast, the agential character of posthumanist subjects arises from their material *affects* – their powers of affecting others, and of affection by others – and the type of assemblages they form when participating in the constitutive relations of power comprising an ecology of activity that includes non-human agencies. The posthumanist task in the era of the Anthropocene, then, is not to restore to a damaged system its essential properties, to recover its authentic or essential character; but rather to regenerate and secure beneficial conditions of relational action within the system, overall conducive to the flourishing of life.

Since environments of diversity and complexity enhance affective potential, it follows that these are the enabling conditions we would wish to encourage. However, as colonial histories demonstrate so starkly, affections are not always mutually beneficial or welcome; they can bring sadness and harm, and may even result in complete destruction. Everything at stake in a complex system of affective assemblages hinges upon a sensitive ethics of communication and a just politics of association, through which the different elements comprising the system can coexist in an overall equilibrium without mutual threat of annihilation, or else can learn to combine successfully for mutual benefit (Bignall 2010). In the foreboding context of our global ailments, characterizing the era of the Anthropocene, posthuman subjects must find ways to orient and assemble appropriate constitutive forces for the systematic orchestration of life-affirming futures, materialized in alternative institutions of productive relationality. As Rosi Braidotti (2019) argues regarding the posthuman condition, ethical knowledge formation calls for a strategically selective response to the perfectly coincident possibilities of subjective exhaustion on the one hand, and the affirmative enhancement of networked complexity on the other; these sit together in parallel as twin vectors of advanced technology today. Anthropocene crises call for 'new arts of living on a damaged planet' (Tsing et al. 2017). Such arts suggest against the simplistic removal of imperial-capitalist humanity from the natural system where it is the cause of such extreme injury; rather, the damaged world requires from humanity a self-conscious and responsible effort of 'exit' from the prevailing mode of systemic agency that materializes as 'the structure itself'; and replacement with an alternative disposition towards affective assemblage. Exit humanism, ex-colonialism, xenofeminism: systemic transformation takes place through the effort to make a definitive break from the constituting forces of assemblage that dominate in a problematic structure, to create a dispositional pathway to the outside, enabling a line of flight to an alternative arrangement.

Connection to other entries:
Collaborative Politics
Ex-colonialism
Norms
Relational Sovereignty
Rights of Nature
Transjectivity

Simone Bignall

POSTHUMAN CARE

The notion of environmental care emerges from ecofeminism, inspired by social psychologist Carol Gilligan's idea of a feminist 'ethics of care' (1982) and is developed by moral philosophy and social theory in ways that exceed the original insight into the social role women play as the traditional caretakers of vulnerable humans. This notion was subsequently expanded from a moral virtue to a political value because in a participatory democracy the task of caring in the public realm helps construct responsible citizenship (Tronto and Fisher 1990; Tronto 1995).

Ecofeminists extended the notion of care to the natural environment and non-human entities, radicalizing it in the process. They foresaw the posthuman turn in several interlinked ways: first, by embracing the natural pole of the foundational nature-culture distinction, allowing for collaborative modes of relation to the non-humans. This move started with the reappraisal of the organic animals, plants and the entire planet, but in the course of time it grew into an epistemology that encompasses also inorganic entities such as technological artefacts, networks, codes, and algorithms (Haraway 1997; Donovan and Adams 1995; 2007; Code 2006).

Secondly, they provided a critique of the power of dominant hierarchical dualisms over both subordinate humans and non-humans. Val Plumwood's critique of ecological reason (1993; 2002) expanded the criticism of the instrumental rationalism of masculine techno-culture to the ecological dimension, adding to the charges of sexism and racism the abuse of the non-humans: 'species-ism'. They developed a geo-political and transnational dimension, exposing the links between militarization, violence and environmental degradation (King 1987). Ecofeminists think transversally as well as intersectionally across axes such as sexism, heteronormativity, racism, colonialism and ableism (Gaard 1993). In all these instances, patriarchal culture is called to accountability for the toxic environmental sphere it created and its disregard of the well-being and the rights of sexualized, racialized and naturalized 'others' (Braidotti 2013).

Thirdly, post-anthropocentric ecofeminist thought connects productively with Indigenous systems of thought and ethical values and their distinctive traditions of naturecultural relations and care for the land (Rose 2017; Bawaka Country et al. 2013). They also expose the links between empire, colonial dispossession and the devastation of the environment, stressing the links between colonial genocide and environmental ecocide (Nixon 2011). In all cases they call for more ethical responsibility and for new forms of ethical care for the non-humans (Whyte and Cuomo 2017). Beyond utilitarianism and profit-making, posthuman care stresses a profound gratuitousness as well as a fundamental obligation.

Feminist studies of techno-culture (Lykke and Braidotti 1996; Bryld and Lykke 2000; Tsing et al. 2017; Lykke 2019) also developed posthuman care by stressing responsibility for technological others. This developed into an affect-driven approach to scientific research and writing that addresses both technological mediation and environmental care. Care for and with technologies have also been addressed by Indigenous thinkers (Carroll et al. 2020; Abdilla et al. 2020).

Posthuman notions of care ethics build on these feminist genealogies and emphasize mutual trans-species interdependence and ontological relationality. Posthuman care highlights relationality and interdependence, challenges anthropocentric and universalist moral notions, and proposes posthuman (speculative) ethics of care for a more-than-human world. It entails caring for non-humans, more-than-humans, dehumanized and other humans alike and thus challenges humanist notions of a bounded individual subject, as well as the anthropocentric bias. A post-binary, cyborg affinity (Haraway 1985) spreads tentacularly (Haraway 2016) across species and organisms. A nomadic transposition beyond the human grounds zoe-egalitarianism (Braidotti 2006); it generates a form of transcorporeality (Alaimo 2010) and requires an ethics of care that is attentive to differences and distribution of power (Puig de la Bellacasa 2017; Martin, Myers and Viseu 2015).

Posthuman care is not without ambivalences and it acknowledges that ethics and practices of care are unevenly distributed and can generate both positive and negative outcomes. It takes into account that discourses of care have been implicated in the projects of colonization and racial oppression (Narayan 1995) and in forms of control of bodies coded as other, such as disabled bodies (Hughes et al. 2005; Kröger 2009). In that, posthuman care aims to critically activate both the role of intersectionality (Raghuram 2019) and inter/dependence (Piepzna-Samarasinha 2018) towards more sustainable and accessible posthuman futures. Posthuman care is significant for re-imagining sustainability in technoecologies (Lorenz-Meyer et al. 2019) and the critical analysis of knowledge production in the posthumanities (Braidotti 2018), in life- and technosciences (Bozalek et al. 2020; Braidotti 2022; Bellacasa 2011; Smith and Willis 2020; Treusch 2020).

The trend in contemporary care politics is to move towards more fluid forms of interrelation across species and organisms and in-between them. A recently launched 'Care Manifesto' (The Care Collective 2020) pleads for universal care as a political principle that needs to be made operative at every level and scale of contemporary societies. It offers a queer-feminist, anti-racist, eco-socialist vision of alternative communities committed to nurture all that is necessary for the flourishing of human and non-human lives.

Connection to other entries:
Critical Posthuman Theory
Empathy Beyond the Human
Intergenerational Justice and Care
Posthuman Agency
Transcorporeality II

Rosi Braidotti and Goda Klumbytė

POSTHUMAN DATA

Datafication runs through our posthuman times. To refer to posthuman data helps to understand both the critical stakes in gendered and racialized practices of artificial intelligence (AI) and the progressive possibilities in affirming different futures. This includes understanding how data-based societies turn both humans and non-humans into sensorial and affective nodes (c.f. Massumi 2015) or data points in a manner which runs contrary to the idea of subjects and objects vested in liberal concepts of society, including law (Lessig 1999; Hildebrandt 2015). As Crawford and Joler (2018) put it, the current form of data extractivism reaches 'into the furthest corners of the biosphere and the deepest layers of human and cognitive and affective being.' Training data is however needed for teaching our smart environments and machines how to behave. How the collected data is to be put in use, whether it is big, personal or relational, determines which forms of futures are prescribed. Very little legislative intervention on which data can be used to create automation has been carried out so far even if change might be on its way in the EU, via the recently proposed Regulation of Artificial Intelligence (EU 2021). As for now, we however find ourselves living under a system where the free flows of information are captured by private property regimes whether via explicit intellectual property right claims or via the contracts and technologies sustaining platform power (c.f. Srnicek 2017). Furthermore, the recent proposals of how to govern data, points at a reaffirming of the human, or as the recent EU proposal suggests: to put *the human* in the centre for evaluating AI, meanwhile keeping the aspects of data as a capitalist resource intact.

A posthuman understanding of data emerges from the view that data extraction runs on capitalist, colonial and sexist practices that link processes of extraction to the bodies from which it was derived and depends upon (Käll 2017b). As such, this puts posthumanist theory in dialogue with the field of critical data and algorithm studies in which it more recently has been demonstrated how both data collection and governance risks reiterating racialized and gendered assumptions. As such studies show, both for example women as well as persons of colour are stereotypically categorized in image data sets or image recognition (e.g. Benjamin 2019; Noble 2018). When knowledge is turned into data and fed into the systems bringing us automated forms of governance, those systems lock in the assumptions of an inequal society, and rebuilds it along the same lines.

Aligned with its affirmative endeavours, a posthuman perspective on data however also shows the capacities that data extraction and use could mobilize different imaginaries, legal realities, and material combinations of bodies and desires. This implies both to put data into use for creating different visualizations of alternative lives and even species to suggest that other desires could be released from the current limited imaginaries capitalism makes of our data. Artists have been particularly active in using data and AI in the wider sense to show how alternative lives and species could be envisioned. For example, in their project, Bhowmik and Hautamäki use GAN (Generative Adversarial Network), where two neural networks (Generative and Discriminative) recreate new species of birds based on a large dataset of extinct and endangered birds of the Baltic Sea to generate new images and species (Bhowmik and Hautamäki 2021). Furthermore, Jenna Sutela's work 'nimiia ïzinibimi' consists of the creation of a book based on an 'invented new language'. This book is based on a new language representing those who lack first-hand access to, or the ability to produce, 'natural' language, drawing upon Sutela's ongoing experiment in machine learning and interspecies communication (Sutela 2019).

A posthuman imaginary of data however also needs to actively engage in questions of (re)distribution of our collective resources in redefining both what a posthuman collectivity implies and which resources it needs to sustain itself. This redefined understanding of joint needs opens up an avenue for an economy based on shared needs and futures rather than for market-based proprietary and affective control. In this manner, a posthuman data future should directly engage in planning intersectional and post-capitalist futures. The need for such collectivist engagement is becoming apparent not only in terms of the environmental crisis threatening to lead into mass species extinction, but also in relation to the risks of not taking care of how non-human–human entanglements come into being, as the COVID-19 pandemic shows. The data on how a virus spreads, how a cure can jointly be created, how a vaccine could be distributed, all depends on collective understandings of who are to collect data, how it should be shared, and how to act upon it. Furthermore, it also visualizes how data such as inventions of vaccines are also always connected to other materialities needed to make the production of, for example, a vaccine possible: factories, raw materials, workers, logistics, etc. In the currently emerging data sharing regime, we can detect openings for a posthuman future when data is treated as a common cause, beyond both the human and humanist ideals, and subsequently as something in need of a joint cure. The COVID-19 virus which is not a conceptual metaphor, but a very material threat to both human and non-human bodies, is not a unique example. Posthumanist understandings of recreating life under, and against, the conditions of Anthropocene directs our thinking just to the questions of what data can be used, and how, transforms planets like the Earth and beyond. A posthuman data plan understands its materialist foundations and the backlashes implied with not taking questions of shared information and the resources needed to materialize it seriously.

Connection to other entries:
Algorithmic Governmentality
New Materialist Informatics
Pattern Discrimination
Postcolonial and Decolonial Computing
Post-humanitarian Law

Jannice Käll

POSTHUMAN FEMINIST AESTHETICS

Aesthetics (contemplations of artistic values) and aesthesis (subjective archives of sensibilities) are interrelated. In Western modernity, art and literature have been privileged arenas for reflections on aesthesis and humanist claims about universalist aesthetic values. Noting that aesthesis materializes in other kinds of relations too, I shall still refer to art and literature here, but emphasize that turning towards a posthuman feminist aesthetics implies a radical disruption of humanist claims to universalism, and a rethinking of aesthesis and aesthetics as embodied and embedded in specific spatio-temporal situatednesses. Therefore, instead of theorizing emerging new posthuman feminist aestheses and aesthetics from the God's eye position, classically criticized by Donna Haraway (1991), I shall take a bottom-up approach. I shall look for potentially shared grounds in two examples which, across differences, suggest that relationships between aesthetics, ethics, politics, onto-epistemologies and aesthesis, are inextricably entangled in posthuman feminist art and literature.

One example is *Hydrofeminist METitations* (Ensayos 2020), a listening series, enacted by the international art and research collective *Ensayos* (2021), during a digital residency at the New Museum in New York. *Ensayos* was founded in 2011 by Chilean curator, researcher and artist Camila Marambio, but the activities are organized by shifting collectives of artists-activists from different parts of the world. The main theme of the *Hydrofeminist METitations* is water – in its specificities, ranging from a creek in Eastern Australia, to peatbogs in Tierra del Fuego (the arctic archipelago, located at the southernmost tip of the Americas). The focus on specificities of water is aligned with feminist scholar Astrida Neimanis' (2017) posthuman phenomenological exploration of a shared characteristic of humans and other planetary beings: that we are bodies of water. Moreover, the *METitations* are inspired by MET, Mechanical Electrical Transduction, 'a sensory mechanism through which cells convert mechanical stimuli into electro-chemical activity, and which accounts for senses of hearing, balance, and touch' (Ensayos 2020).

The *METitations* invite audiences into a new posthuman eco-aesthesis, which implies a shift from a specifically delineated human perspective to a 'we', comprising all planetary critters existing as bodies of water in each their specific way. The framing also invites listeners to a reflection – meditation – on the relation of the new aesthesis to specific sensory mechanisms, also to be contemplated as posthuman. MET is based on sensory mechanisms, shared by all critters whose mode of experiencing the world is based on hearing, balance and touch.

The posthuman feminist aesthetics, enacted in the *METitations*, is inextricably linked to activism, ethics and politics. To illustrate this, I shall dwell with the peatbogs of Tierra del Fuego, a key protagonist of the third *METitation* (Ensayos 2020). The perspective of peatbogs is voiced, among others, by Indigenous writer, scholar and activist Hema'ny Molina Vargas, president of the Selk'nam Corporation of Chile. The Corporation is an indigenous organization, gathering descendants of the Selk'nam people, a tribe that was indigenous to Tierra del Fuego before colonization and deportation/killing of the island's indigenous population began in the late nineteenth century. Today, the Selk'nam is claiming indigenous rights to return to the island to revitalize their culture and kinship with it. In the *METitation*, Vargas poetically explores her

embodied experience of intimate connectedness with the peatbogs of the island's arctic landscapes, and calls for ecopolitical action to protect them. In a poetic-political manifesto, Vargas tells how embracing the peatbogs has made her develop a new aesthesis, and understanding of their key ecological importance. Planetwide, peatbogs fulfill a crucial ecological task in terms of decreasing the toxicity of the atmosphere through a binding of CO_2 and transforming it to living matter. Against this background, Vargas experiences peatbogs as the liver of the earth, the organ which helps to decompose bodily waste products. Linking onto-epistemology, politics, ethics, aesthetics and aesthesis, Vargas's eco-poetic and decolonial manifesto explores her experience of the earth as a living body of which humans are but one minor part. She aligns this experience with the ways in which her Selk'nam ancestors co-existed with the land, and links to the ethico-political urgency of protecting peatbogs against capitalist extractivism.

While the *METitations* cross-cut borders between art, activism and research, my second example of posthuman feminist aesthetics – a short poetic novel *Havbrevene* [*The Sea Letters*], by Danish writer Siri Ranva Hjelm Jacobsen (2018) – stays within the sphere of literature. But it shares with the *METitations* the dissolution of boundaries between human subject and planetary embodiment. The novel is a meditative correspondence between two seas, the Mediterranean, the younger sister, and the Atlantic, the elder sister, planning to flood the earth because they feel that the experiment which an originally unitary planetary seascape made in terms of creating earth critters, humans in particular, have failed. The failure came about due to human technological *hubris,* represented by the mythic architect Daidalos, who constructed wings for his son Ikaros. Inventiveness turned into destruction, when Ikaros was killed, using his wings to fly too close to the sun.

Across situated differences, I experience a resonance in the posthuman aesthetics of the novel and the *METitations*. Both spell out a key posthuman feminist theme: that humans are existentially embedded in the planetary body. Moreover, they articulate an ethico-political protest against modern human estrangement from and destruction of the planet's body. But instead of speaking from the conventional god-trick position, where the human 'I' sets itself aesthetically and ethico-politically apart, while speaking *about* the world, both artworks voice critique in an affirmative form, exploring a new aesthesis, while speaking *from the inside of* the watery planetbody.

Connection to other entries:
Art and Bioethics
Convergences
Cosmic Artisan
Hydrofeminism
Transcorporeality II
Weird

Nina Lykke

POSTHUMAN INTERNATIONAL LAW AND OUTER SPACE

While scholarship on posthuman theory and international law is a relatively new and emerging field, it is one that is taking shape fast, as exemplified by the many entries on law in this Glossary. Posthuman theory, gender theory and critical environmental law scholarship are especially useful in recasting the debate and thinking through the development of outer space law.

On the critical side, legal scholars argued that the law is fundamentally anthropocentric, prioritizing human interests over all others and casting non-human animals and the material world as objects to be exploited for human, and in particular human economic, interests on this, as on other planets (Jones 2022). While many of the core legal texts on outer space were drafted and agreed upon decades ago, such as the Outer Space Treaty of 1967 and the Moon Agreement of 1979, scientific and technological advances, alongside a new-found will to visit, exploit and dominate space have brought these legal instruments back to the forefront of legal and political debate.

Critical environmental law scholars have noted that international law combines uncritical anthropocentrism with patterns of human exceptionalism. This results in upholding binary oppositions between subjects and objects and downgrading the objects to the status of exploitable resources (Jones 2021; Otto and Jones 2020; Grear 2017). International law is characterized by this constant privileging of human subjects and human interests, including state economic interests, as the ultimate justification for environmental exploitation. Whether it is being protected – as a venerable site – or exploited – as a valuable resource – non-humans and the environment are rendered as objects, albeit differing in status among themselves.

The objectification of the environment within international law not only limits the effect of the legal measures undertaken to protect it under the existing logic of the law, but it also introduces and thus rationalizes other forms of discrimination. For instance, Zylinska argues (2018) that the apocalyptic narratives which surround the Anthropocene are expressions of masculinist and Eurocentric panic. They also show the inability of the dominant social categories to confront vulnerability and fear without denial, scapegoating or aggression.

This deficit in relational competence and ethical care for others can be seen, for example, in the logic of the billionaire tech giants who propose selected human migration to Mars as the solution to climate change. Mars is envisaged as the solution, the place to go once we realize that the resources of planet Earth have been depleted. This applied transhumanist project combines analytic post-anthropocentrism with normative neo-humanism, declaring Gaia defunct and proposing the extension of the old extraction economy to other planets, through massive technological intervention. Human enhancement is an integral part of such an intervention, which is defended as the humanist pursuit of the perfectibility of the human species via science and technology.

The economic-minded transhumanists follow the legacy of humanism in another significant way: by actively disregarding the colonial nature of the policy they propose. Actively deploying the terminology of colonization, venture capitalists such as Elon Musk and Jeff Benzos are indifferent to the echoes of European colonialism in their proposed elite, capital-intensive, white male utopia on Mars (see Storr 2021).

This is where creative international law responses have been made, for instance, by posthuman legal theorists, to counter-act the omissions and slippages that mark the attempts to legalize intergalactic mining and extraction practices. For instance, feminist scholars have called for a feminist founding constitution for Mars, noting the need to avoid the perpetuation of past and existing inequalities (Braidotti 2022; Yoshida 2018; Jones 2018a; McNeily 2018). A feminist constitution for Mars is a great idea on the one hand, but like any universalist project it is not very realistic in that, in founding a constitution, decisions will have to be made about how things are decided, how things are owned (or not) and who by. Moreover, while a feminist constitution may seek to resist traditional modes of property and power (O'Donoghue and Houghton 2019a, 2019b), on another level, this seems impossible in the context of, ultimately, the colonization of Mars. After all, whether this colonization is led by feminists or not, it remains colonial and therefore is inherently anti-feminist from a critical feminist perspective (Jones 2018a).

Let us keep in mind that, under existing legal provisions, outer space is deemed to be part of the global commons. This means it is held in common by all of humanity and it therefore cannot be used for commercial exploitation (The Outer Space Treaty 1967; The Moon Agreement 1979). Such a provision seems promising, potentially providing a new way of understanding property. However, this alternative vision is already being challenged before we have even properly gotten to Mars. The US, for one, has made recent attempts to shift this long-held view in international law that outer space is part of the global commons. In 2020, following an Executive Order by President Trump a few months earlier which called for the inclusion of commercial partners in space exploration and encouraging exploration of space mining (US Federal Register 2020), NASA released the Artemis Accords (2020). The Accords aim to 'establish a common set of principles to govern the civil use of outer space', seeking to 'facilitate exploration, science, and commercial activities for the benefit of humanity'. The Accords propose a series of bilateral agreements in which 'partner nations' agree to follow US-drafted rules (Ibid.).

The move away from ideas of shared cooperation and ownership, towards a property-based model which sees outer space as the next commercial frontier, blatantly contradicts the transhumanist capitalists' claim that they are motivated by ethical concern for the future of humanity. They rather appear to work to uphold and perpetuate the anthropocentric nature of international law, whereby matter, outer space, is seen as an object to be exploited for economic benefit. Given, however, that the underlying anthropocentrism of international law, has caused and justified vast environmental degradation, it is evident that anthropocentric, capitalist outer space laws and the great colonization of space cannot provide the solution to the journey towards destroying the planet that humanity is on course to complete. To try to present this project as compatible with humanism, moreover, only adds insult to injury.

It may be more effective, as Zylinska notes, to exit the humanist script altogether, while embracing the post-anthropocentric mode, to propose instead a 'feminist counterapocalypse' in the here and now (Zylinska 2018, 53). Nietzschean in character, this counterapocalypse introduces patterns of repetition with a difference, seeking to 'interrupt the habit' of the eternal return of the apocalypse, that is to say the flat replication of practices that have already failed on earth (Keller 2004,

19). Zylinska's counterapocalypse finds resolution in theories of posthuman relationality, that challenge the epistemic basis of the law itself and explode its contradictions. If humanity and its non-human companions are to move beyond the same old story of masculinism, sexism, colonization, racism, speciesism and so on, the rejection of anthropocentrism needs to be brought in line with the critique of humanism and more especially of its contemporary extra-galactic transhumanist crusaders.

Connection to other entries:
EcoLaw
Geoengineering
Post-humanitarian Law
Rights of Nature

Emily Jones and Rosi Braidotti

POST-HUMANITARIAN LAW

Law is divided into a range of areas contingent on the issues covered as well as the relations sought to be regulated. International law – the legal field to which post-humanitarian international law aims to contribute – is a broad set of different laws regulating issues that cut across national borders affecting relations between nation states. Post-humanitarian international law departs from the existing international laws of war and conflict known as International Humanitarian Law (IHL). Post-humanitarian law therefore seeks to engage with these laws on conflict (and hence has a more specific focus than Posthuman Law which refers to law more broadly). The ethical and normative move from IHL towards a post-humanitarian version is guided by the realization that warfare is already a posthuman practice inclusive of, for example, advanced and semi-autonomous weapons systems – such as drones – operating in collaboration with artificially enhanced more-than-human warfighters (Arvidsson 2018, 2020, Bourke 2014, Wilcox 2017b). The latter are part of militarized visions of e.g. the neuro- and tech-enhanced humans embedded within the state apparatus of governance, violence, and surveillance (Heathcote 2018, Jones 2018b, Noll 2014). If law is to order violence and warfare in any meaningful way it must be able to recognize contemporary warfare practices. It must, moreover, be able to recognize all the different entities that warfare and other violent eruptions expose to lethal danger if it is to offer any protection to these. Hence, other forms and figurations than those already recognized and ordered by IHL must be taken into account. While the problem is recognized by some legal scholars the vision of a post-humanitarian international law is yet to become materialized and gain normative force.

In order to achieve its aims, post-humanitarian international law seeks to do away with some of the central tenants of modern law. *First*: it emulates and follows that which it seeks to order – just as life and death defies nation-state borders, so must the law. The state-based modern law is therefore shifted towards what is known as transnational law (Zumbansen 2020). The defining character of the latter is that it orders actions and events that transcends national borders without hinging on the nation state as its main organizational unit. *Second*: 'The human as law' telos is decentred and becomes one among many entities recognized by the law. Still, the human is held responsible on account of a privileged position and, to varying degrees,

culpability (Philippopoulos-Mihalopoulos 2017). Rather than adding ever-more objects to an increasing array of laws specializing in protection of objects of 'minor' importance (in relation to the human), the post-humanitarian international legal vision is one of offering recognition on non-hierarchical basis (Davis 2017: 451). *Third*: The exclusive recognition of human agency – and states as its extensions – is exchanged for a wider recognition of agents and agency, both digital and material (Käll 2017a).

Drawing on Rosi Braidotti's posthuman feminist theory (Braidotti 2019, 2013) post-humanitarian law takes seriously the ontological shift needed in order to move away from IHL, towards a law worthy of our time and condition. To this end post-humanitarian law offers a framework of norms applicable during situations of war, conflict as well as other instances of violent eruptions. The latter include guerrilla warfare, 'natural' disasters such as volcanic eruptions, pandemics caused by a mutating virus spreading throughout the globe, and cybernetic as well as human–artificially intelligent warfare (Arvidsson and Sjöstedt forthcoming). Beyond the scope proper to IHL, post-humanitarian international law expands to conditions currently governed, in part, by a range of other laws: international relief and disaster law, (international) environmental law, the law of the seas, space law, animal protection law, refugee law and more (see Arvidsson and Jones 2022). Each of these fields of law seek to order situations in which potentially lethal forces are set in motion in relation to conflicting claims of being and becoming in the same place at the same time. Yet, none of the fields of laws are able to recognize, describe (Orford 2012), properly address or order violent forces set in motion in the posthuman condition.

A central tenant of the ontological shift entailed in the move from IHL to a post-humanitarian law is the possibility to move beyond the human as law's ultimate genesis, telos, primary object of protection as well as custodian of all things worthy of recognition. Post-humanitarian law thus builds on a critique of both humanism and anthropocentrism. The law that post-humanitarian international law seek to supersede is that *of* the Anthropocene, as Anna Grear puts it: 'law as coloniality and neo-coloniality – law complicit in ongoing forms of eco-violence, economic predation and the unparalleled imposition of precarity on humans and non-humans alike' (Grear 2020: 3). Posthuman and new materialist legal scholars have increasingly criticized the *anthropos* of the law of the Anthropocene 'for whom all other life systems exist as objects' (Grear 2015: 225. See also: Chapeaux et al. forthcoming). The urge towards law and its scholarship is to hold humans responsible, on account of their privileged position, while affording normative regulation and distribution of fair and equal standing to non-human and more-than-human entities and eruptions alike. Post-humanitarian international law is a response to that call. Other attempts towards similar inclusions of posthuman ethical ends in terms of law and warfare include the scholarships of Emily Jones (2018b) and Gina Heathcote (2018).

Connection to other entries:
Postcolonial Drone Scholarship
Posthuman International Law and Outer Space
Swarm Warfare

Matilda Arvidsson

POSTHUMAN NURSING

Posthuman nursing is a response to the way in which health and well-being have come to be technologically mediated and commodified in recent times. Biopolitical authority has shifted from the church, to medicine, to the State, to the self and now to the laboratory. Within quantified neoliberal healthcare, everything is monetarized and subjects are held responsible for their own health in an increasingly data-driven system. Nursing has developed alongside these changes to integrate them into codes of conduct. Professional practices and paradigms of care such as person-centred care (McCormack and McCance 2010). These axioms of care are now so common-place that practitioners lose the broader picture, so that the quantified neoliberal subject is unchallenged.

Person-centred care emerged in healthcare in the 1990s and quickly became the dominant global paradigm in health systems. Person-centred care emphasizes the rationality and decision making of the service user of care. The concept pushes to consider patients as cultural and social beings, exceeding symptoms, illness or their materiality. This approach shifts from one narrow perception to another – from a medical subject to a rational agent. The explicit power relations of healthcare providers are obscured by giving them the appearance that they are choices to be made by an appropriately advised and educated patient but excludes the materiality, vulnerabilities or possibilities of their situations. This does not mean that such power relations stop existing nor that the existence of such power relations are necessarily nefarious. Nor does this mean that this advocates for neglecting a patient's perspective.

The professionalization of nursing has fixed an idea of a nurse in the contemporary collective and legislative imagination. Nursing codes of conduct, which are components of a professionalized workforce, enshrine the sacrificial logic of the nurse as a care-taker, into nursing practice. In this way, the process of the professionalization of nursing has created the idealized nurse. As the Vitruvian man is an advanced capitalist version of the ideal human (Braidotti 2013), the Vitruvian nurse is produced within the professionalization of nursing as an axiomatic mechanism to govern care. The idea of a self-sacrificing, uniformed, female nurse who's subjectivity is restricted by the desire to care for others. Contemporary health systems maintain these ideas with iconography such as Florence Nightingale. This is colonial, patriarchal and reproduces problematic knowledge production systems i.e. the white European male mutates into the white European female nurse, and is the perfect nurse that is the benchmark of 'good care'. Diverse feminine histories are overwritten to create care as a branded commodity.

Nursing navigates and (re)negotiates the histories and materialities of a space. In order to approach nursing with critical posthumanism, there are three posthuman assumptions to be made (Braidotti 2013): First, all matter is one but not the same. Still, there is a difference in how matter assembles and this is not to negate the existence of individuality in humans nor the human itself. Second, perceiving the world in dichotomous ways (either or), limits us in understanding its complexity. Thus, humans are deeply reciprocal, inter- and intradependent of humans and more-than-humans. And, third, just as there is no central design or centre in the human

itself, there is no centre in the assemblage of human life. Rather, humans live with other humans and more-than-humans and make worlds, while doing so. This approach can (re)configure two central concepts in contemporary nursing practice; person-centred care and professional practice.

Posthuman nursing resists the trend towards neoliberal healthcare by challenging us to continue to ask questions about caring for ourselves, caring for others and caring for our environments. Posthuman nursing draws upon posthuman theory by stressing that caring for humans is implicated in the human, and the more-than-human. For example, consider a patient with a chest infection; the nurse may administer intravenous antibiotics three times a day, in order to reduce the amount of bacteria in the patients' lungs. The nurse is working at the convergence of their own being, the patients being, the powders and liquids to mix the drugs, the hospital environment, the needles, the hospital bed etc. The care of the patient in this scenario, is also the care of the bacteria in their chest – the materiality of the environment is worked with to reduce the number of bacteria so that they return to a level that does not threaten the 'ongoingness' of the patient. It is highly uncommon or unlikely that a treatment would eradicate the bacteria, moreover, return to a sympoetic state where multispecies can exist together (Haraway 2016).

Posthuman nursing is situated in broader feminist histories of care ethics, approaching nursing with the work of scholars such as Wynter, Plumwood, Gilligan, Young, Bird Rose and most recently Puig de la Bellacasa, to understand that *self-determination does not mean self-sufficiency* (McKittrick 2015; Plumwood 1993; Gilligan 1982; Rose 2012;

Puig de la Bellacasa 2017). Much like when Copernicus said that the sun does not go round the earth, the world does not orbit a single person (Smith and Willis 2020), posthuman nursing implicates people and nurses in their situation; however, within dynamic constellations. Posthuman nursing works with materiality, relationships and accountabilities for the positions we inhabit. Practicalities of care and nurse work can help us understand worldmaking with posthuman philosophies and knowledge production. Nurse work is an opportunity to make the posthumanism perceptible by demonstrating the affirmative ethics of situated and affective material practices that are implicated in relationality and materiality.

Connection to other entries:
Empathy Beyond the Human
Intergenerational Justice and Care
Posthuman Care
Transcorporeality II

Jamie B. Smith

POSTHUMAN PUBLICS

Posthuman Publics is a feminist, relational, speculative convergence of art, science, technology and public space. It is informed by laboratories established as test sites of creative practice on the edges of remediating post-industrial urban sites. Posthuman Publics can creatively reveal human and non-human entanglements of public space that enable us to understand public space as more than just a back-drop to our lives. Interdisciplinary creative collaborations constitute territories where human and non-human entanglements offer new

knowledges of public space for and of our times.

Doreen Massey defines space as 'the sphere of coexistence of a multiplicity of trajectories ... always and ever open, constantly in a process of being made' (Massey 2005: 9). Posthuman Publics invites interdisciplinary practitioners to attune to the multiplicity of trajectories of public space. Massey affirms – 'the way we think about space matters' (2005: 9). Already a convergence, Alaimo's 'transcorporeality means that all creatures, as embodied beings, are intermeshed with the dynamic, material world, which crosses through them, transforms them and is transformed by them' (Alaimo 2018: 435).

Thinking through Posthuman Publics, I consider the multiplicity of trajectories through Alaimo's convergent thinking: transcorporeality and the experimental capacity the laboratory offers to ephemeral creative practices of the public sphere.

The *Posthuman Glossary* (Braidotti and Hlavajova 2018) maps a cartography of art/science collaborations. In 'Art and the Anthropocene', Heather Davis posits art as a 'polyarchic site of experimentation for living in a damaged world' (2018:64). In 'Biological Arts/Living Arts', Oron Catts describes the relationship of artists to scientific laboratories as he maps out a lively and diverse field of creative practices that work in a multiplicity of ways with 'life and living systems as both subject and object' (Catts 2018: 67). On vibrant matter, Jane Bennett asserts 'the locus of agency as always a human and non-human collective' (448).

In relation to public art practices, Patricia Phillips's article 'Temporality and Public Art', suggests 'temporary practices stimulate the idea of a research laboratory' (1989: 331). In 'Cartographies of

Environmental Arts', Jussi Parikka creates a cartography of how the laboratory can 'frame artistic activity' while 'recreating situations where transdisciplinary knowledge is circulated' (Parikka 2018:54). He contends 'the laboratory maps across planetary space and becomes one way of articulating what forms of knowledge are necessary for us to 'scale up' to respond to the particular difficult, complex and multilayered problems of the Anthropocene (55). Posthuman Publics shape interdisciplinary laboratories in and of the public realm, where art/science/technology activisms create 'sympoeitic practices for living on a damaged planet'. (Tsing et al. 2017: M31)

Posthuman Publics draws inspiration from the work of Eben Kirksey, Thom Van Dooren and Ursula Münster and the lively 'collaborative associations' they have ceded and nurtured through Multispecies Ethnography (van Dooren et al. 2016: 3). They describe Multispecies Ethnography as standing apart from Animal Studies through a focus on:

> the multitudes of lively agents that bring one another into being through entangled relations that include, but always also exceed, dynamics of predator and prey, parasite and host, researcher and researched, symbiotic partner, or indifferent neighbour.
>
> **van Dooren et al. 2016: 3**

I expand the multispecies thinking with a specific focus on public space, where 'the idea of public is the genesis and subject for analysis.' (Phillips 1989: 332)

Recently published 'The Feral Atlas'; an interdisciplinary project by Anna Tsing, Jennifer Deger, Alder Saxena Keleman and Feifei Zhou, offers new ways of thinking through 'feral ecologies' exploring 'relationships between ferality and imperial and industrial infrastructure' (Tsing et al. 2021). These projects create an already interdisciplinary international network for Posthuman Publics.

Through Posthuman Publics, I have come to know Noctiluca scintillans as my companion species (Haraway 2003). As bioluminescent dinoflagellates, the conditions for their bloom are the warming waters of climate change, the effluent of industry and human habitation, and excesses of nitrogen present in the wake of the Anthropocene. I am literally immersed in a trans-corporeal assemblage with and through my companion species.

As a practicing public artist, I have been engaging in trans-corporeal entanglements of the biosphere. From the shores of an industrial harbour to science laboratories, locally and internationally, I have learned to understand my companion species' lifecycle, I have learned to think with and listen to their glow. I feel their 'shimmer' as we co-constitute a shoreline's affect, lit up by thousands of glowing single-celled organisms. Their presence nomadic in nature, reliant on the wind and the tide, the Noctiluca scintillans, cloudy red waters by day, glow blue in the evening's crashing waves, this is quite literally the 'shimmer' of climate change.

I borrow the term 'shimmer' from Debra Bird Rose (2017: G51). She describes the 'shimmer of the biosphere' as the shimmer of life: 'an aboriginal aesthetic that calls us into this multispecies world', translated from an Indigenous Australian term *Bir'yun* from the cosmology of the Yolngu people (Bird Rose 2017: G53). The humanist colonial project has devastating, lasting impacts for traditional owners of Australia. In an article commissioned as a provocation for the first iteration of Posthuman Publics, Simone Bignall talks about ethical decolonial alliances for our times; 'Commonly motivated in resistance to an intolerable present shaped by colonial humanism, a shared impetus is to forge decolonial alliances between the divergent positionalities described by Continental feminist posthumanism and aboriginal traditions of non-humanist knowledge and environmental governance' (Bignall 2020: 5). Such alliances are critical to the work of Posthuman Publics.

Posthuman Publics explores how interdisciplinary laboratories create attentive registers for the abstraction of ordinary experiences and spaces that allow artists and audiences to co-constitute the possibility of something other. Triggering fleeting transformative acts of imagination, or moments for recuperation within and through ephemeral public practice, Posthuman Publics is an experiment in 'staying with the trouble' (Haraway 2016) while 'living and dying on a damaged planet' (Tsing et al. 2017).

Connection to other entries:
Feminism and Oceans
Low Tropic Theory
Posthuman Feminist Aesthetics
Transcorporeality II

Fiona Hillary

POSTHUMANISM AND DESIGN

The world is in flux. Everything must be redesigned. It is high time for a rethinking of the category of the human in the field of design (Forlano 2016, 2017b). For the past several decades, human-centred design methods – with a focus on individual needs and customized solutions – have dominated the field, closely tied to making products and services that are 'desirable, feasible and viable' within the frame of neoliberal capitalism. This focus on the human in contrast to earlier periods of tech-driven or designer-driven design was an important shift in the early 1990s. And, there are many areas – such as architecture and healthcare, for example – in which human-centred design may still provide significant benefits and improve lives, despite the well-known tendencies towards increased inequality and wealth accumulation.

Computer scientists have recently adopted the language of human-centredness in order to sell their research on artificial intelligence, making the claim that they seek to benefit humanity rather than increase bias and inequality. Yet, the human at the centre of design is currently being questioned from a variety of perspectives, which have prompted discussions about alternative modes of thinking and being. These include: the Anthropocene, cyborg theory (Haraway 1991), posthumanism (Braidotti 2013), more than human, other than human (Todd 2015) and beyond the human (Jackson 2020).

Posthumanism has great potential to orient the design field towards more relational and hybrid ways of thinking, thereby reconfiguring, challenging and expanding the category of the human inherited from Western, European Enlightenment philosophy. Specifically, much of what is understood to be 'human' (and distinct from non-human or animal) over the past several hundred years is coded as white, male, wealthy, young, heterosexual and able-bodied. As the field of design aspired to be more scientific and research driven, it also reified abstract, rational and universal conceptions of the human (Rosner 2018). While designers aspire to truly understand the humans at the centre of their designs, in actuality, too much of the world is designed around default settings.

Posthumanism – from actor-network theory to object-oriented ontology, feminist new materialism, non-representational geography and, even, perhaps transhumanism – is useful for describing and understanding the nature of living with emerging technologies such as artificial intelligence that are (in some instances such as my own (Forlano 2020, 2017b, 2018)) deeply embedded in our bodies, participating in the shaping of our minds, and creating the infrastructures that mediate our experiences of the world. At the same time, it offers ways of thinking differently about the ongoing and intensifying climate crisis and our relationship with the world of microbes, plants and animals and the natural world. Both of these topics explode the field of human-centred design by moving away from the sole focus on the discrete individual's needs and towards a consideration of our role as participants in socio-technical and ecological systems, deeply complicated and entangled ways of living with the world around us.

Posthumanism opens multiple ways to question our relationship with knowledge production (Wakkary 2020), technologies such as the robots, internet of things, machine learning and artificial intelligence (DiSalvo and Lukens 2011; Frauenberger 2019; Giaccardi and Redström 2020), smart cities and ecologies (Heitlinger et al. 2018) and multispecies relationships (Galloway and Caudwell 2018; Smith et al. 2017).

But, in design's rush to embrace posthumanism, it risks orienting towards a new kind of abstract, totalizing and universalizing language that serves mainly to exclude (Todd 2015). The posthuman should not be a new 'centre' around which the design field should orient. In fact, this seems to contradict the most important argument within posthumanism: that it is our relations with the world that matter most. As such, there can be no posthuman-centred design or posthuman design, only a rich dialogue with posthumanism in the field of design that allows us to question our assumptions. Rather than conquering the world with new paradigms of design, we must seek to deliberately decentre, unsettle and destabilize the category of the human itself.

Scholars from feminist technoscience, critical race theory and critical disability theory have offered necessary critiques of both the category of the human as well as the potential harms of merely replacing the white/male/wealthy/young/heterosexual/able-bodied human with a similarly white/male/wealthy/young/heterosexual/able-bodied figure of the posthuman. A closer look at ideas about the social construction of race (Dixon-Roman 2016), gender (Wajcman 2007) and disability (Kafer 2013) allows for a deeper understanding of the ways in which notions of the human as well as those of the posthuman are limiting. Many people's lives have never been included within the walls that have been drawn around the human. We can learn much from scholars, artists and activists that have been fighting for their humanity, ultimately for the benefit of all.

Alongside these concerns it is essential to consider the role of power, politics and participation within the field of design in ways that align with feminism (D'Ignazio and Klein 2020), justice (Costanza-Chock 2020) and the desire for pluriversal worlds

(Escobar 2018). Who benefits from the discourse of posthumanism in the field of design? Who continues to be left out? What has changed as we have rushed to find new centres for the field of design? Our institutions of education and publishing in the field of design (as well as many other fields) remain – to a very large extent – white, male, wealthy and able-bodied. Posthumanism embraces multiplicity but we must also resist its capture into systems of domination and oppression in the field of design.

Connection to other entries:
Convergences
Critical Posthuman Thought
New Materialist Informatics
Postcolonial and Decolonial Computing
Posthuman Data

Laura Forlano

PROXY REASONING

The lacklustre term, 'proxy' is a kind of connector that, as an untranslated loan word, populated languages other than English with the emergence of the World Wide Web in the 1990s. A proxy server sits between an individual computer and a web page, providing services or limiting what one can see. Proxies remain a key element of network architecture, but are also a form of reasoning prevalent in a data-driven society and thus a key instrument of a certain kind of technological arrangement of the world.

The origin of the word 'proxy' lies in administration. The simplest form of proxy – a substitute, retains a two-way connection to what it stands in for, which endows

it with a capacity to act on their behalf. Similarly, the terms 'proxy data' or 'proxy variable' name a piece of data that is used to measure something that cannot itself be directly measured. The reasons for the impossibility of direct instrumental measurement could be qualitative (how to measure conscientiousness?), structural (real data not available), ecological (the cost of processing all data too high), cosmological (data about the future non-existent) or legally enforced. Hence, proxy variables are widely used instead. The decision on the kind of proxy data that would stand in for something that cannot be measured is based on disciplinary knowledge, historical practice, personal judgement or 'intuition'.

In statistics, for example, GDP can be used as a measure of the economic health of the nation. The use of GDP as a proxy variable is standard practice in the discipline of economics. It has been criticized as overly focused on economic growth, both harmful to the planet and unrepresentative of people's lives. In data analytics-driven fields, which now seem to include every sphere of action, but most notably policing, healthcare, insurance, finance, advertisement and retail, the use of proxy data is widespread. Given that our societies are structurally racist, patriarchal and ruled by capital, it is not surprising that historical practices, cultural habits and personal opinions that determine and use proxies return racist, sexist and discriminatory computational judgements.

The examples are innumerable. Sweeney's investigation of the delivery of online ads offering prison data when Black-associated names are entered in a search engine, but not for White-associated ones, is an example of the operation of name as a proxy variable for race (Sweeney

2013). There is significant work documenting discrimination against Black people in terms of accessing loans based on the use of their neighbourhood postcode as a proxy variable for financial stability as well as critical investigations of the use of predictive models in the prison-industrial complex, such as recidivism prediction (Angwin et al. 2016). The use of proxy variables in these examples is rooted in historical practices, the use of newly invented algorithms and supported by an infrastructure. This includes separate companies offering databases linking names to ethnicity and gender or historical records of insurance claims. It extends to practices of policing and imprisonment as well as an infrastructural cohesion across industries.

The use of proxy variables as a source of discrimination is widely discussed in in the critical data research community. One of the problems preventing a quick remedy is that excluding proxy variables that can lead to discrimination would not prevent a machine learning algorithm from inferring certain information about people on the basis of other characteristics. Proxy variables will emerge even when not directly specified (for instance, age could be inferred from the length of work experience, health records, etc.).

Proxy reasoning is not only based on past correlations used to make judgements about the present. Its main vector of operation is future-oriented. Prediction relies on large amounts of proxy operations, taking some activity of some people as an indication of the future likelihood of another activity of that same people – or the future activity of another group of people, related to the control group by – again – another proxy operation.

A knee-jerk reaction to the ever-expanding infrastructure of proxy reasoning is a total rejection of technology. Historically, a large proportion of European philosophy framed technology as instrumental, rationalizing, objectifying and thus deprived it of existential value. Indeed, the currently dominant logic of proxy reasoning is dreadful: it is about extending instrumental measurement not only to areas where it's not possible, but also in space and in time. A critical response to proxy reasoning is of utmost importance (Noble 2018; O'Neil 2016). It can't, however, proceed by a full rejection of inference that is key to the use of proxies. This would be defeatist. Medicine, climate research and many other forms of enquiry that could contribute to a survivable world use proxy variables in their analysis. It has been argued that the operations of the proxy, i.e. relating things to each other, expressing one thing through another and inference, are habitual capacities of language (i.e. metaphor) and reasoning (logic). Moreover, the logical operation of proxy is not limited to human reasoning. Elephants use the sound of fallen fruit as a proxy for its ripeness and the availability of food to dine on. There are arguments in botany to extend the animal capacity to infer the likely reason for an event (abduction) and to expect related things to happen (foresight) to plants that exhibit learning behaviour, and are able to anticipate on the basis of past experience (Trewawas 2015).

There are larger questions concerning the alternative framing of technology that could account for proxy reasoning that extends from Haraway's notion of the cyborg to technofeminism, and the propositions of Afrofuturism to software studies (Haraway 1991; Sollfrank 2019; Eshun 1998; Fuller 2008). While proxy reasoning embedded in the current techno-capitalist complex may seem to have a chilling grip, Heidegger cannot have been right. Things have always been technical. What can make technology so deadly are the alliances it enters into and therefore the question of technology is a question of struggle rather than of essence.

The proxy has the cunning capacity to be right in the middle – a glue that sticks things together. As a shifter, the proxy can and must be deployed for other purposes, turned against its crippling use, manoeuvred to work as an ally.

Connection to other entries:
Algorithmic Governmentality
Pattern Discrimination
Posthuman Data

Olga Goriunova

Q

QUEER DEATH STUDIES

Queer Death Studies (QDS) is an emerging field which takes research on death, dying and mourning in new directions, inspired by feminist, posthumanist, decolonial, anti-racist, queer and trans theorizing. What distinguishes QDS from conventional Death Studies such as death sociology or anthropology of death is an overall critical focus on the framing of death and extinction in the contemporary world through Anthropocene necropolitics (Mbembe 2003, Lykke 2019) and necropowers of post/colonialism, racial and extractivist capitalism. Death is approached as an ethico-political issue that is embedded in global power structures. QDS pays attention to systematic, necropolitical productions of death, in dialogue with theoretical-political critiques emerging from political movements for social, environmental and planetary justice and change (Geerts and Groen 2021). Moreover, QDS is based on critiques of the dichotomous divides, characterizing Western modernity, and is marked out through a critical focus on normativities and exclusionary notions of the human, casting the death of those who differ from the normative human subject in terms of gender, racialization, class, geopolitical situatedness, able-bodiedness, and species as less grievable or not counting at all (Butler 2004). In short, QDS aligns itself with critiques of the intra-acting multiplicity of hierarchizing divides between appropriate and in/appropriate/d others (Minh-ha 1989), articulated by social, environmental and planetary justice movements.

With critique of necropowers and necropolitics as an ethico-political framework, QDS aims to queer death. The verb-form 'queering' is understood in a broad, open-ended sense as strange-making, defamiliarizing, where the critical defamiliarization implied may lead to an opening of other, more affirmative horizons, for example a focus on the entanglement of growing and decomposing, life and death as non/living (Radomska 2017), death as vibrancy (Lykke 2022), living well with the dead (Shildrick 2020) or embracing death (MacCormack 2020b). As the field has been unfolding among others through the Queer Death Studies Network (started in 2016), the strange-making is linked with three moves, entangling queering, decolonizing and posthumanizing (Radomska, Mehrabi and Lykke 2020).

Decolonizing death involves critically dismantling the violent necropowers of colonization, racial and extractivist capitalism, which made death become 'life's quiet companion' (Lehman 1997) for racialized and Indigenous people worldwide. However, decolonizing also signals an affirmative turn towards pluritopic hermeneutics (Tlostanova and Mignolo 2009), a hermeneutics which does not universalize Western modern frameworks such as conceptualizations and imaginaries of death as a final endpoint within a chrononormative linear temporality, but instead opt for geo- and corpopolitically grounded knowledge seeking, based on indigenous cosmo-ontologies, philosophies and sensibilities, which critically-affirmatively shift the meanings of death.

Posthumanizing death refers to the systematic problematization of the planetary-scale mechanisms of annihilation of the more-than-human world in their ontological, epistemological and ethico-political dimensions. It involves critical analyses of the human/nonhuman divide and power differentials that have allowed for the reduction of the nonhuman to mere resource and instrument for human endeavours. Furthermore, the posthumanizing move entails unpacking philosophical and cultural meanings of extinction and the ways in which it fundamentally disrupts life processes in relation to time, death and generations (e.g. Rose 2012); it draws attention to environmental violence, environmental grief, as well as nonhuman death manufactured en masse through anthropocentric habits of consumption and mechanisms of extractivism. Consequently, posthumanizing death takes seriously the issues of responsibility, accountability and care for/in dying more-than-human worlds, while remaining grounded in radical critiques of human exceptionalism (Haraway 2008).

Frequently entangled with decolonizing and posthumanizing, the move of queering encompasses both: (1) open-ended deconstructing of normativities and processes of normalization in various forms (e.g. Chen 2012, Eng and Puar 2020), and (2) deconstructing and undoing of heteropatriarchy, heteronormativity, binary gender and sexualities governed by reproductive biopowers or, in other words, the 'normative heterosexual matrix' (Butler 1990). In consequence, queering death ranges from challenging modern Western ontologies of death and conceptualizations of the life/death threshold, embedded in Christian and Cartesian dualisms, to the critical focus on the ways in which misogyny, trans- and queerphobia lead to 'social death', and how violence and hate crimes towards non-normative individuals seek to render their lives and deaths 'non-grievable'.

The power of the three moves of QDS: queering, posthumanizing and decolonizing death lays in their entangling with one another, which is of key theoretical, methodological and ethico-political importance in approaching intersecting structures of global necropolitics, emerging out of (post)colonial violence, extractivist and neoliberal capitalisms and the intertwined systems of oppression: racism, sexism, speciesism, classism and ableism, to name a few.

Connection to other entries:
Crip Theory
Existential Posthumanism
Intergenerational Justice and Care
Posthuman Care
Posthuman Feminist Aesthetics
Undead
Vibrant Death

Marietta Radomska and Nina Lykke

R

RACIALIZING ASSEMBLAGES

In the 1980s and early 1990s, Black feminist scholarship began to push for the importance of using a lens that took into account the multiple forms of oppression that shape social lives differently (hooks 1984; Lorde 2017). As a theory developed to understand the matrix of oppression and the multiplicity of difference, intersectionality was a black feminist intervention to subvert the hegemonic configurations of race, class and gender as well as other discursive formations of 'difference' (Crenshaw 1991; Collins 2000). It was an intentionally humanist theory with a specific focus not just on oppression but the prosthetic social products of identity and difference. As a result, others have turned to assemblage theory (see Deleuze and Guattari ([1980] 1987)) in order to account for the complex, more-than-human and non-static process of being with/in social events, acts and situations (Haraway 1985; Puar 2007, 2012; Weheliye 2014).

Assemblage theory has provided a posthumanist lens for rethinking and rereading the processes that bring about emergent racialized events, acts and situations. For instance, Jane Bennett (2005) argues that assemblages are 'a web with an uneven topography: some of the points at which the trajectories of actants cross each other are more heavily trafficked than others, and thus power is not equally distributed across the assemblage' (445). Donna Haraway (1985) understands the body as unstable assemblages that cannot be partitioned into the multiplicity of identity formations. And, Jasbir Puar (2012) most clearly argues for and articulates how assemblage theory can be put to work to sharply account for the multiplicity of forces of power and oppression in a social event or situation. Puar argues that assemblages have the theoretical virtue of (a) not treating the human body as a separate and unique phenomenon but rather directly connected to all matter beyond it; (b) deconstructing the human/non-human division by acknowledging the bodies that live within and outwith the human body such as bacteria and bodies of water; (c) understanding that the meaning of a substance is not only from signification but rather a *doing* in matter, a *mattering*; and (d) social categories such as race, gender and class are situated in events, acts and situations rather than characteristics of human subjects. More specifically, Puar pushes a posthumanist pragmatist reading of the racializing processes and forces of an assemblage.

As work that engages Puar and builds on the scholarship of black feminist literary studies, Alexander Weheliye develops what he calls racialized assemblages. In *Habeas Viscus* ('you shall have the flesh', 2014), Weheliye seeks to more adequately account for the processes of power and racializations of the body/flesh. For Weheliye, racialization is not to be reduced to race or racism but is the very process of differentiation and hierarchization that produces the discursive formations of race, gender, class, sexuality and dis/ability among other structural relations of difference. He argues that posthumanist and anti-humanist theories assume that everyone equally occupies the space of humanity, without accounting for the ongoing historicity of socio-political relations and the ways in which political violence has been constitutive of the hierarchy of humanity. In particular, Weheliye puts to work Sylvia Wynter's (2001) sociogenic principle and Hortense Spillers' (2003) theory of the flesh so as to develop a theory of racializations that accounts for the ways in which socio-political relations and violence mark the flesh and discipline the ontologies of humanity into full humans, not-quite-humans and non-humans.

As a way of developing a theory of racialization that is situated in a system of socio-political relations and accounts for the anchoring of difference in the ontogenic flesh, Weheliye draws from Wynter's (2001) sociogenic principle. As a further development of Fanon's (1967) sociogeny, Wynter incorporates ideas from neurobiology to provide a theoretical route to explain how racializations become part of the ontologies of the body via neurochemical processes that reconfigure the experience of the self. Thus, the physiognomy of the body are shaped by the sociogenic. As a product of socio-political forces, race is then not inherent to physiognomical ontologies but rather those ontologies become racialized assemblages through their encounters of racialized events, situations or acts. Weheliye further states

Consequently, racialization figures as a master code within the genre of the human represented by Western Man, because its law-like operations are yoked to species-sustaining physiological mechanisms in the form of a global color line— instituted by cultural laws so as to register in human neural networks—that clearly distinguishes the good/life/fully-human from the bad/death/not-quite-human.

2014: 27

As a way of drawing a distinction between the legal constitution of the body and the social designations of the flesh, Weheliye also engages Spillers' (2003) theorizing of the flesh. As Spillers insightfully states 'before the "body" there is "flesh," that zero degree of social conceptualization that does not escape concealment under the brush of discourse or the reflexes of iconography …' (as quoted by Weheliye 2014: 39). Prior to the legal constitution of the body is the formation of the flesh, a formation that is bound by the markings or traces of political violence designating a hierarchy of humanity. The traces of political violence of the flesh are what Spillers refers to as 'hieroglyphics of the flesh' that are produced from the instruments or acts of violence such as whips, police brutality, mass shootings or more subtly from the silence in speech acts. Spillers argues that the 'hieroglyphics of the flesh' are transmitted to future generations and is concealed in what is narrativized to be pathological or biological explanations of hierarchies of difference. 'Racializing assemblages translate the lacerations left on the captive body by apparatuses of political violence to a domain rooted in the visual truth-value accorded to quasi-biological distinctions between different human groupings' (Weheliye 2014: 40). It is the political violence and disciplining of the flesh that designates bodies as full humans, not-quite-humans and non-humans; rendering certain bodies as exceptional and others as disposable (Weheliye 2014).

Connection to other entries:
Ex-colonialism
(De)constructing Risk
Ontologized Plasticity
Pattern Discrimination

Ezekiel Dixon-Román

RELATIONAL SOVEREIGNTY

In 1977 Michel Foucault famously claimed we need 'a political philosophy that isn't erected around the problem of sovereignty ... We need to cut off the King's head: in political theory that has still to be done' (1980: 121). At this time, Foucault (2003) was developing his alternative theorization of power operating as a diffuse network of force relations, in which truth is not a function of essence or of right but rather is a weapon wielded for partisan victory in a never-ending battle for ascendency. His distinctive genealogical approach to the analysis of power has become a critical edifice supporting subsequent posthumanist efforts to redefine the focus, nature and scope of political action.

Foucault takes issue with the modern conceptualization of sovereignty, theorized by Bodin in the sixteenth century and subsequently reframed in Humanist terms by Hobbes and Machiavelli, which has since lain at the heart of Western political philosophy and the theory and practice of human rights. The Westphalian system, predicated on this notion of sovereignty, remains the normative basis for international relations and law-making between states. Here, sovereignty refers to the essential qualities of a law-making power with exclusive jurisdiction (or 'effective government' (Montevideo Convention 1933 Article 1(c)) over a defined territory (Ibid., Article 1(b)): the sovereign state is conceived as such when it is uniform and undivided (Charlesworth 1997, 261), and as a coherent power it enjoys a fundamental right of non-interference in its internal affairs (Nicaragua Case ICJ 1986). Although the law-making activity is proper to a sovereign power, insofar as jurisprudence relies upon a unified centre of rational selfhood with coherent moral agency as the effective basis of judgement, capability and integrity, the principle of sovereign identity also corresponds with the legal personality and political subjectivity implied by human rights. Foucault's gripe with the sovereign model of power is twofold. Firstly, he contests the notion that power is located centrally and rationally 'in the King's head', rather than extending across the unruly field of a densely interactive social network and exercised through multifarious practices in the affective relations that constitute such networks. Secondly, he rejects the 'repressive' hypothesis that power is a sovereign imposition. Far more than a curtailing force, for Foucault power is primarily productive and generative of a social order.

The critique of sovereignty has typically preoccupied posthumanist political philosophy after Foucault. Schematically, two contrasting approaches attend to this critical task. The first is exemplified by the deconstructive philosophy associated with Jacques Derrida, which is aligned also with a post-Lacanian critique of the humanist subject. A broadly 'deconstructive' or 'destituent' approach is thus also evident, for example, in the work of Judith Butler, Giorgio Agamben, Ernesto Laclau and Chantelle Mouffe? Deconstruction proceeds by contesting the self-sufficiency of the concept, demonstrating its constitutive reliance upon others. Accordingly, an identified concept that presents as sovereign, independent, exclusive, uniform and unified, rather is revealed as reliant upon a relational context; this fundamental reliance on the other must even so be disavowed if the subject is to present as essential in its given and rightful properties. The relational chain of signification through which meaning is conferred attests that identity is never in fact essential and predetermined, but rather is unstable, always in process, never finished, fundamentally incomplete or lacking. The self is thus not sovereign, but rather is always-already undone, essentially void, striving for a form of completion and satisfaction that never arrives. There is no sovereign; the throne is empty; and politics is nothing but the effort to mask this constitutive absence through techniques of glorification that manufacture the political illusion of subjective presence and coherence (see Agamben 2011).

Yet, while it is effective as a conceptual strategy for 'cutting off the King's head', the method of deconstruction is nonetheless problematic from the perspective of groups whose political existence is a site of historical resistance and struggle. This is the case for colonized Indigenous peoples, for example, whose sovereignty and political identity as First Nations has been denied or eroded. Feminist theorists, too, have criticized the political consequences of a deconstructive approach to political subjectivity, since this would apply not only to the apparently gender-neutral (but normatively male-identified) humanist subject of the Enlightenment, but also to feminist political selfhood at a time when the majority of the world's women have yet to achieve status equal with that of men. Rather than the destabilization of their political foundations, queer subjectivities of all persuasions may require the firm acknowledgement and affirmation of their equal sovereign humanity.

An alternative posthumanist approach that is constructivist (rather than deconstructive) arguably provides a preferred platform for the critique of sovereignty. Drawing inspiration from the Spinozist philosophical lineage evident in the affirmative philosophy of Deleuze and Guattari, the constructivist feminist posthumanism of Rosi Braidotti, Donna Haraway and Karen Barad, amongst others, results in the rich re-visioning of political life involving intimate and strategic processes of assemblage. Constructivist posthumanism accepts the loss of absolute sovereignty and fixed identity in the aftermath of anti-essentialist philosophy. But it does not mourn this loss or celebrate the consequent void that arises. Nor does it seek to suture the wound by insisting on the enduring viability of humanist conceptualizations of the sovereign subject. Instead, constructivist posthumanism heightens emphasis on the relational nature of selfhood and the ways in which the affective exercise of power relations enables a 'nomad' conceptualization of political subjectivity-in-process, accompanying an understanding of sovereignty as shared, negotiated, multiple and overlapping. When subjectivity is a creative process dependent upon input and interpretation by others, then power must be re-conceived as a relational exercise. In turn, freedom is best understood as a practice of strategic negotiation or the 'governmentality' of an affirmative ethics that disposes relations towards beneficial outcomes for interdependent subjects-in-formation.

Connection to other entries:
Collaborative Politics
Feminism and Oceans
Norms
Posthuman Agency
Rights of Nature

Simone Bignall

RIGHTS OF NATURE

One of the core tenants of posthuman theory is its focus on understandings of the agency of matter (Bennett 2010; Barad 2007; Braidotti 2013). However, the application of this theoretical work remains challenging. In parallel, over the past few decades, nature has begun to be recognized as having rights in certain contexts. The call for the environment to have legal rights, allowing it to bring claims in law on behalf of 'itself', could potentially foster a more posthuman legal system in which nature, itself, is recognized as a lively agent.

Rights of Nature (RoN) provisions have been applied in different contexts in different ways. One core theme which emerges, however, is the role of Indigenous peoples. For example, Indigenous peoples played a key role in the recognition of RoN in Ecuador's 2008 constitution (Eisenstadt and Jones West 2019). The constitution 'celebrates' nature which is defined as 'Pachamama', referring to the sacred deity revered by Indigenous peoples of the Andes (Republic of Ecuador 2008, Preamble). In New Zealand, Indigenous

peoples also played a central role in the recognition of RoN. Here, RoN have been recognized through two agreements with local Māori activists, (the Whanganui *iwi* in relation to the Whanganui River or Te Awa Tupua and the Tūhoe *iwi* in relation got the Te Urewera forest) (Te Awa Tupua Act 2017; Te Urewera Act 2014). However, Indigenous people have not been involved in all instances of RoN recognition. For example, Indigenous groups are not involved in the proposed 'right of nature' Bill in the Philippines. Further, not all Indigenous peoples support a RoN approach. Some Australian Nations have, for example, rejected the approach, calling instead for stronger Indigenous environmental governance through 'Caring for Country' (Marshall 2020). It is, however, clear that Indigenous legalities have been central in the recognition of RoN (O'Donnell et al. 2020).

In 2008, Ecuador became the first country to recognize RoN constitutionally. Ecuador's constitution outlines nature rights as being inherent to the Earth, a status that applies nationally. This national coverage differs from other provisions, which focus on specific ecosystems. For example, in New Zealand, the Whanganui River and the Te Urewera forest have had their legal personality recognized. Here, the laws define the boundaries of the two ecosystems and thus provisions apply to these two specific areas – not nationwide. The latter is a more common approach to the application of RoN. From a posthuman perspective, recognition of RoN within a bounded area alone runs the risk of failing to recognize the ways in which humans, non-humans and environments are interconnected beyond those boundaries. A posthuman informed approach to RoN must ensure these connections are adequately accounted for within the law (Jones 2021).

RoN provisions differ but they do share at least one key commonality: the linking of the health and well-being of the environment to that of the people who live there, allowing people to bring legal claims on behalf of nature. In coming to the Te Awa Tupua agreement (2017), for example, the Whanganui *iwi* argued that they are connected to the environment they live in and that the river is alive. The Act recognizes the river as a legal person and the river and the people are deemed to be inseparable (Article 69(2)). To uphold the river's interests, a guardian body (Tu Pou Tupua) must be appointed and is authorized to speak on behalf of the river. Similarly, in Ecuador, the constitution (2008) states that humans are an inherent part of nature, and in the US, RoN provisions frame nature as being integral to human welfare (e.g. City of Pittsburgh 2010). The focus on community rights could be seen as a human-centred approach. However, posthuman theory calls, not for the displacement of culture for or by nature but, rather, for the need to focus on the nature-culture continuum (Haraway 1991; Åsberg 2017). By drawing out the entanglements between humans, non-humans and the environment, a more reciprocal dynamic can be centred.

There are two central models of RoN recognition: models that recognize rights (as in Ecuador) and provisions that recognize nature's legal personality. In New Zealand a legal personality model has been used. This is because the *iwi* do not emphasize the concept of rights because, to *iwi*, nature is not property but is a living entity (Te Awa Tupua Act 2017, Article 13(a)). Accordingly, the concept of guardianship is promoted. This preference, in

part, explains the difference between provisions in New Zealand and, say, Ecuador. The different models result in different procedures. Unlike Ecuador's RoN laws, New Zealand's laws do not award inherent rights. Rather, legal personality is instilled. This grants the river and the forest (through their guardians) procedural access rights in New Zealand's legal system but does not give them special rights per se. The natural systems thus have the mediated right to petition the court or to receive reparations, for example, but do not have the right to be protected in and of themselves.

The differences between the design of RoN provisions impacts what happens when RoN clash with other rights. Ecuador, being one of the first states to recognize RoN, has some of the most developed jurisprudence in this area. Under the Constitution of Ecuador, nature rights are recognized but are not absolutely protected: the Constitution (2008) situates sustainable development as core, seeking to balance environmental needs against development needs (Article 395). Central, however, is Article 395.4, which states that, 'In the event of doubt … it is the most favorable interpretation of' the 'effective force' or RoN provisions 'that shall prevail'. This, however, is not always the outcome, and RoN laws have, since 2008, developed within a highly politicized context (Kauffman and Sheehan 2019, 349). Environmental damage in Ecuador remains rampant, particularly in relation to industrial activity and oil extraction (Eisenstadt and Jones West 2019). Many provisions have yet to be adequately applied. Nevertheless, there are signs of real progress. Several cases have established a standard that killing any animal that is part of an endangered species constitutes a RoN violation (Judgment No. 09171-2015-0004). Other Judgments have concluded that government construction projects cannot impede the ability of ecosystems or species to regenerate (Judgment No. 11121-2011-0010). The disruption of migration and breeding patterns has also been ruled as violating RoN (Judgment No. 269-2012) and RoN laws have been ruled to be transversal, sometimes challenging other rights, including property rights (Judgment No. 166-15-SEP-CC). However, the setting of standards in Ecuador took considerable effort and that this struggle is still very much ongoing (See Kauffman and Sheehan 2019: 357).

In New Zealand, the Te Awa Tupua Act (2017) does not derogate from existing private rights in the Whanganui River. The Act states that any actor, public or private, must 'have particular regard to' the interests of the river (Article 15(3)) and must recognize the values of the Te Awa Tupua, which include treating the river as a living entity (Article 13). The New Zealand system has been set up so that 'decisions on how to balance the rights of ecosystems against the rights of other legal persons (e.g. individuals and corporations) . . . will still need to be made' (Kauffman and Sheehan 2019: 354). Standards will likely develop over time, much as in Ecuador. These Acts, therefore, while being key for Māori rights,

are carefully constructed to ensure that they are framed around the neo/liberal, settler-colonial legal order, avoiding the outright prioritization of RoN over, for example, corporate rights to exploit nature (Otto and Jones 2020). It remains to be seen how a court would rule in the instance of a clash between rights.

RoN have much in common with posthuman theory. RoN have the potential to provide a more integrated account of the environment, with RoN laws directly challenging 'the values of dominant political and economic systems, which view humans as separate from nature . . . [and] treat the elements of nature as objects for human exploitation . . .' (Kauffman and Sheehan 2019: 356). This aim very much aligns with posthuman theory and with its call for a greater understanding of the connection between human and nonhuman entities. However, crucially, the effectiveness of RoN in reaching these aims will depend on how nature and its rights are defined.

Connection to other entries:
EcoLaw
Geontopower
Intergenerational Justice and Care
Posthuman Agency

Emily Jones

S

SIDE CHANNEL ATTACK

A signature quality of research in the posthumanities is the attempt to expand the range and kind of factors worked together in coming to an understanding of the world. Diverse sorts of experience, data, agency, subjecthood and methodology become part of this attempt. Indeed, the separation of method, data and findings are themselves subject to shifts and reversals. This glossary entry proposes the side channel attack as providing a method or technique attuned to posthuman dimensions. More broadly, recognizing side channel attacks can be a way into understanding and reworking politics in the posthuman era.

A side channel attack is typically a hacking technique in which information derived from monitoring and analysing the normal functioning of a technology can be used to access supposedly secure data from within it. In security studies, one of the key points of entry into a technology is often the 'excess' that it produces in the form of incidental emissions. TEMPEST systems, for instance, read the electromagnetic radiation from computer screens, cables or circuits to work out what data is circulating on them (Young 1996). Even something as innocuous as the sound emissions from physical locks being turned have been used to work out the location and size of their tumblers in order

to reverse engineer the proportions of the necessary key (Ramesh, Ramprasad and Han 2020). Basically, any exchange of energy results in some overspill that can be recouped as information.

Collectively, these kinds of approaches are known as side channel attacks. If the channel is the intended form of communication, like a message on a computer, or the designed function of an object like a lock, the side channel attack reads it from an unexpected angle. Cultivating sensitive means to capture these signals is a core activity for hackers and others. A side channel attack, thus, finds a use for anything generated as surplus to the ostensive function of a system. Such systems can be technical, but they might also be evolved or designed in biological settings, different types of vaccine for instance use particular aspects of the target virus to reroute or disarm it. By extension, side channel attacks indeed may not be intentional. They can also be the results of the haphazard iterations of evolution.

Further, side channel attacks may be ideological or stylistic. Identifying an unknown author by their linguistic tics for instance is one tool of the digital humanities, but also a forensic means to track persons making ransom demands or justifying anonymous direct action. In such cases, it is best to keep your communiques short and neutral if they are to be made at all. Indeed, any communication or interaction opens up an 'attack surface' for such enquiries. As characteristics such as gait, face, emotion, and in farm-animals, skin patterns, become vectors for the identification of individuals, the art of being indiscernible becomes harder – or requires greater elegance.

In her discussion of the 'Material Witness' artist and theorist Susan Schuppli (2020) discusses ways that media often incidentally record the conditions in which they are made. A photographic film, for instance, may bear traces of chemical or radioactive contamination from the site of a recording. Additionally, things not designed as media end up as archives of information: for instance, arctic ice cores store logs of climatic gases. In this argument, mediation becomes a more general condition of matter. Finding the route into the archive that is the world is a practice of perceptual cunning or of aesthetic openness – which may amount to the same thing.

Such side channel attacks are the essential structure that the late Michel Serres (2007) describes in his remarkable work, *The Parasite*. Information theory, where a message passes from A to B without complication, is shown to always be contingent upon interruption. Bits of noise come into the system of any communication. Unintended crumbs can be snaffled from the table of any banquet. Consequently, the movement of a value, of signal, noise, food, wealth, from A to B or back always elicits a third entity, starting with the channel of communication, but proliferating into others. This can arise as a purely symbiotic relation, or one that gnaws at the foundation of stability or usurps it setting in play another sequence of unfoldings. For Serres, there is an art of jiggling the wires, of mapping the proliferating trifurcations in any relation. The side channel thus is a way of detecting a route to a result beyond a binary.

To follow Serres and Schuppli then, in the case of the side channel attack on the lock: what gives which game away? The scraping of the key in the lock, or the microphone hidden nearby which itself may be found and become an indication of surreptitious intent? Little tweaks or deformations of a chain of events lead across landscapes budding with unexpected consequences.

Jesse Darling's multi-part artwork, *The Ballad of Saint Jerome*, (2018) retells the story of Saint Jerome and the lion. Having encountered a lion with a thorn in its paw, and after removing the wounding item, the fourth-century saint becomes the saviour of the now lame lion, almost its captor. The privilege of doing good becomes the power to dominate or to extract the tribute of gratitude. Saint Jerome and his medical kit is the paternalistic figure that orders nature along humanizing lines, becoming a debt-collector. In Darling's retelling of the tale, the lion must repurpose medical equipment to deflect the predatory benefactor. Here, the side channel attack is mounted through compulsory gratitude, but then also through the repurposing of equipment.

Can the idea of the side channel attack be opened up to its own method? Of course – this is inevitably the case. Indeed, one might turn the approach of an attack into a mode of unexpected collaboration. This is something the Dadaist Walter Serner (2020) also suggests in his guide for the con artist, where one is advised to use the desires of those who oppose you to achieve your own ends. To follow Serres further, working with side channel attacks can be a part of a wider disposition towards objects and ideas, persons and processes, recognizing their openness to interpretation. For instance, designing systems that allow for, indeed encourage, multiple overlapping use-cultures is key to the good design of urban spaces (Sendra and Sennett 2020). Here, the 'excess' is the capacity for an object, say a piece of street furniture or a street corner to be an element in multiple kinds of composition, especially those of which the designer had no anticipation.

Connection to other entries:
Cosmic Artisan
The Distributed University
Parasitology
Pattern Discrimination
Proxy Reasoning
Surface Orientations

Matthew Fuller

SURFACE ORIENTATIONS

Surface orientations is a concept and methodology for approaching digital modelling and mapping platforms as 'lure for feelings' that intensify experience and provide a form of orientation within these constructed worlds (Whitehead 1978). They involve a critical distancing from the regimes of visuality embedded within such platforms by questioning the ability to make faraway places visible or to make them knowable. They instead emphasize experience and the intensification of narratives related to other possible worlds. A turn to surface resists the volumetric concerns of sensing technologies currently being deployed to colonize further into and beyond our planet, while rejecting technological imaginaries that claim to reveal new depths such as those of the deep ocean. Surface orientations provide

another way of apprehending faraway places beyond the remote sensed view of satellites while not eliding the computational. In taking a posthumanist stance, surface orientations necessarily involve the production of transversal relations that exceed the affordances of proprietary technology, and explode the myth of a unitary perspective of a planet we all inhabit but experience differently. As a material practice surface orientations takes seriously the question of what a malfunctioning satellite might sense; as a critical practice it might engage with the remote sensed view by exaggerating error and reinserting friction into the smooth experience of zooming in and out of places in platforms such as Google Earth.

Surfaces have always been crucial to the act of mapping and to its politics. Historically, the importance of surfaces emerged in cartographic disputes over the geometries of flattening a sphere onto two-dimensions to produce a navigable territory. The urge to lay claim to the world understood as globe has meant that navigation has always been central to cartography, and cannot be disentangled from colonial invasions and the seafaring voyages of slavery. Such navigation requires an external datum traditionally provided by the horizon or the stars, which, in contemporary times, is provided by the ping of our phones to the satellites orbiting overhead. These offer a relation to a known object from which a position can be triangulated and then pinpointed on an already existing map. Orientation is different, however; it does not require an external datum in the same way. Here, I am thinking with Sara Ahmed's notion of orientation where she writes that bodies and objects are affected by the orientations they take towards each other through sharing space, and that these orientations depend on certain tendencies and social norms. Ahmed is writing about queer lives but her insight into how orientations act both as 'straightening devices' as well as providing 'fleeting moments', where something slips and other inhabitations are possible, is also applicable in relation to digitally produced worlds (Ahmed 2006: 563 and 565). Thus surface orientations offer an alternative to cartographic practices understood through the paradigm of navigation and colonization embedded in humanist ideas of an externalized and objective perspective.

As visual and spatial practices embrace digital technologies of seeing, the question of how to situate ourselves without the horizon as datum seems to have gone unasked. To map a multiple subject requires a located yet composite point-of-view on a world that, on the one hand gives us information overload, and on the other produces a sense of complete visibility and knowability through forms of data analysis. The challenge posed in the horizonless worlds of platform visuality is that relationships between space and time are to be produced by the viewer (or the user) themselves as they navigate through and across platforms (Mende 2019). Yet, this navigation occurs in a totalizing world that resists any outside meaning beyond the closed and often obscure circuits produced through the exchange and analysis of data across platforms. Recent debates in visual culture have discussed what a machine or a platform sees (as opposed to what it makes visible). These range from Trevor Paglen's (2014) exploration of machine vision that does not produce images that can be seen by what he refers to as 'meat-eyes', to the question of how visuality transforms in relation to algorithmic production. Here,

the notion of 'image ensembles' emerging across hardware, software and various external inputs produces new forms of seeing but also new opacities (MacKenzie and Munster 2019: 6). This opacity sits uncomfortably next to the claim to make faraway places visible or to reveal the processes that are producing and transforming territories. It suggests that the pertinent political question may not be what we can see but how we see and what this does to our ability to act. If navigation is a key mode through which we can critically engage with new forms of the visual, then in relation to the image ensembles described above, the question of how to navigate through opacity seems to be crucial, knowing also that opacity is in certain contexts for certain people a mode of survival (Glissant 1997). Here the notion of surface orientations returns as an embodied form of engaging with the images being produced through remote sensed and other technologies. As computational techniques are becoming malleable and their deployment ranges from the seemingly benign context of agriculture to that of border security, the agency of maps as tools is far from straightforward and they can only be approached as part of an assemblage of humans, technologies and environments.

Surface orientations, then, questions the centrality of a notion of agency in relation to maps that asks quite simply what use-value they have as objects in the world (Corner 1999). While thinking through the operative nature of maps, mapmaking as surface orientation would consider itself a practice of 'distributed cognition' (Hayles 2008), as well as questioning mapping as a practice that makes hidden truths visible, or one that bestows agency. Instead, we might approach mapping and visual regimes in their encounter with multiple and contradictory subjectivities, and through their technological, historical and computational complicities. This could allow a form of orientation within what at first sight appear to be the closed and smooth worlds of digital mapping platforms. Along the way some things may become visible or invisible and certain moments of agency might appear, but this mode of thinking and working with maps as visual regimes privileges the production of affective relations and intensities over use-value, in order to glimpse other possible worlds.

Connection to other entries:
New Materialist Informatics
Pattern Discrimination
Postcolonial and Decolonial Computing
Postcolonial Drone Scholarship
Side Channel Attack

Nishat Awan

SURROGACY

How could a person possibly be pregnant with *someone else*'s baby? But also: how could they possibly be pregnant with their *own*? In the (post)humanistic context, 'surrogacy' denotes the material-semiotic framework of legitimation for various anthrogenetic practices; the way of organizing nature that rationalizes the rationing of property and belonging. It defines, for example, 'the similarities and differences between making kin and making babies' (Hamilton 2019), the repressed fact that everybody has many mothers, and the structures of exploitation against which reproducers all over the world are still

struggling in the tradition of 'wages against housework' and 'family abolition' (Lewis 2019). Like its more palatable sibling-terminologies 'care' and 'kin' (or better: kith), then, surrogacy discourse has the potential to shift conversational foci 'from the quantity of humans made to the quality of relations available under capitalism' (Dow and Lamoureux 2020: 484). The issue 'is not an absence of relations but how to redistribute them' (Strathern et al. 2019: 159).

Surrogacy, as a lens, can make visible (and thus denaturalize) contingent ways of imagining and organizing the relationalities that subtend given economic, cultural and social productions of human beings, from wet-nursing to outsourcing to inter-species astronaut ventures. (We are not addressing here definitions of 'surrogates' as test vectors and applications in, e.g. biochemical, computational and engineering settings). By proposing proxies and stage-managing natural otherness, surrogacy both makes and unmakes, rehabilitates and troubles, geographies of subject- and object-hood; giving birth to 'unexpected country' or, alternatively, displacing it (Haraway 2011). It was Donna Haraway's *Primate Visions* (1989) that initiated this vein of theorization, with its deep dive into the myriad multispecies surrogacies embedded in the heart of Western humanism (notably, the knowledge productions of colonial primatology, museology, the Space Race and white feminism).

Posthumanists drawn to the problem of surrogacy today are likely to be sceptical, in a somewhat Harawavian mode, about the extent to which 'reproduction', as a fantasy of self-valorizing self-replication, ever even occurs in human biology or culture. Not all surrogates are (made visible as) surrogate mothers. Conversely, thinkers in-and-against surrogacy might consider the extent to which products of surrogated human labours can be regarded as human (or: more human than 'traditional' products, perhaps). Recent contributions to a putative 'surrogacy studies' have made inroads in this direction. For instance, for Kalindi Vora and Neda Atanasoski in *Surrogate Humanity* – their important theorization of race and so-called automation – the relationship-category 'surrogacy' describes, far more broadly, technology's consolidation of the liberal subject under colonial capitalism: a subject that cannot exist 'outside of the surrogate–self relation through which the human, a moving target, is fixed and established ... [and] whose freedom is possible only through the racial unfreedom of the surrogate' (Atanasoski and Vora 2019: 5).

In the commercial gestational surrogacy industry, cellular co-imbrications between proletarian and bourgeois humans multiply geographically, even as kinship between gestator and gestatee is systematically blocked and denied. The commodity sold by surrogacy clinics, in this respect, is un-kinship, as much as it is kinship. The epigenetic landscapes of alienation and sorrow, traceable back to 'surrogacy', yawn ever wider. But what might the transformative affordances be, of such seemingly sharp contradictions and un-oedipal apertures in the fabric of capitalist nature-cultures – for example, for the future (or lack thereof) of private nuclear households currently inscribed as 'natural'? Is the positive supersession of classed surrogacy-relations synonymous with children's liberation?

Approaching surrogacy as a philosophical conundrum may or may not contribute to reviving the felt urgency of well-worn polymaternalist insights of revolutionary Black feminisms, Indigenous feminisms and crip feminisms: 'To be a good relative means being a good relative to everyone' (Denetdale 2020; TallBear and Willey 2019; Kafer 2019). But, whether named as such or not, surrogacy politics is fundamentally a matter of multispecies economy: a politics of the matrixial writ large, in the sense of chimerical co-gestationality developed by Astrida Neimanis in her posthuman feminist phenomenology (2013). It was with a communist 'hydrofeminism' (or: 'comradely amniotechnics') in mind that I proposed: 'Our wateriness is our surrogacy ... the bed of our bodies' overlap' (Lewis 2019: 162). Lest this be misunderstood as a romantic observation: there is nothing affirmatively queer or utopian about contemporary surrogacy™. Discourses that single out the (racist, exploitative) commercial gestational surrogacy industry for moral condemnation, however, reinscribe the same romanticization of (racist, exploitative) 'natural' reproduction that the commercial gestational surrogacy capitalizes upon and shores up.

The civilizing desire to 'rescue' surrogates is inextricable from the desire to make their communities as a whole go away and never 'come knocking' on the doors of the rich (Lewis 2019). The alternative, class- and family-abolitionist possibility of multiplying and proliferating surrogacies – of seeking to become surrogates for surrogates *for surrogates* such that authorship could truly only be co-authorship – seems indigestible for now. But perhaps critical thinkers can contribute in a small way to their societies' ability to recognize surrogacy-workers as desiring subjects rather than tragic and inert unfortunates. According to the latter myth, the surrogate is a serviceable and threatening reproducer – standing in, qua object, for a subject

– standing in overfamiliarly in the place of another, proper (i.e. proprietary), body. Indeed, the racialized, ambivalent figure of the surrogate is constantly being reinvented anew. Yet there was nothing new about the 'New Reproductive Technologies' of the 1980s, as Black feminist radicals pointed out; nothing new, either, about the groups whose flesh they made bioavailable. The cyborg figure of the surrogate is at least as old as the Old Testament narrative of Hagar, the Egyptian woman whom Alys Weinbaum describes as a 'fugitive foremother' of Black feminism, an 'insurgent slave' forced to 'surrender her body for reproductive use' by Sarah and Abraham (Weinbaum 2019: 22). The late twentieth-century emergence of the so-called 'assisted reproduction' sector of capitalism, by commodifying some surrogacies, made them more visible and, in so doing, aggressively naturalized the idea of a prior, unmarked realm of somehow *unassisted* reproduction.

Through co-gestating *Full Surrogacy Now* (Lewis 2019) in the wake of its publication, I have come to understand surrogacy as a concept every bit as impossible and necessary as the human, which it co-constitutes. The simultaneously fictive and factual, descriptive and speculative name for the dystopian *and* utopian relations of production at the heart of Earthly anthrogenesis, 'surrogacy' offers a window onto a contradiction in the landscape of the present. The fissure in question is vulnerable, I believe, to slow explosive action on the part of comradely gestators desirous of a classless, post-white, regenerative, sympoietic earth. While a dystopian reality of deep and extensive surrogacy™ is with us 'now' (a synonym for it would be *reproductive stratification*), there is an imminent utopian sense of 'full surrogacy' that

bespeaks a vision of communized care, queer multispecies mutuality, symbiogenetic xenohospitality and gestational justice: 'we are the makers of one another, and we could learn collectively to act like it' (Lewis 2019: 19).

Connection to other entries:
Crip Theory
Endomaterialities
Posthuman Care
Racializing Assemblages
Transcorporeality II

Sophie Lewis

SWARM WARFARE

The swarm threatens to engulf, to terrorize, to consume, but also to move, communicate and create as 'more-than-one'. Whether a swarm of 'killer bees', a swarm of zombies, or a swarm of immigrants, or the swarming of a riot, the swarm represents the threat of the multitude, the racialized horde set to overwhelm sovereign power: the intelligence and creativity of the many in relation versus the *one* of the sovereign. The swarm as not quite a singular entity but also not disconnected units either poses a challenge for anthropocentric understandings of governance and also, in our contemporary world of the climate crisis, digital and social media, and rise of far-right politics, a unique challenge to understanding the imbrication of the human, technological, animal and ecological. Governance of the multitudes, as Mbembe theorizes, (2019: 86) either in fixing such populations spatially or disaggregating them, forcing them to scatter, is a core component of the necropolitical war machine: this war machine now aims to use 'swarms' as part of its own tactics. Swarming, thus, is a 'a dynamic structure, a topological system of inter-individual communication that has deeply affected the governmentality of the present.' (Vehlken 2019: 23) As such, 'the swarm' represents a posthuman figuration that defies strictly top-down or bottom-up understandings of power.

Arquilla and Ronfeldt (2002) famously argued in a RAND study 'Swarming and the Future of Conflict', that swarming is to be the future of war fighting tactics in the US, and that successful swarming would rest upon controlling the flows of information needed to support these swarms. Swarms of micro-machines are being developed in the US, the UK, China, Russia, Turkey. A swarm arms race is occurring, with states seeking to develop war fighting technologies that aim to mimic the kind of collective action and intelligence that bees, ants, birds, termites and other creatures exhibit. The US Navy is testing 'SwarmDiver' that consists of underwater drones, while DARPA's OFFSET program of swarming drones is imaged to be preparing for urban warfare. 'Swarms' here could serve as a new generation of drones: apart from the singular, individualized machines controlled by operators and linked to complex communication and control systems, the intention with drone swarms is to allow for greater autonomy and communication of information *within* the swarm robots to adapt to conditions more quickly in order to accomplish complex tasks with less human involvement. Such developments represent efforts to move beyond AI work that situates the human as the highest form of intelligence to emulate, and toward recognizing and attempting to duplicate and

control other forms of intelligences that animals demonstrate in collective forms. These forms of self-organization and collective intelligence are derived from both animal life but only possible through their medication with the technologies of computer simulation: that is to say, with the 'bio' in the 'biomimetic' mediated through the technological (see Vehlken 2019 and Thacker 2004). The figuration of the swarm is increasingly displacing the individualized human body as the model of artificial life. Here, we see something of a blurring between man/machine as in the more familiar drones as well as the 'cyborg' figuration that has shaped generations of critical scholarship on the 'posthuman' broadly defined, but a blurring across all lines of the human/animal/machine triumvirate (Wilcox 2017b).

'Swarm' is more than a metaphor, it is a materialist figuration that also speaks to a posthuman ontology of the world: not a world nearly demarcated between different states, between citizens and non-citizens, or between friends and enemies, nor between categories such as humans, animals, machines. 'Swarms' speak to a world whose ontologies are those of 'becoming' rather than 'being' and also a world in which the humanities cannot remain separate from engineering, zoological, geological, nor ecological sciences (see for example Braidotti 2019). The development of 'swarming' artificial intelligence takes place in a world in which the living beings that inspire such technologies are themselves under threat by ecological damage and destruction caused by humans, including the climate crisis. The emergent and systems effects of ecological damage can be seen in the example of honeybees: Jake Kosek, for example notes the ironies of militaries developing swarm technologies to combat threats in world in which the colony collapse of honeybees threatens over a third of world agricultural production (2010). The ironies of the 'swarm' are also evident in role of digital technologies and social medial in particular that are factors in the spread of 'fake news' and conspiracy theories, including the denial of climate science. Byung-Chul Han (2017:11–12) characterizes the '*digital swarm*' as the contemporary manifestation of the masses crowds that are made of up of digital individuals as anonymous profiles, that display collective patterns of movement like the aforementioned animals: volatile, unstable, fleeting.

If 'swarm warfare' represents the forefront of militaristic responses by wealthy state governments to manage threats, uprisings and challenges to sovereign power, as well as to further extend the reach of state power in oceans (by underwater swarming drones) by appropriating the self-organizing capabilities of swarms and reproducing them in machines, perhaps forms of resistance and political action might similarly be inspired by 'the swarm' as well. 'Swarm warfare' also speaks to how modes of resistance to empire, to capitalism might be envisioned. Here we might posit the 'swarm' as a less individualistic descendant of the 'cyborg' that is both potentially oppressive and emancipatory: William Connolly finds inspiration in the 'swarm' for thinking about political activism in a world of intersecting, self-organizing systems and processes: the ability to leverage specific forms of knowledge and act locally so as to set off political effects across geographical scales and sites of interconnectivity (2017). Afrofuturist work, such as that of Octavia Butler, has been a key site of reinvention and re-envisioning forms of life outside of the machine/human/animal categories that are foundation to anti-black racism. Zakiyyah Iman Jackson (2020: 127–158), for example, analyses Butler's *Bloodchild* as providing an examination of humanity's constitution and embeddedness in dynamic processes of non-human bodies including those of insects and bacteria in ways that displace the anti-black foundations of the human/animal distinction. 'Swarm warfare' opens a terrain for thinking about forms of collective becoming that transcend human/animal/machine distinctions and that help us situate and theorize modalities of power in a posthuman age.

Connection to other entries:
Ontologized Plasticity
Parasitology
Postcolonial Drone Scholarship
Post-humanitarian Law

Lauren Wilcox

SYNDEMIC

The term 'syndemic' is a portmanteau combining the ideas of synergy and epidemic (Hartman et al. 2020). The syndemic concept appears increasingly relevant and appropriate as a way to consider many interlinked human tragedies occurring during the recent global COVID-19 emergency, as well as other mutually intensifying links among public health risks tied to social and environmental problems (Adamson and Hartman 2020: np). Many of these risks are addressed, directly or indirectly, by the Sustainable Development Goals (United Nations), including: poverty, hunger, health and well-being, education, clean water and sanitation, reduced inequalities, sustainable cities and communities, responsible consumption and climate action.

The discriminatory practices targeting ethnic and racial minority communities that have long subjected these groups to the direst effects of polluting industries in North America are, in many cases, the same ones that have put African-Americans, Latinx-Americans and Indigenous Americans at heightened risk for COVID-19. Statistically the overall toll of COVID-19 globally was still far from complete in early 2022, in the midst of unprecedented waves of infection from the Omicron variant two years after the initial outbreak. However, existing data in the US analysed by APM Research Lab in March 2021, after the first year of the pandemic, revealed the age-adjusted mortality rates of Black Americans, Latinx-Americans, Pacific Islanders and Indigenous Americans was profoundly higher at this point in time when compared with whites. These general conclusions were strongly corroborated by researchers in the Annals of Internal Medicine in December 2021, based on analysis of Center for Disease Control data from the first nine months of the COVID-19 pandemic. Their analysis found that there were 'profound racial/ethnic disparities in US excess death rates in 2020 during the COVID-19 pandemic' portending 'severe widening of racial/ethnic disparities in all-cause mortality as longer-term data are released.' Noting that 'racial/ethnic inequities continue' even after the beginning of vaccinations in spring 2021, the authors cautioned that continued inequities 'will further drive mortality disparities if not addressed with urgency and cultural competence, as has

been done by tribal communities.' A key takeaway from the study was the conclusion that the 'disproportionate effect of the pandemic on Black, AI/AN, and Latino communities has been devastating and highlights the urgent need to address long-standing structural inequities' (Shiels et al. 2021, 1693).

Increased mortality rates are linked to underlying health conditions such as diabetes, cancer and hypertension, which in turn are often linked to historic traumas and accumulated stressers. For example, long-term food insecurities linked to high rates of Type 2 diabetes among the Navajo in the American Southwest, or the Diné as they call themselves, can also be traced back to 'The Long Walk' which interrupted traditional hunting, gathering, agricultural and pastoral traditions (Adamson 2015: 9–10). In 1864, Kit Carson, who is remembered in mainstream American history as a 'hero', but by the Diné as a murderous villain, rounded up 8,000 Diné and forced them to walk more than 300 miles from their homes to a desolate military fort in southern New Mexico. Many died during the march and many were murdered. Those who survived had only brackish river water to drink, which caused severe intestinal problems, and exacerbated diseases. When they were finally allowed to return home, they were never allowed to return completely to their traditional foodways, as government-distributed processed foods continued to be staples in their diets (Greenaway 2019: np).

Today, the Navajo Nation remains a 'food desert' with only thirteen full-service grocery stores on its 27,000-square mile sovereign territory. As a result, many Diné people rely heavily on convenience stores that tend not to sell healthy, fresh, immune system-building food (Greenaway 2019:

np). Eating the sorts of processed foods and sugared drinks often sold in such establishments is known to contribute to higher rates of Type 2, or juvenile-onset diabetes which is seven times more common in native youth than in the general US population (Lakhani 2020: np). These accumulated stressers help to explain why, in 2020, the Diné were the population with the most infections per capita in the US (Sternlicht 2020: np). Infrastructural injustices such as these persist among socio-economically disadvantages urban populations as well.

This continuing history of food injustice together with industrial pollution from mining sites, is exacerbated by lack of easy access to clean water, electricity, housing and quality healthcare. As long-time Chicago activist Orrin Williams has noted, higher rates of diabetes and lack of access to quality food are often persistent in cities predominantly inhabited by African-American communities (Williams 2006: 121). Improving community health, he concludes, will take a 'whole systems approach to developing healthy and sustainable communities' that recognizes the links between food injustices and other systemic injustices (121).

Williams's observations and the disproportionate effect of the pandemic on Black, AI/AN, and Latino communities undergird the groundwork and main arguments put forward in a 2019 Report of The Lancet Commission on the mutually intensifying links between obesity, malnutrition and climate change. This report provides a reasonable basis for understanding the present COVID-19 pandemic, arguably, as a 'global syndemic' – a relatively new term that the authors of the report define as a 'synergy of epidemics' that 'co-occur in time and place ... [and] interact with each other to produce complex' pathological conditions 'that share common underlying societal drivers.' (Swinburn et al. 2019: 791). The term syndemic was coined by medical anthropologist Merrill Singer in the 1990s (Ellis 2019: np). Singer's original use of the term denoted a sense much more specific than the one applied in the 2019 report of The Lancet Commission. While noting this difference himself, Singer has also recognized the value of expanding the concept to help 'reframe' discussions concerning the root causes, both ecological and social, underlying linked epidemics.

In the COVID-19-affected world of the early 2020s, the syndemic concept helps to illuminate the entangled, rhizomatic connections between climate change and contagions of various kinds, both biological (in the conventional sense of epidemiology) and psychosocial. For example, such synergetic factors can exacerbate the effects of poverty and increased food insecurities, with significant feedbacks that ultimately compound the effects of malnutrition and other health crises impacting specific groups of people at a particular time and place. Early in the coronavirus pandemic, recognition of the connections between racism, police violence and climate injustice were also amplified in the US through the 'unbearable grief of black and brown mothers' (Meadows-Fernandez 2020) after the deaths of George Floyd and other shocking cases in the African-American community (Breonna Taylor and Daunte Wright to name only two). For too many people, such lived conditions exacerbate the links between pathologies of climate change, environmental degradation, pollution, racism, violence and compromised human health. In turn public debate and political agendas have been profoundly affected by an expanding understanding of social justice, environmental justice and climate justice movements led by African, Latinx and Indigenous communities in the Black Lives Matter and Food Sovereignty/Justice Movements (See Adamson 2015).

Such movements have played driving roles in a developing social consciousness of the realities and effects of police racism, discrimination and violence in light of their underlying structural commonalities and entanglement with other forms of social inequity clearly affecting public health, well-being, life expectancy and relative quality of life, often in mutually reinforcing ways. Especially when they have aligned in spirit and strategy with other activist movements such as the youth-led, climate action focused Fridays for Future, some of these movements, as transformative agents, have come to reverberate far outside the borders of the local, regional or national contexts in which they originated.

The concept of syndemic may prove to be a useful lens through which to approach these and other entangled connections among public health vulnerabilities, pathologies of the body politic and the systemic social-environmental challenges facing the world in the twenty-first century.

Connection to other entries:
Emergent Ecologies
Empathy Beyond the Human
Intragenerational Justice and Care
Parasitology
Posthuman Care
Viral

Joni Adamson and Steven Hartman

TOXIC EMBODIMENT

Earth-dwellers currently inhabit an avalanche of over a hundred billion tonnes of human-emitted chemical substances a year, harming people and life in general. Some scientists even suggest we inhabit a toxic planet, saturated with chemical waste in a chain of events unlike anything in the Earth's history (Paulsen et al. 2021; Nature Geoscience 2017). The World Health Organization estimates that one in four people on earth die every year from diseases related to air, water and soil pollution, chemical exposure, climate change and ultraviolet radiation; these deaths mainly resulting from human activities. Our toxic emissions might well be the heaviest human impact on the planet, and also the least regulated or even understood. Existential risks around health today encompass a much wider set of issues as we intra-act with antibiotics, nanoparticles and untested chemical cocktails through the food we eat, its packaging, the make-up some wear, the latest furniture we sit in. *Toxic embodiment* refers to this now ubiquitous condition, where differentially situated human and non-human bodies, land- and waterscapes are immersed in the naturalcultural intra- and interactions with toxic assemblages. Substances like endocrine disruptors, neurotoxins, asthmagens, carcinogens and mutagens flow through and accumulate in exposed environments and the always porous bodies of both human and non-human kinds. The concept of toxic embodiment addresses the postnatural mutuality of environed embodiment and embodied environment, building on posthumanist feminist and environmental theorizing (see Braidotti and Bignall 2018; Margulies and Bersaglio 2018), and engendering understandings of 'trans-corporeality' (Alaimo 2008; 2010; 2016) and 'slow violence' (Nixon 2011).

Toxic embodiment also speaks to the impossibility of purity of any kind in the posthuman and postnatural setting of the Anthropocene. We are all entangled in our shared relationship to chemical substances that make us up, and break us down. Life is chemical, as is death. Amongst chemists, the issue of how *toxic* something is – is infamously just a matter of quantity and concentration. Paracelsus, the sixteenth-century Swiss chemist (alchemist) and natural philosopher, expressed the basic principle of toxic embodiment (Ball 2006): 'All things are poison and nothing is without poison; only the dose makes a thing not a poison.' Often this is abbreviated into 'the dose makes the poison'. Substances with toxic properties cause noticeable harm only in high enough concentration. What used to be poison to all living creatures on planet Earth billions of years ago: oxygen, is to most contemporary organisms today a core element of the air we breathe. Even water, like any chemical substance, can become toxic to the body, if ingested or absorbed by the body in too high a concentration. Toxic embodiment is thus a relational and situated concept, depending on a variety of factors like concentration, mode or duration of exposure. In feminist and queer environmental-, post- and more-than-human humanities, toxic embodiment gathers under-researched aspects of human and non-human environmental health, asking political questions around exposure and vulnerability, *to whom* and how it matters. What is benign, even pleasurable to some, is toxic to others. In tending to a wider concern of effects in humans as societal and cultural beings, and across other species, toxic embodiment invokes a transcorporeal ethic that 'turn from the disembodied values and ideals of bounded individuals toward an attention to situated, evolving practices that have far-reaching and unforeseen consequences for multiple peoples, species and ecologies' (Alaimo 2008: 253).

In the present context, the question of toxic embodiment embraces extensive existential concerns around health, environmental degradation, global politics and co-existence in a situation where the concentration of, and exposure to, toxins are reaching new levels and have unfathomable consequences for diverse populations. Plastics seep hormone-like substances into bodies, non-human animals are born and bred, fatally toxic, and disposed of in laboratories, industries leak waste into rivers and oceans, and the weather itself carries pollution and traces of contaminants to the Polar Regions, especially to the Arctic, into seal, reindeer and human breast milk (Massart et al. 2005; Fournier et al. 2021). The modern

transcorporeal transits of toxicity spares nobody and no place, even while far away from the source of origin (Mishra et al. 2021), which makes toxic embodiment a matter of scale, relationality and transition.

Transdisciplinary research from across environmental sciences and environmental humanities (Neimanis, Åsberg and Hedrén 2015; Cielemecka and Åsberg 2019) points to the seriousness of the questions of bioaccumulation, that is, the processes by which toxic substances, industrial waste or human-made chemical compounds, gradually accumulate in living tissues (Mackay and Fraser 2000). With a focus on black diaspora and poor communities, critical environmental scholars of race and gender have asked if toxicity is *coloniality made material*, embodied and lived experience (Agard-Jones; DeLoughrey 2013; Murphy 2017). Simultaneously, insights from queerfeminist research and environmental policy research (e.g. Chen 2012; Ah-King and Hayward 2014; Di Chiro 2010) draw attention to the problematic framing of toxicity in the media and popular imagination. Gendered, racialized, ableist and heteronormative patterns of mainstream environmentalism expose often perceived 'feminization of nature' as a threat. Castrating chemicals, low sperm counts, and reproductive and genital neoformations, is shown as the ultimate risk scenario. Alarmist views to toxic embodiment should therefore also draw our critical attention. What are the normative views to gender and embodiment that get reproduced when toxic exposure is narrated? What would even a clean, detoxed or pure body be? The notion that toxicity (or toxic people) must be purged from our lives (detoxed) in order to return to some pristine or pure state of being points to a whole range of assumptions that need re-appraisal in everyday life. Toxic embodiment begs the question: How are we complicit ourselves in the first place, with our consumerist lifestyles and taken-for-granted, even normative, intoxications (say, coffee, cars and social media)? What can we live with, and without? What is the dosage effect on peoples, species and ecologies that the individual consumerist might experience as mundane, even pleasurable, intoxication? Considering dosage and scale, our own involvement and mortal embodiment, how can we learn to live, and die, better on this damaged, yet still pleasurable, planet of chemical substances?

In sum, the analytical theme of toxic embodiment establishes a postdisciplinary field of enquiry that critically attends to the contemporary material and discursive interweavings of toxicity and human and non-human bodies and environments (cf. Cielemecka and Åsberg 2019).

Connection to other entries:
Endomaterialities
Crip Theory
Humus Economicus
Queer Death Studies
Transcorporeality II
Vibrant Death

Cecilia Åsberg

TRANSCORPOREALITY II: COVID-19 AND CLIMATE CHANGE

Transcorporeality, as articulated in *Bodily Natures: Science, Environment, and the Material Self* (Alaimo 2010), emerged from a study of environmental health and environmental justice movements that detect and contend with invisible toxins that intensify racial and economic inequality. Whereas predominant models of environmentalism seek to protect a nature that is 'out there', transcorporeality contends that the ostensibly external world is already the very stuff of the human, as substances, many of them harmful, permeate and affect our material selves. Transcorporeality is a mode of new materialist posthumanism, as it contends with material agencies and intra-actions that erode the boundaries of the human figure, positioning everyone, including non-human species, at the crossroads of body, place and substance. The transcorporeal subject is a creature of the Anthropocene, a being immersed in profoundly altered ecologies and risky anthropogenic materialities. Modes of epistemology, ontology, ethics and politics that assume a human subject detached from and exerting control over an external material world are relics of Western thought, colonialism and capitalist commodification. Granted, these relics remain terribly effective in terms of amassing the wealth of the few, and yet they are unable to adequately address current environmental crises that permeate our very selves.

Shifting from environmental health and environmental justice movements that focus on invisible chemical toxins, to the COVID-19 pandemic and the ravages of climate change, underscores how 'natural disasters' reveal patterns of social injustice that are deeply embodied. Marco Armiero, writes in 'Something I have learned from COVID-19': 'The embodied experience of transcorporeality in the dramatic form of COVID-19 calls for rethinking our understanding of the daily, familiar environment and its invisible/invisibilised relationships to the wider world' (2020). Rejecting a levelling impulse that obscures inequalities, Armiero stresses that such structures are deeply interwoven with human health and well-being: 'No, through COVID-19 I have not discovered how much we are all the same, but, on the contrary, the extent to which inequalities are inscribed in our lives and deaths' (2020). Bjørn Kristensen, in 'Welcome to the Viralocene: Transcorporeality and Peripheral Justice in an Age of Pandemics,' similarly argues, in an essay published before vaccines were developed, that the concept of 'transcorporeality matters in this age of pandemics because in so many ways the real disease we are facing is not viral in nature but rather is a deeply political and economic affliction upon already marginalized bodies that is made apparent through the presence of the virus' (2020). The shameful global disparities in vaccine availability magnify Kristensen's argument. I would not cast the virus as less real than politics and economics, but would instead stress a new materialist onto-epistemology of intra-action, as developed by Karen Barad, to account for the ways that multiple realities come into being through and with each other, not separately. Accounting for why African-Americans have been dying at higher rates from COVID-19, for example, demands analyses that consider the intertwined impacts of histories of racism, ongoing racist violence, economic inequalities, racial geographies of housing and labour, and perhaps the thorny questions of epigenetics. Such questions confuse the divides between the natural sciences, the social sciences and the humanities, suggesting the need for the posthumanities, and more specifically, what Lucinda Cole has termed the medical posthumanities (Cole 2021). Transcorporeality, as a method for the medical posthumanities would trace the interconnections between health disparities, systems of racial and economic injustice, and various environmental/material agencies, broadly conceived. Meanwhile, in the stark pandemic landscapes of the US, the unmasked faces of COVID deniers and vaccine refusers perform an aggressive mode of capitalist individualism, reasserting their 'rights' to consider themselves as magically self-contained, rigidly independent, impermeable actors. The masked face, by contrast, signifies a recognition of exposure as a state of being and a willingness to engage in precautionary measures as an ethics of interdependence.

Living through the extreme heat, drought and wildfires in the Western US has made climate change painfully immediate. When the skies were dark with smoke, the air was off-the-charts dangerous to breathe, and grey ash rained down for many days, it was impossible to ignore the transcorporeal sense of immersion within the changed climate. What was in that ash and smoke? Not just the ashes of trees, but (I guessed, having no way of actually knowing) the toxic particles of burned houses, cars, and other human buildings and possessions, piling up like snow in my yard. That was last summer. This summer, breathing wildfire smoke for weeks has become normalized, though I worry for the unhoused people and all the wildlife that have no refuge from the dangerous air. In 'Climate Change and the "Thick Time" of Transcorporeality', Astrida Neimanis and Rachel Loewen Walker propose the concept of 'weathering' to bring climate change, which is often understood abstractly, closer to home. 'We can grasp the transcorporeality of weathering as a spatial overlap of human bodies and weathery nature.' (2014: 560). With the concept of weathering they 'seek to cultivate a sensibility that attunes us not only to the "now" of the weather, but toward ourselves and the world as weather bodies, mutually caught up in the whirlwind of a weather-world, in the thickness of climate-time.' (561) Published in 2014, this sense of weathering already seems closer to home as so many people, in different regions, are feeling the impact of climate change more directly and dramatically.

To consider COVID-19 and climate change through the lens of transcorporeality may seem to reinstall the human at the centre of knowledge. But weathering these storms requires that we foster modes of subjectivity, epistemologies, ethics and politics, in which we recognize ourselves as immersed within multispecies ecologies, networks, assemblages and climates. We need modes of thinking as the stuff of the world, of performing insurgent exposure, and of responding ethically and politically to our participation within global networks of destruction, oppression and extinction. This entails an engagement with scientific captures, informed speculation about scientific information, the practice of musing upon the limits of our knowledge, and the determination to somehow proceed in the midst of uncertainty, loss and change. Will the necessary science ever be done that could tell us how much the wildfire smoke itself – along with the loss of habitat, extreme heat and persistent drought – has or will contribute to species extinction? Imagine the birds and the mountain lions trying to breathe, within the surreal landscapes of climate change, landscapes brought about not only by the rapacious exploits of settler colonialism

and capitalism – so tempting to make these seem merely historical or abstract – but by the ordinary activities of ordinary people. Tracing transcorporeal connections can be disheartening and exhausting. Take heart. Rosi Braidotti casts exhaustion as potentially affirmative, in that it 'marks the demise of the sovereign subject position,' as a 'practice that aims at deactivating the despotic attachment to power' (2019: 181). In the midst of pandemics, climate change and the sixth great extinction, would it be possible to let that sovereign subject position go and instead, create affirmative, collective, multispecies modes of transcorporeality, orienting ourselves toward sustaining life in this world?

Connection to other entries:
Convergences
Critical Posthuman Theory
Posthuman Care
Syndemic
Viral

Stacy Alaimo

TRANSJECTIVITY

Posthumanism does not do away with the human. Rather, it does away with the notion of the human as autonomous, exceptional, a mind in a body and yet separate from it, in charge and in control, a mind/body separate from others and separate from nature, empowering it to engage in exploitative behaviour. This is the notion that posthumanism criticizes and dismisses, a notion inherited from centuries of humanist philosophizing. But the human being itself is there to stay and we need to theorize it in a way that allows us to better understand it. Critical posthumanism does not wipe the theoretical ground clean either. As the heir of feminist theory, postcolonial studies, affect theory of a Deleuzoguattarian kind, phenomenology and postphenomenology, it incorporates and pushes further key insights provided by these, putting them in conversation in a post-anthropocentric context. The renewed attention to materiality afforded by material feminists provide another set of key insights that allow us to grasp that bodies are more than subjectivized embodiment (Neimanis 2017). I elaborate the concept of transjectivity on this fertile ground.

Transjectivity is a compound word that enmeshes the transsubjective and the transobjective. All beings exist in a web of subjective relations: to themselves, to individual others, to collective others. One's being is shaped by these encounters as well as socio-cultural factors such as ideologies, religion, language, social imaginaries. The operations of power that constitute a subject, as delineated by Foucault (1982) and Butler (1990) for example, are part of the transsubjective constitution of the human. These operate along with and permeate the relation to oneself and intersubjective relations to others, as Beauvoir potently explains in *The Second Sex*: individual female human beings interiorize patriarchy's construct 'woman' and become the women they are expected to be (Beauvoir 2011). They relate to themselves, to others, and to society as a whole as women. They make themselves such. The woman a female human becomes is a transsubjective assemblage of all these relations.

In addition to transsubjective constitution, we are also materially constituted, what I capture with 'transobjectivity', the parallel term to 'transsubjectivity'. Material feminists have insisted on the importance of understanding the materiality of our beings, our bodies, and the fact that we are consistently permeated by the materiality in which we are thanks to quantum entanglements of particles (Barad 2007), biochemical processes that allow the creation and exchange of molecules (Frost 2016), the porosity of membranes, and the dynamic and vibrant unfolding of matter and material relations (Bennett 2010). Transjectivity posits that transsubjective and transmaterial webs of relations and constitution are constantly unfolding and dynamically becoming. A self emerges in the midst of this dynamic bundle that we are as bodies, as a moment of coalescence that goes on to be undone the next moment through the ongoing transjective constitution of itself. Transjectivity retains and recombines traces of the transcorporeal (Alaimo 2010, 2016), the cyborg (Haraway 1991), the holobiont (Haraway 2016), the mangle (Hekman 2014), and the zoe/geo/techno framed subject (Braidotti 2019).

All beings are transjective and all beings are radically entangled in their subjective and material relations. All beings exercise agentic capacity (Coole 2005, Coole and Frost 2010) while some may also exercise agency in the traditional sense. However, to say this is not to posit any kind of symmetricality in the relations or the power of action: there are many different quantitative and qualitative degrees of entanglements and affect that circulate through those and my impact on the constitution of another transjective being may not match the impact that other being has on me. With that said, all beings are constituted through their manifold entanglements. What this means for us humans is the discovery of our ontological vulner-ability

– our capacity to wound or be wounded – which really amounts to affect-ability, the ability we have to affect and be affected, materially and subjectively. Because our beings are porous in manifold ways, we are under constant threat of being undone and are in fact undone through any new relation, entanglement, affect or shift thereof. But being undone is a doing. The threat opens up potentiality. At the same time we are undone, we emerge as a self that continues to change: a dynamic assemblage that is making itself and is being made.

Embracing transjectivity as an ontological notion requires that we devise an ethics of flourishing that rests upon a recognition of ontological vulner-ability/affect-ability and its impact on self-constitution. Every relation I enter into, every action I carry through, every belief or ideology I uphold are not only contributing to shape me but all beings with whom I am entangled. As such, my responsibility toward others, be they human or more-than-human, is magnified. Because the mesh of entangled relations we are cannot be disentangled, we need to exercise care (Puig de la Bellacasa 2017).

The fundamental ethical insight offered by transjectivity is that no being can thrive and flourish on their own. This means that one must open oneself to one's relations and perform one's exposure (Alaimo 2016) as transjective being. This also means that as one enters in relations with other beings, one must do so with understanding, care and respect for them as transjective beings. As humans, we have the capacity to understand ourselves as transjective and therefore, our responsibility toward others is coupled with a heightened response-ability. As the kind of being that can know and reflect on one's own being as transjective, we have a duty to exercise our agentic capacity in the least negative way. While we cannot ever entirely predict the range and impact of our actions or relations, we can and should adopt a humble and careful attitude. This is the transjective ethos needed for our troubled times.

Connection to other entries:
Collaborative Politics
Convergences
Critical Posthuman Theory
Posthuman Agency
Posthuman Care
Racializing Assemblages
Relational Sovereignty
Transcorporeality II

Christine Daigle

U

UNDEAD

Perhaps as a response to the experience of collective death in multiple worlds, the undead are now characters that haunt contemporary imaginaries, and have become generative figures in the (post) humanities. The undead swarm through a multitude of movies, graphic novels and video games, as a series of funhouse mirrors that reflect different facets of the present human condition. Beyond the flat represent-ations of the undead as digital others – enemies that can be clicked away and killed without remorse on our smartphones and Xboxes – the living dead have complex underpinnings. They come in a variety of flavours, and it is perhaps helpful to look at what this variety is made of. Jeffrey Jerome Cohen (1997) writes that 'the monster is difference made flesh, come to dwell among us'. But the undead are not so much monsters, as they are foreboding constructs, embodi-ments of dark possibility, the fear and fascin-ation we feel towards realities that could come to be. So, what are the meanings of the identities inhabited by the living dead?

The classic undead are the vampire, the ghost and the zombie. A vampire is a seductive incarnation of extractivism and capital, an immortal being that eroticizes sucking out your blood and turning you into more of itself. A vampire doesn't give anything back, not even a reflection ... a black hole of desire and hunger.

The ghost – a spirit without a body – can be seen as both the attenuated human, and as the restless craving for temporalities that can no longer be accessed: frustration, longing and howling. The ghost wants to turn the clock back, a return to former glory.

Like the slogans of recent American electoral campaigns: 'Make America Great Again'; 'Build Back Better'. But we can only build on what is ahead of us. The white ghost howls, but time moves forward.

Zombies are an unthinking and raven-ous multitude. As opposed to the vampire and the ghost which are extraordinary, the zombie is ordinary. Ghosts and vampires have individual desires and idiosyncrasies, but zombies are a collective, zombies are never alone. They are legion. A multitude of bodies without agency, shells, husks, less than human ... Movies and novels are filled with scenes of victims who willingly offer up their necks to join the ranks of the immortal. Zombie bites, however, are not sexy. It is hardly attractive to lose one's mind, and sense of self, while becoming infected with an uncontrollable rage. We know the names of our ghosts and vampires, but zombies never get a name. They inhabit an uncomfortable space of being disposable in death, and probably being also disposable in life.

Taken together these figures of the undead invite us to reflect, with a sense of horror, about what the human has become.

The undead herald a coming apocalypse, or perhaps a new era of posthuman flourishing that is yet to come. Horror is a map of what we fear. As our unconscious anxieties are elevated to the forefront of consciousness, audiences respond with fascination and ghoulish delight. Horror can offer catharsis in times of trouble and even open up wounds to begin the process of healing.

The undead play a big role in apocalyptic imaginaries. But, both horror movies as well as cute spin-offs for kids in the virtual world of Minecraft, have lost sight of what is actually at stake in end time imaginings. Many worlds have already ended. Indigenous and previously enslaved peoples have long been living with apocalypse after terrifying encounters with inhuman monsters. The undead have started to cross the threshold into the real world. Horrific images of the undead emerged during the pandemic: hundreds of restless bodies floated along the Ganges River in India, and thousands of minks that had been culled, emerged from their graves. And in Siberia, as the permafrost melts, 30,000-year-old viruses that are still infectious have been found amongst the methane fumes. Comfortable middle-class lifestyles may well be under threat, but not from hordes of people displaced by colonialism and capitalism. Violence is not the right response to the undead. Instead, we need renewed commitments to intergenerational responsibility and care.

Outside of the undead that are like us, there are the undead that we ourselves have created. Products of this consumer culture will outlive us, with a relentless haunting presence. All the novel entities that have been introduced into the world, ghost nets haunting the oceans, toxic spills, radium isotopes with a half-life decay of 1,600 years, making buried bones glow in

the dark. Pick up a piece of sun-bleached plastic from the shore. Peel the brittle flakes with your fingernail as if you were scraping a palimpsest, uncovering layers of meaning from this petroleum product that cannot die. Perhaps it is your own 'fossil kin' – your own ancestor from the Palaeozoic that has been unearthed, reanimated and weaponized (Todd 2021).

Once upon a time death was simply an intergenerational gift. Ecological communities – associations of predators and prey, omnivorous scavengers, parasites and hosts – have always depended on ongoing intergenerational cycles of life and death. The food web is premised on reciprocity among species. New kinds of undead entities and agents emerged with industrial production. The catastrophe of modern progress, as described by Walter Benjamin (1968), has disrupted these regenerative processes. Piles of debris are still growing skyward, with wreckage that is very slow to decay. Life and death have been uncoupled (Rose 2011). The undead products of modernity are turning away from the living. Life is becoming non-life on a planetary scale (Povinelli 2016).

In the words of Jeffrey Jerome Cohen, 'Apocalypse signals giving up on the future instead of committing to the difficult work of composing a better present' (2012). Instead of revelling in the horror of the apocalypse, Cohen suggests that we disentangle the undead from nightmares about the end times. We can embrace the undead as generative figures that illustrate aspects of the world that are needy of care.

Recognizing how we ourselves are becoming undead is an important first step as we contemplate reparative work that is urgently needed. It is easy to lumber along, unthinking, within a modern world that continues to generate wreckage in the name of progress. It is time to rethink how to care for our dead and our forgotten ancestors. We must rearticulate intergenerational cycles of life and death. It is important to advocate for responsibility in technology and design. We must learn to create and make things that can die.

Connection to other entries:
Queer Death Studies
Toxic Embodiment
Vibrant Death
Weird

Julieta Aranda and Eben Kirksey

V

VIBRANT DEATH

Vibrant Death (Lykke 2022) is a figuration which reontologizes death in conversation between vitalist materialist, spiritual materialist and immanence philosophical perspectives – with a posthuman phenomenology of mourning as lens. The reontologization is critically turned against dualist (Christian and Cartesian) conceptualizations and modern Western imaginaries of death. It rejects the ways in which the human corpse, as a result of the dualist mind/body divides, is constructed as a piece of base, inert machinelike matter, left by the immortal soul and/or the rational subject. Lykke (2022) also argues that the way in which human corpses are cast as abject (Kristeva 1982) is a consequence of the mind/body divides. Critically turning away from these historical constructions, the unfurling of the figuration of vibrant death takes another route, sustained by Spinoza's monism and concept of *conatus* (1996), by political philosopher Jane Bennett's concept of vibrant matter (2010), and by an immanence philosophical understanding of life and death as a flat continuum rather than an opposition (Braidotti 2006, 2013; Deleuze and Guattari 1987). Against this backdrop, the figuration is built on the presuppositions that neither should dead and living bodies be understood as ultimately different, nor are human bodies (dead or alive) to be seen as exceptional, and decisively different from non-human ones.

To flesh out the implications of these presuppositions, Lykke (2022) reflects on death and the dead human body through a posthuman phenomenology of mourning, materialized through autophenomenographic analyses and poetic explorations, carried out from the position of enunciation of a mourning 'I', and entangled with philosophical contemplations. The methodological entrance through the mourning 'I' is chosen as an alternative to the conventional philosophical subject position: the sovereign 'I'. While death per definition can be reflected only in anticipation, it is argued that the liminal position of the one who deeply mourns the loss of a beloved, and who, in a symphysizing (bodily empathizing) mood and mode, experiences the passed away loved one as an intimate, co-present companion, still opens potentials for a different approach than that of the sovereign 'I'. The latter cannot escape its resistances to the idea of its own death, and these resistances will unavoidably interfere with the sovereign philosopher-subject's contemplations. By contrast, the mourning subject may take another approach due to hir potential desire to die as a way of becoming-one with the dead beloved. Against this background, Lykke (2022) explores the theme of love-death as part of the unfolding of the figuration of vibrant death.

However, instead of approaching the love-death theme from a conventional stance in a romantic-humanist aesthetics, it is queered and posthumanized. It is suggested that a poetic and spiritual-material co-becoming with the material remains of the dead beloved, metamorphosed through cremation and spreading of the ashes over the sea, can be an entrance to the awakening of other queer and posthuman sensibilities towards a symphysizing with the inhuman, conative forces and material agencies of the world. To further sustain the argument and unfurl the figuration of vibrant death, pluriversal conversations (Tlostanova and Mignolo 2012) are established with the spiritualist materialism of queer, feminist and decolonial philosopher Gloria Anzaldua (1987; 2015) and her spelling out of the agencies of spiritmattering matter (Schaeffer 2018). Through such pluriversal conversations, and the autophenomeno-graphic and poetic analyses, it is spelled out how the co-becoming opens radically changed horizons. The thresholds between life and death are redefined as cyclical/spiralling shape-shifting rather than embedded in a chronological timeline. The establishing of ongoing, non-nostalgic relationships between the living and the dead is another outcome of the changed horizons, based on a Deleuzoguattarian inspired distinction (Deleuze, and Guattari 1987) between molar mourning of the human subject that was, and molecular mourning related to the vibrant assemblages of spectrally and materially metamorphosed remains of the dead beloved.

The figuration of vibrant death is shaped up through an individual story of mourning (Lykke 2020). But it is also collectivized as a figuration, offering a critical-affirmative, posthuman ethics of death as vibrant. This is an ethics that requires recognition of death not as a final endpoint on a linear chrononormative timeline, but entangled with life within a continuous process of cyclical/spiralling shape-shifting. Against the background of this cyclicity, an ethics of vibrant death distances itself from the exceptionalizing and elitist claims to the possibility and desirability of human immortality, embedded in (illusory) transhumanist beliefs in the potentials of human technoscientific powers. Moreover, an ethics of vibrant death is defined as planetary in its perspective, insofar as it poses a radical challenge to the global necropolitics of post/colonial, extractivist, racial capitalism, when it requires that all deathbound critters (non-human and human) on the planet, rather than being subjected to necropowers, should be allowed a vibrant death. This is a death which implies both a vibrant merging with the dynamic inhuman forces, *zoe* (Braidotti 2006) that makes up the world, and a cyclical/spiralling shape-shifting re-emergence.

Connection to other entries:
Posthuman Feminist Aesthetics
Queer Death Studies
Transcorporeality II
Undead

Nina Lykke

VIRAL

It is April 2021, the second spring of the COVID-19 pandemic. Lisbon is experiencing an abnormal cold wave and I text my father about the heater he's installing. I read the news. I watch a YouTube video of two people talking about fiction and narrative and I feel envious of how COVID-free their thoughts are. I read the news. I discover a story published online about an imaginary travel to China and I wonder when will my next travel be, knowing I should not wish to travel again. I read the news. I refill the birdfeeder with seeds, compensating for how some (humans) eroded the resources of many (humans and non). I read the news. I let the cats out, feeling I shouldn't be letting the cats out while the birds are eating. I read the news. I stare out of the window and wonder, again, what on earth is going on.

This is a list of some of the things I did instead of writing this entry. I am sharing it with you because they matter. They are symptoms, manifestations of a state of sufferance, agitation and dispersion that punctuates the present. As symptoms, they can be transmitters too, accentuating the condition they are trying to eliminate. Hence their paradoxical stance, for while easing the pain, they sometimes propagate its cause. Another important example of this dual nature of symptoms can be found in such gestures as coughing and sneezing. The body, while attempting to clean its breathing passages, violently propagates pathogens by releasing aerosols, some of which may find a new host. But despite being exemplar and sometimes painful vectors of transmission, symptoms can be healers too. Sneezing and coughing effectively expel irritant particles. Similarly, the above-mentioned gestures of everyday pandemic life are also means of searching for solace and attunement to change and the unknown, gestures of both connection and disconnection to the distress and loss caused by the global propagation of the disease COVID-19 and the resulting propagation of information and misinformation about the SARS-CoV-2, a virus that went viral, which is what viruses do.

So, viral symptoms can be manifestations of a malaise, vectors of transmission, and healing attempts. They are one of the tangible expressions of a real situation that has, and is, causing so much fear, insecurity and grief to so many and in so many ways. Followingly, I would like to propose the term viral as a movement, speed and intensity and consider its potential for being a long-term means of regeneration, thanks to its intrinsic relationship to causality and its capacity to activate planetary threads of intersectional transmission. This proposal is not metaphorical. This is a time for concrete figurations that make recovery possible and that appear when thinking is insufficient, planning redundant, and ideas scarce. Suffering subjects are not mere occasions to think about and to learn from. So this proposal concretely aligns itself with virality as a propagation force, a turbulence, and an agent of diffusion to investigate its possible positive outcome.

Viral processes are not human-made. Even if the evolutionary history of viruses is hard to tell, it is known that their inception is aligned with that of early life, preceding and conditioning the origins of much of the current and previous lifeforms on the planet, including that of animals. Viruses have adapted to these multiple living modes too. While metabolic processes were slowly allowing bodies to became bodies, viruses learned to mutate, adapt and propagate with and through these bodies that were becoming bodies. In doing so, viruses also modulated these bodies to their own vices, strengths and weaknesses, making them both porous and resistant to them. Viruses and living organisms constituted one another, participated into one another's narratives, existences, immunities, inceptions and extinctions. It was also through bodies that viruses learned to move and transmit, that is, to become viral. In doing so, they trained bodies to both support and stimulate virality.

Bodies that learned to whisper, speak, shout, inhale and exhale. To aerosol. To cough, sneeze, spit, sweat and touch. To fomite. To drink, eat, regurgitate, urinate and defecate. To be waterborne. To breast-feed, bleed, lubricate, ejaculate and host. To vector. To sit-and-wait. Bodies know how to sit-and-wait. Viruses know how to sit-and-wait better.

Viral processes are not human-made but they can be human-accelerated. Even if evolutionary stories of viruses are hard to tell, it is said that their present-day action is aligned with that of contemporary life-forms, having adapted to so much life in the planet but largely adapting it too. While contemporary metabolic processes are slowly weakening the bodies of many bodies, and contemporary capitalist processes are quickly eroding the diversity of biodiversity. Viruses have learned to mutate, adapt and propagate faster with and through these bodies that are becoming less bodies, these habitats that are becoming less habitats, these spaces that are becoming more crammed. Where everybody consumes everybody else quicker, everybody gets everywhere faster, and everybody touches everybody else more. No wonder viral became another word for the quickly consumed, the rapid, the overloaded.

But by existing through contact, flow and movement, the viral flow undermines basilar concepts of the Western ecological modernity. It attests the degree to which organisms are interconnected, interdependent, intersected. It troubles the obsolete concept of species (Sodikoff 2020). By jumping, flowing and hovering from one organism to another while being able to call a home to each of them, the viral flow makes visible the fertile hybridity that characterizes life in its multiple configurations. By lingering, permeating, spilling and sitting-and-waiting in airports, train stations, offices, markets, factories and schools, the viral flow blurs the function and functionality of spaces that were considered aseptic, controlled, lifeless. It turns operations, enterprises and organizations into feasts of triumphant permutation.

The viral flow 'is you calling me in a world we can't control' (Gumbs 2021). The viral flow turns transmission into awareness and regeneration. By rendering commonality visible, it conjures transformation. May this awareness be as persuasive, contagious and diffused as the viral turbulence that made it perceptible.

Connection to other entries:
Parasitology
Syndemic
Transcorporeality II

Filipa Ramos

W

WEIRD

Posthuman thought raises questions about the 'human' as a stable category and with a homogenous body at the centre of the universe and challenges the assumption that 'human' is hierarchically dominant over other categories such as 'non-human', 'environment', and 'nature'. Such questions also occupy the weird: a restless, slippery form of narrative, which for the better part of a century has grappled with the deepest anxieties about being human in deep time. 'Weird' comes from the Old English *wyrd*, which means 'fate' or 'destiny', but since the nineteenth century (if we look past the more colloquial use of the adjective as a synonym to 'odd'), 'weird' more often means '[p]artaking of or suggestive of the supernatural; of a mysterious or unearthly character; unaccountably or uncomfortably strange; uncanny' (OED Online 2020). Authors like Algernon Blackwood, Shirley Jackson, Clark Ashton Smith and H. P. Lovecraft established the weird as a distinct literary category; Lovecraft, in particular, 'explicitly adopted, defended, and defined the weird tale' (Noys and Murphy 2016: 118). Gathered around the magazine *Weird Tales* (1923–), their nightmarish stories formed the 'pulpy underside of literary modernism' (Marshall 2016: 633). In the twenty-first century, the weird has seen a popular and critical resurgence, with a considerable number of 'weird' special journal issues, genealogies and edited collections in circulation since the 2010s in particular (c.f. Sederholm and Weinstock 2016; Luckhurst 2017; Canavan and Hageman 2016; Greve and Zappe 2019 and 2020; Carroll and Sperling 2020). Ann and Jeff VanderMeer's seminal collection *The Weird* (2011) contains stories by authors ranging as widely as Lovecraft, Franz Kafka, Daphne Du Maurier, Ben Okri and Octavia E. Butler, and is a testimony to the hybridity of the weird and speaks to its influence as a literary mode or register rather than (merely) a subgenre of fantastic fiction.

Explaining the weird is tricky business, though. Lovecraft's famous 'atmosphere of breathless and unexplainable dread of outer, unknown forces' (Lovecraft 2011: 1043), resonates with contemporary characterizations of the weird, which are similarly interested in atmosphere and affect over plot. Most definitions consider the weird to be a type of horror, and many compare and contrast the weird to other aesthetic registers such as the uncanny, the sublime, the fantastic and the eerie. In the broadest sense, the weird expresses an urgent feeling of 'estrangement of our sense of reality' (Noys and Murphy 2016: 117; Joshi 1990: 118). Recent scholarship stresses the weird's category slippage (Luckhurst 2017: 1046; VanderMeer 2008: xi), and resistance to fantastic conventions; archetypes like vampires or ghosts are uninteresting because of their ordinary horror (VanderMeer and VanderMeer 2011, xvi; Fisher 2016: 15). Other definitions frontload the weird's 'obsession with the numinous under the everyday' (Miéville 2009: 511), and its critique of anthropocentrism (MacCormack 2016: 200–201, Marshall 2016: 633–634).

Chronologically, it is common to divide the weird into 'old weird' (*c.* 1880–1940) and 'new weird' (1980 and onward). The new weird marks a countermovement to the old weird and involves a conscious rejection of Lovecraft's racism and misogyny (Kneale 2019: 94–95; MacCormack 2019: 61). New weird writing is more political and experimental, radically bending and challenging old weird tropes such as the indifference of the cosmos (which played into a misanthropic worldview). Although certain authors are closely associated with the new weird, like China Miéville and Jeff VanderMeer, 'their' weird has become a genre-hopping, transmedial mode of storytelling, with films, TV series, video games and graphic novels engaging the weird to express 'upheaval and crisis' (Miéville 2009: 513).

The new weird is often used with(in) other genres and modes to address topics like ecology and climate change, gender and sexism, and race and postcolonialism. Take, for example, Jordan Peele's horror film *Us* (2019) in which people across the United States are hunted, killed and replaced by their *doppelgängers*, who have lived underground for generations, abandoned after a failed government experiment. Peele's movie reads as a call to make visible and talk about the violence of the past, shifting the critical stakes of the weird from cosmic to historic and from misanthropy to racism: what might be called 'common weirdness' (Brinkema 2020: 129).

As Emily Alder notes, 'Weird tales, though at times reactionary, can offer radical new forms of knowledge—ecological, philosophical and spiritual, for example—and model new sets of relations between selves and others' (2020: 3).

It is perhaps not strange, therefore, that the weird has become an important concept for the growing interest in representations of the non-human, different forms of subjectivity and agency, and ecological crisis. Directions include posthumanism and new materialism, as seen in Benjamin Robertson's monograph on VanderMeer's fiction (Robertson 2018; see also Kortekallio 2020), and narrative theory and ecocriticism – most notably in Jon Hegglund's suggestion of a 'weird narratology' (2020: 34). Cultural critics and philosophers like Donna Haraway (2016) and Timothy Morton (2016) evoke a weird aesthetic in their discussion of the 'dreadful graspings, frayings, and weavings' of the Anthropocene/Chthulucene (Haraway 2016: 33), while thinkers within speculative realism consider the weird a productive access point for their object-oriented ontologies (see Harman 2012; Thacker 2011). Recent contributions to queer and feminist studies seek to reclaim Lovecraft's monsters as examples of the weird's 'inherent queerness' (MacCormack 2019: 61; see also Sperling 2017). Likewise, contemporary weird narratives express 'a new sensibility of welcoming the alien and the monstrous as sites of affirmation and becoming' (Noys and Murphy 2016; 125). The weird thus presents a promising platform for questioning tradition, tropes and truths – perhaps particularly in the Anthropocene moment.

Like posthuman theory, the weird seeks to poke (tentacular, slimy) holes in our conceptions about the human, revealing that 'human' and 'nature'; 'inside' and 'outside'; 'self' and 'other' – along with so many other (non-Indigenous) conceptualizations – were in fact always already deeply unstable and intricately interwoven. As part of the posthumanist toolbox, then, weird is when the planetary leaks into the individual and becomes crisis – global and personal; personal *because* it is global: weird is failing to metabolize the dread of being human and recognizing that this failure can be productive.

Connection to other entries:
Critical Posthuman Theory
Linguistic Incompossibility
Posthuman Feminist Aesthetics

Gry Ulstein

Cumulative Bibliography

Aaltola, E. (2018), *Varieties of Empathy: Moral Psychology and Animal Ethics*, London and New York: Rowman and Littlefield International.

Abbas, A. (1997), *Hong Kong: Culture and the Politics of Disappearance*, Minneapolis: University of Minnesota Press.

Abdilla, A., N. Arista, K. Baker, S. Benesiinaabandan, M. Brown, M. Cheung, M. Coleman, A. Cordes, J. Davison, K. Duncan, S. Garzon, D. F. Harrell, P. L. Jones, K. Kealiikanakaoleohaililani, M. Kelleher, S. Kite, O. Lagon, J. Leigh, M. Levesque, J. E. Lewis, K. Mahelona, C. Moses, I. Nahuewai, K. Noe, D. Olson, 'Ō Parker Jones, C. Running Wolf, M. Running Wolf, M. Silva, S. Fragnito, H. Whaanga (2020), *Indigenous Protocol and Artificial Intelligence Position Paper*, Honolulu: Indigenous Protocol and Artificial Intelligence Working Group and the Canadian Institute for Advanced Research.

Adams, C. and J. Donovan (eds) (1995), *Animals and Women*, Durham: Duke University Press.

Adamson, J. (2015), 'The Ancient Future: Diasporic Residency and Food-based Knowledges in the Work of American Indigenous and Pacific Austronesian Writers,' *Canadian Review of Comparative Literature*. 42(1): 5–17.

Adamson, J. and S. Hartman (2020), 'From Ecology to Syndemic: Accounting for the Synergy of Epidemics,' *Bifrost Online*, 8 June, https://bifrostonline.org/joni-adamson-and-steven-hartman/ [accessed 22 February 2022].

Adas, M. (2015), *Machines as the Measure of Men*, Ithaca: Cornell University Press.

Agamben, G. (2011), *The Kingdom and the Glory*, Redwood City: Stanford University Press.

Agamben, G. and S. Wakefield (2014), 'What is a Destituent Power?', *Environment and Planning D – Society and Space* 32(1): 65–74.

Agard-Jones, V. (in preparation), *Body Burdens: Toxic Endurance and Decolonial Desire in the French Atlantic*.

Agius, C. (2017), 'Ordering without bordering: drones, the unbordering of late modern warfare and ontological insecurity,' *Postcolonial Studies*, 20(3): 370–386.

Ah-King, M. and E. Hayward (2014), 'Toxic Sexes—Perverting Pollution and Queering Hormone Disruption,' *O-zone: A Journal of Object-Oriented Studies* 1: 1–12.

Ahmed, S. (2006), *Queer Phenomenology: Orientations, Objects, Others*, Durham: Duke University Press.

Ahmed, S. (2017), 'Making Feminist Points, *Feministkilljoys*, 11 September 2013, https://feministkilljoys.com/2013/09/11/making-feminist-points/ [accessed 1 March 2021].

Akama, Y., A. Light and T. Kamihira (2020), 'Expanding Participation to Design with More-Than-Human Concerns', in C. Del Gaudio (ed), *16PDC Participatory Design Conference: PDC 2020, Participation(s) otherwise : proceedings of the 16th Participatory Design Conference: June 15–19, 2020 Manizales, Colombia – Universidad de Caldas*, 1–11, New York: The Association for Computing Machinery.

Alaimo, S. (2008), 'Trans-Corporeal Feminisms and the Ethical Space of Nature,' in S. Alaimo and S. Hekman (eds), *Material Feminisms*, 120–154, Bloomington Indiana University Press.

Alaimo, S. (2010), *Bodily Natures: Science, Environment, and the Material Self*, Bloomington: Indiana University Press.

Alaimo, S. (2016), *Exposed: Environmental Politics and Pleasures in Posthuman Times*, Minneapolis: University of Minnesota Press.

Alaimo, S. (2018), 'Trans-corporeality' in R. Braidotti and M. Hlavajova (eds.), *Posthuman Glossary*, 435–438, London: Bloomsbury Publishing.

Alder, E. (2020), *Weird Fiction and Science at the Fin de Siècle*, London: Palgrave MacMillan.

Alhassan, A. and P. Chakravartty (2011), 'Postcolonial media policy under the long shadow of empire,' in R. Mansell and M. Raboy (eds), *The Handbook of Global Media and Communication Policy*, 366–382, London: Blackwell Publishing.

Ali, S. M. (2016), 'A brief introduction to decolonial computing,' *XRDS: Crossroads: The ACM Magazine for Students*, 22(4): 16–21.

Ali, S. M. (2021), 'Decolonising Computing?' *OpenLearn*, 3 March, https://www.open. edu/openlearn/science-maths-technology/computing-ict/decolonising-computing [accessed 2 March 2021].

Allinson J. (2015), 'The necropolitics of drones,' *International Political Sociology*, 9(2):113–127.

Alpaydin, E. (2016), *Machine Learning*, Cambridge: MIT Press.

Althusser, L. (1970), *For Marx*, London: NLB.

Amaro, R. (2022), *The Black Technical Object: On Machine Learning and the Aspiration of Black Being*, Boston: MIT Press.

Amaro, R. (2018), 'Afrofuturism,' in Rosi Braidotti and Maria Hlavajova (eds.), *Posthuman Glossary*, London: Bloomsbury Academic.

Amin, K. (2014), 'Temporality', *TSQ: Transgender Studies Quarterly*, 1 (1–2): 219–222.

Amoore, L. (2020), *Cloud Ethics: Algorithms and the Attributes of Ourselves and Others*, Durham: Duke University Press

AMP Research Lab Staff (2021), 'The Color of Coronavirus: COVID-19 Deaths by Race and Ethnicity in the US,' *American Media Public Research Lab*, 5 March, https://www.apmresearchlab.org/covid/ deaths-by-race [accessed 22 February 2022].

Andrews, K. and L. Gruen. (2014), 'Empathy in Other Apes,' in H. L. Maibom (ed), *Empathy and Morality*, 193–209, Oxford and New York: Oxford University Press.

Andrews, R. G. (2020), 'A chunk of Yellowstone the size of Chicago has been pulsing. why?', *National Geographic*, 19 March, https://www.nationalgeographic. com/science/article/chunk-yellowstone-size-chicago-has-been-pulsing [accessed 28 May 2021].

Angwin, J., J. Larson, S. Mattu, and L. Kirchner (2016), 'Machine Bias: There's Software Used Across the Country to Predict Future Criminals. And It's Biased against Blacks,' *ProPublica*, https://www. propublica .org/article/machine-bias-risk-assessments-in-criminal-sentencing [accessed 20 January 2022].

Anzaldua, G. E. (1987), *Borderlands/La Frontera: The New Mestiza*, San Francisco: Aunt Lute Books.

Anzaldua, G. E. (2015), *Light in the Dark/Luz en Lo Oscuro: Rewriting Identity, Reality,*

Spirituality, Durham: Duke University Press.

Aouragh, M., S. Gürses, H. Pritchard, and F. Snelting (2020), 'The Extractive Infrastructures of Contact Tracing Apps,' *Journal of Environmental Media*, 1(2): 9.1–9.9.

Apprich, C., W. H. K. Chun, F. Cramer, and H. Steyerl (2019), *Pattern discrimination*, Minneapolis: University of Minnesota Press.

Armiero, M. (2020), 'Something I have learned from COVID-19', *whitehorsepress*, 14 July, https://whitehorsepress.blog/2020/07/14/something-i-have-learned-from-covid19/ [accessed 6 December 2021].

Arough, M. (2012), *Palestine online: Transnationalism, the Internet and the construction of identity*, New York: IB Tauris.

Arquilla, J., and D. Ronfeldt (2002), *Swarming and the Future of Conflict*, Santa Monica: RAND Corporation.

Arvidsson, M. (2018), 'Targeting, Gender, and International *Posthuman*itarian Law and Practice: Framing The Question of the Human in International Humanitarian Law', *Australian Feminist Law Journal*, 44 (1): 9–28.

Arvidsson, M. (2020), 'The swarm that we already are: artificially intelligent (AI) swarming 'insect drones', targeting and international humanitarian law in a posthuman ecology', *Journal of Human Rights and the Environment*, 11(1): 114–137.

Arvidsson, M. and E. Jones (eds) (forthcoming), *International Law and Posthuman Theory*, Abingdon: Routledge.

Arvidsson, M. and B. Sjöstedt (forthcoming), 'Ordering Human-Other relationships: International Humanitarian Law and Ecologies of Armed Conflicts in the Anthropocene', in V. Chapeaux, U. Natarajan and F. Mégret (eds), *The Routledge Handbook of International Law and the Anthropocene*, Abingdon: Routledge.

Åsberg, C. (2017), 'Feminist Posthumanities in the Anthropocene: Forays into the Postnatural', *Journal of Posthuman Studies*, 1(2): 185–204.

Åsberg, C. and R. Braidotti (eds) (2018), *A Feminist Companion to the Posthumanities*, Cham: Springer.

Åsberg, C. and M. Radomska (2021), 'Environmental violence and postnatural oceans: Low trophic theory in the registers of feminist posthumanities', in M. Husso, S. Karkulehto, T. Saresma, A. Laitila, J. Eilola and H. Siltala (eds), *Gender, Violence and Affect: Interpersonal, Institutional and Ideological Practices*, 265–285, London: Palgrave.

Atanasoski, N. and K. Vora (2019), *Surrogate Humanity: Race, Robots, and the Politics of Technological Futures*, Durham: Duke University Press.

Ball, P. (2006), *The Devil's Doctor: Paracelsus and the World of Renaissance Magic and Science*, London: Heinemann.

Banerji, D. and M. R. Paranjape (eds) (2016), *Critical Posthumanism and Planetary Futures*, New Delhi: Springer.

Barad, K. (2007), *Meeting the Universe Halfway: Quantum Physics and the Entanglement of Matter and Meaning*, Durham: Duke University Press.

Barad, K. (2010), 'Quantum Entanglements and Hauntological Relations of Inheritance: Dis/continuities, SpaceTime Enfoldings and Justice to Come,' *Derrida Today*, 3(2): 240–268.

Barad, K. (2014), 'Diffracting Diffraction: Cutting Together-Apart', *Parallax*, 20(3): 168–187.

Bardawil, F. A. (2020), *Revolution and Disenchantment: Arab Marxism and the Binds of Emancipation*, Durham: Duke University Press.

Barrett, R. and D. Worden (2014), *Oil Culture*, Minneapolis: University of Minnesota Press.

Bateson, G. ([1972] 2000), *Steps to an Ecology of Mind.* Chicago and London: Chicago University Press.

Baucom, I. (2005), *Specters of the Atlantic: Finance Capital, Slavery, and the Philosophy of History*. Durham: Duke University Press.

Bawaka Country including S. Suchet-Pearson, S. Wright, K. Lloyd and L. Burarrwanga (2013), 'Caring as Country: Towards an Ontology of Co-becoming in Natural Resource Management', Asia Pacific Viewpoint, 54: 185–97.

Bayard de Volo L. (2016), 'Unmanned? Gender recalibrations and the rise of drone warfare', *Politics & Gender*, 12(1): 50–77.

Beauvoir, S. de. (2011), *The Second Sex*, New York: Vintage.

Beck, U. (1992), *Risk Society: Towards a New Modernity*, London: SAGE Publications.

Beckman, U. (2016), *Culture, Control, Critique*. London: Rowman and Littlefield.

Bellacasa, M. P. de la (2013), 'Encountering Bioinfrastructure: Ecological Struggles and the Sciences of Soil,' *Social Epistemology*, 28(1): 26–40.

Bellacasa, M. P. de la (2015), 'Making time for soil: Technoscientific futurity and the pace of care,' *Social Studies of Science*, 45(5): 691–716.

Bellacasa, M. P. de la (2017), *Matters of Care: Speculative Ethics in More than Human Worlds*, Minneapolis and London: University of Minnesota Press.

Bellacasa, M. P. de la (2020), 'When the Word for World is Soil. Notes on the Troubles of Ecological Belonging' [lecture], *The Shape of a Circle in the Mind of a Fish: The Understory of the Understory*, Part of the General Ecology project, Serpentine Galleries, 5–6 December. Available online: https://www.youtube.com/watch?v=bfNSPx24f2I (accessed 12 March 2021).

Bendell, J. and R. Reed, (2021), *Deep Adaptation*, Cambridge: Polity Press.

Benjamin, R. (2019), *Race After Technology*, Medford: Polity Press.

Benjamin, W. (1968), *Illuminations*, Berlin: Schocken.

Ben-Moshe, L. (2018), 'Weaponizing disability', *Social Text*, https://socialtext-journal.org/periscope_article/weaponizing-disability/ [accessed 1 February 2021].

Bennett, J. (2005), "The Agency of Assemblages and the North American Blackout", in *Public Culture*, 17(3), pp. 445–465.

Bennett, J. (2010), *Vibrant Matter: A Political Ecology of Things*. Durham: Duke University Press.

Bennett, J. (2018), 'Vibrant Matter' in R. Braidotti and M. Hlavajova (eds), *Posthuman Glossary*, 447–448, London: Bloomsbury.

Bentley, M. (2018), 'Fetishised data: Counterterrorism, drone warfare and pilot testimony,' *Critical Studies on Terrorism*, (11)1: 88–110.

Berardi, F. (2015), *And: Phenomenology of the End*, New York: Semiotext(e).

Berkes, F. (2012), *Sacred Ecology*, London and New York: Routledge.

Berlina, A. (2017), 'Part One: Introduction', in A. Berlina (ed.), *Viktor Shklovsky: A Reader*, 53–63, London and New York: Bloomsbury.

Berne, P. and Raditz, V. (2020), 'To Survive Climate Catastrophe, Look to Queer and Disabled Folks', in A. Wong (ed), *Disability Visibility: First-Person Stories from the Twenty-First Century*, 232–235, New York: Vintage Books.

Bhandar, B. (2018), *Colonial Lives of Property: Law, Land, and Racial Regimes of Ownership*. Durham: Duke University Press.

Bhandar, B. and R. Ziadah (eds) (2020), *Revolutionary Feminisms: Conversations on Collective Action and Radical Thought*, London: Verso.

Bhowmik, S. and J. Hautamäki (2021), 'Panic Breeder,' *DEEP FAKE Exhibition*, https://issuu.com/isabelbeaversstudio/docs/deep_fake_v4_final/s/11622876 [accessed 10 February 2022].

Bignall, S. (2010), *Postcolonial Agency: Critique and Constructivism*, Edinburgh: Edinburgh University Press.

Bignall, S. (2014), 'The Collaborative Struggle for Excolonialism', *Settler Colonial Studies* 4(4): 340–356.

Bignall S. (2020), Posthuman PUBLICS [unpublished manuscript], RMIT University.

Bignall, S., S. Hemming and D. Rigney (2016), 'Three Ecosophies for the Anthropocene: Environmental Governance, Continental Posthumanism and Indigenous Expressivism', *Deleuze Studies* 10(4): 455–478.

Bignall, S. and D. Rigney (2019), 'Transforming Colonial Systems: Indigeneity, nomad thought and posthumanism', in R. Braidotti and S. Bignall (eds) *Posthuman Ecologies: Complexity and Process after Deleuze*. London: Rowman and Littlefield: 159–182.

Blanchette, J.-F. (2011), 'A material history of bits', *Journal of the American Society for Information Science and Technology*, 62(6): 1042–1057.

Blohm, H., S. Beer and D. Suzuki (1987), *Pebbles to Computers: The Thread*, Oxford: Oxford University Press.

Bloom, P. (2017), *Against Empathy: The Case for Radical Compassion*, London: Vintage.

Boers, S. N. (2018), 'Sculpting Body Parts: How the Arts Contribute to Ethical Reflection', *Journal of Medical Ethics Blog*, https://blogs.bmj.com/medical-ethics/2018/10/29/sculpting-body-parts-how-the-arts-contribute-to-ethical-reflection/ [accessed 20 January 2022].

Boers, S. N. (2019), 'Organoid Technology: An Identification and Evaluation of the Ethical Challenges', unpublished PhD thesis, https://dspace.library.uu.nl/handle/1874/380204 [accessed 20 January 2022].

Boers, S. N., and A. L. Bredenoord, (2018), 'Consent for Governance in the Ethical Use of Organoids', *Nature Cell Biology* 20(6): 642–645.

Boers, S. N., J. J. M. Van Delden, and A.L. Bredenoord, (2019), 'Organoids as Hybrids: Ethical Implications for the Exchange of Human Tissues', *Journal of Medical Ethics* 45(2): 131–139.

Boers, S. N., J. J. M. van Delden, H. Clevers, and A.L. Bredenoord, (2016), 'Organoid Biobanking: Identifying the Ethics. Organoids Revive Old and Raise New Ethical Challenges for Basic Research and Therapeutic Use', *EMBO Reports*, 17(7): 938–941.

Boes, T and K. Marshall (2014), 'Writing the Anthropocene', *Minnesota Review*, 80: 60–72.

Bonilla, Y., and Hantel, M. (2016), 'Visualizing Sovereignty: Cartographic Queries for the Digital Age', *archipelagos: a journal of Carribean digital praxis*, issue 1, May 2016, https://doi.org/10.7916/D8CV4HTJ.

Bostrom, N. (2003), 'Are you living in a computer simulation?', *Philosophical Quarterly*, 53(211): 243–255.

Bostrom, N. (2005), 'In Defence of Posthuman Dignity', *Bioethics*, 19(3): 202–214.

Bostrom, N. (2011), 'A History of Transhumanist Thought', in Michael Rectenwald and Lisa Carl (eds.), *Academic Writing Across Disciplines*, London: Pearson Longman.

Bou Akar, H. (2018), *For the War Yet to Come: Planning Beirut's Frontiers*, Stanford: Stanford University Press.

Bourke, J. (2014), 'Killing in a Posthuman World: The Philosophy and Practice of Critical Military History', in B. Blagaard and I. van der Tuin (eds), *The Subject of Rosi Braidotti: Politics and Concepts*, London: Bloomsbury.

Boyle M. J. (2015), 'The legal and ethical implications of drone warfare', *The International Journal of Human Rights*, 19(2): 105–126.

Bozalek, V., M. Zembylas and J. C. Tronto (2020), *Posthuman and political care ethics for reconfiguring higher education pedagogies*, London: Routledge.

Braidotti, R. (1994), *Nomadic Subjects: Embodiment and Sexual Difference in Contemporary Feminist Theory*. New York: Columbia University Press.

Braidotti, R. (2002), *Metamorphoses*, Cambridge: Polity.

Braidotti, R. (2006), 'Posthuman, All Too Human: Towards a New Process Ontology', *Theory, Culture & Society*, 23(7–8): 197–208.

Braidotti, R. (2006), *Transpositions: On Nomadic Ethics*, Cambridge: Polity Press.

Braidotti, R. (2013), *The Posthuman*, Cambridge: Polity Press.

Braidotti, R. (2016), 'Posthuman Critical Theory', in D. Banerji and M. R. Paranjape (eds.), *Critical Posthumanism and Planetary Futures*, New Delhi: Springer India.

Braidotti, R. (2018), 'A Theoretical Framework for the Critical Posthumanities', *Theory, Culture & Society*, 36(6): 31–61. (Published online May 2018.)

Braidotti, R. (2019), 'Affirmative Ethics and Generative Life', *Deleuze and Guattari Studies*, 13(4): 463–481.

Braidotti, R. (2019a), *Posthuman Knowledge*, Cambridge: Polity Press.

Braidotti, R. (2019b), 'A Theoretical Framework for the Critical Posthumanities', *Theory, Culture & Society*, 36(6): 31–61. (Published issue November 2019.)

Braidotti, R. (2022), *Posthuman Feminism*, Cambridge: Polity Press.

Braidotti, R. and S. Bignall (2018), *Posthuman Ecologies: Complexity and Process after Deleuze*, London: Rowman and Littlefield.

Braidotti, R. and M. Hlavajova (eds.), (2018) *Posthuman Glossary*, London: Bloomsbury.

Braidotti, R. and M. Fuller (eds) (2019), 'Transversal Posthumanities,' special issue of *Theory, Culture & Society*, 36(6).

Braidotti, R., V. Bozalek, T. Shefer, and M. Zembylas (eds) (2018), *Socially Just Pedagogies. Posthumanist, Feminist and Materialist Perspectives in Higher Education*, London and Oxford: Bloomsbury Academic.

Braverman, I. (2018), 'Law's Underdog: A Call for More-than-Human Legalities', *Annual Review of Law & Social Science*, 14: 127–44.

Bredenoord, A. L., H. Clevers, and J.A. Knoblich (2017), 'Human Tissues in a Dish: The Research and Ethical Implications of Organoid Technology,' *Science*, 355(6322): eaaf9414.

Brinkema, E. (2020), 'Get Out, Race, and Formal Destiny (On Common Weirdness),' in J. Greve and F. Zappe (eds), *The American Weird: Concept and Medium*, 121–138, London: Bloomsbury Academic.

Brown Weiss, E. (1992), 'In Fairness To Future Generations and Sustainable Development,' *American University International Law Review*, 8(1): 19–26.

Bryld, M., and Lykke, N. (2000), *Cosmodolphins: Feminist cultural studies of technology, animals and the sacred*, London: ZED Books.

Britton, L., G. Klumbyte and C. Draude (2019), 'Doing thinking: revisiting computing with artistic research and technofeminism', *Digital Creativity*, 1(1): 1–16.

Browne, S. (2015), *Dark matters: On the surveillance of blackness*, Durham: Duke University Press.

Brunton, F. (2018), *What Algorithms Want: Imagination in the Age of Computing*, Cambridge: MIT Press.

Buchanan, A. and R. Keohane (2015), 'Toward a Drone Accountability Regime,' *Ethics & International Affairs*, 29(1):15–37.

Buck, H. (2019), *After Geoengineering: Climate Tragedy, Repair, and Restoration*, London: Verso.

Burg, S. van der (2009), 'Taking the "Soft Impacts" of Technology into Account: Broadening the Discourse in Research

Practice,' *Social Epistemology* 23(3–4): 301–316.

Butler, J. (1990), *Gender Trouble. Feminism and the Subversion of Identity*, London and New York: Routledge.

Butler, J. (2004), *Precarious Life: The Powers of Mourning and Violence*, New York: Verso.

Butler, J. (2010), *Frames of War: When Is Life Grievable?*, London: Verso.

Calvino, I. (1997) *Invisible Cities*, Vintage Classic,

Chace, C. (2016), *The Economic Singularity: Artificial Intelligence and the Death of Capitalism*, Three Cs Online Publishing.

Canavan, G. and A. Hageman (eds) (2016), 'Global Weirding,' *Paradoxa*, 28 (1).

Canguilhem, G. (1978), *On the Normal and the Pathological*, Dordrecht: D. Reidel Publishing Company.

Cárdenas, M. (2016), 'Pregnancy: Reproductive Futures in Trans of Color Feminism,' *TSQ: Transgender Studies Quarterly*, 3 (1–2): 48–57.

Carroll, J. S. and A. Sperling (eds) (2020), 'Weird Temporalities,' *Studies in the Fantastic*, 9 (1).

Carroll, S. R., I. Garba, O. L. Figueroa-Rodríguez, J. Holbrook, R. Lovett, S. Materechera, M. Parsons, K. Raseroka, D. Rodriguez-Lonebear, R. Rowe, R. Sara, J. D. Walker, J. Anderson, M. Hudson, M. (2020), 'The CARE Principles for Indigenous Data Governance,' *Data Science Journal*, 19(1): 43.

Catts, O. (2018), 'Biological Arts/Living Arts' in R. Braidotti and M. Hlavajova (eds), *Posthuman Glossary*, 66–68, London: Bloomsbury Publishing.

Chakradhar, S. (2017), 'Put to the Test: Organoid-Based Testing Becomes a Clinical Tool,' *Nature Medicine* 23(7): 796–794.

Chakravartty, P. and M. Mills (2018), 'Virtual Roundtable on Decolonial Computing,' *Catalyst: Feminism, Theory, Technoscience* 4(2): https://catalystjournal.org/index.php/catalyst/article/view/29588/23451

Chalmers, D., M. Burgess, K. Edwards, J. Kaye, E.M. Meslin, and D. Nicol (2015), 'Marking Shifts in Human Research Ethics in the Development of Biobanking,' *Public Health Ethics* 8(1): 63–71.

Chamayou, G. (2015), *A Theory of the Drone*, New York: The New Press.

Chan, A. S. (2018) 'Decolonial Computing and Networking Beyond Digital Universalism,' *Catalyst: Feminism, Theory, Technoscience* 4(2): https://catalystjournal.org/index.php/catalyst/article/view/29844/23496 [accessed 5 March 2021].

Chandler, E. (2017), 'Reflections on Cripping the Arts in Canada,' *Art Journal*, 76(3–4): 56–59.

Chandler, E. (2018), 'Disability Art and Re-Worlding Possibilities,' *A/b: Auto/Biography Studies*, 33(2): 458–463.

Chapeaux, V., U. Natarajan, and F. Mégret (eds) (forthcoming), *The Routledge Handbook of International Law and the Anthropocene*, Abingdon: Routledge.

Chapelle W., T. Goodman, L. Reardon and W. Thompson (2014), 'An analysis of post-traumatic stress symptoms in United States Air Force drone operators,' *Journal of Anxiety Disorders*, 28(3): 480–487.

Charlesworth, H. (1997), 'The Sex of the State in International Law,' in N. Naffine and R. Owens (eds), *Sexing the Subject of Law*, 251–268, London: Sweet and Maxwell.

Chen, M. (2012), *Animacies: Biopolitics, Racial Mattering, and Queer Affect*, Durham: Duke University Press.

Chen, M. (2015), 'Unpacking Intoxication, Racialising Disability,' *Medical Humanities*, 41(1): 25–29.

Chen, N. J. and cárdenas, M. (2019), 'Times to Come: Materializing Trans Times,' *TSQ: Transgender Studies Quarterly*, 6(4): 472–480.

Cheney-Lippold, J. (2019), *We Are Data: Algorithms and the Making of Our Digital Selves*, New York: New York University Press.

Choat, S. (2017). 'Science, Agency and Ontology: A Historical Materialist Response to New Materialism' (2017) *Political Studies* 1

Cochet, Y. (2011), 'The Collapse: Catabolic or Catastrophic? Seminar of the 27th of May', momentum institute, 1 June 2011, https://www.institutmomentum.org/the-collapse-catabolic-or-catastrophic/ [accessed 10 February 2022].

Chun, W. H. K. (2021), *Discriminating Data. Correlation, Neighborhoods, and the New Politics of Recognition*, Cambridge: MIT Press.

Cielemecka, O. and C. Åsberg (2019), 'Toxic embodiment and feminist environmental humanities,' *Environmental Humanities*, 11(1): 101–107.

Citton, Y. (2020), 'Collapsology as a Horizon,' *Electra*, 9: 87–104.

Clare, E. (1999), *Exile and Pride: Disability, Queerness, and Liberation*, Cambridge: South End Press.

Clarke, A. (1998), *Disciplining Reproduction: Modernity, American life sciences and the 'problem of sex'*, Berkeley: University of California Press.

Clemens, R. (2022), 'Languages are so like their boots': Linguistic Incompossibility in Flush,' *Comparative Critical Studies* 19(2): 259–280.

Clough, Patricia T. (2008) 'The Affective Turn: Political Economy, Biomedia and Bodies,' *Theory, Culture & Society* 25(1): 1–22.

Code, L. (2006), *Ecological Thinking: The Politics of Epistemic Location*, Oxford: Oxford University Press.

Cohen, J. J. (1997), 'Monster Culture (Seven Theses),' in Cohen, J (ed.) *Monster Theory: Reading Culture* (1st edn, 7) University of Minnesota Press.

Cohen, J. J. (2012), 'Undead (A Zombie Oriented Ontology)'. *Journal of the Fantastic in the Arts*, 23(3): 397–412.

Cohen, J. J. (ed.) (2013), *Prismatic Ecology: Ecotheory Beyond Green*, Minnesota: Minnesota University Press.

Cole, L. (2021), 'Zoonotic Shakespeare: Animals, Plagues, and the Medical Posthumanities,' in K. Raber and H. Dugan (eds), *Routledge Handbook of Shakespeare and Animals*, 104–115, London: Taylor and Francis.

Collins, P. H. (2000), *Black Feminist Thought: Knowledge, Consciousness, and the Politics of Empowerment*, 2nd Edition, New York: Routledge.

Colman, F. (2015), 'Digital Feminicity: Predication and Measurement, Materialist Informatics and Images,' Artnodes, 14: 7–17.

Colman, F., V. Bühlmann, A. O'Donnell and I. van der Tuin (2018), *Ethics of Coding: A Report on the Algorithmic Condition*, Brussels: European Commission.

Connolly, W. E. (2017), *Facing the Planetary: Entangled Humanism and the Politics of Swarming*, Durham: Duke University Press.

Coole, D. (2005), 'Rethinking Agency: A Phenomenological Approach to Embodiment and Agentic Capacities,' *Political Studies*, 53: 124–142.

Coole, D. and S. Frost (eds) (2010), *New Materialisms: Ontology, Agency and Politics*, Durham: Duke University Press.

Coplan, A. (2004), 'Empathetic Engagement with Narrative Fictions,' *The Journal of Aesthetics and Art Criticism*, 62(2): 141–152.

Coplan, A. (2011), 'Understanding Empathy: Its Features and Effects,' in A. Coplan and P. Goldie (eds), *Empathy: Philosophical and Psychological Perspectives*, 3–18, Oxford: Oxford University Press.

Cornell, S. (2015), 'Processes of Native Nationhood: The Indigenous Politics of Self-Government,' *The International Indigenous Policy Journal*, 6(4): 1–27.

Corner, J. (1999), 'The Agency of Mapping,' in D. E. Cosgrove (ed), *Mappings*, 214–253, London: Reaktion Books.

Costanza-Chock, S. (2020), *Design Justice*, Cambridge: MIT Press.

Couldry, N., and U. A. Mejias (2019), *The Costs of Connection: How Data Are*

Colonizing Human Life and Appropriating It for Capitalism, Redwood City: Stanford University Press.

Coulton, P. and J. G. Lindley (2019), 'More-Than Human Centred Design: Considering Other Things', *The Design Journal*, 22(4): 463–481.

Couture, V., J.-C. Bélisle-Pipon, M. Cloutier, and C. Barnabé (2017), 'Merging Arts and Bioethics: An Interdisciplinary Experiment in Cultural and Scientific Mediation,' *Bioethics*, 31(8): 616–30.

Cover, R. (1983), 'Nomos and Narrative,' *Harvard Law Review*, 97(4): 4–68.

Cowing, J. (2020), 'Occupied Land Is an Access Issue: Interventions in Feminist Disability Studies and Narratives of Indigenous Activism', *Journal of Feminist Scholarship*, 17(17): 9–25.

Crawford, K. (2021), *Atlas of AI: Power, Politics, and the Planetary Costs of Artificial Intelligence*, New Haven: Yale University Press.

Crawford, K. and V. Joler (2018), 'Anatomy of an AI System,' *The Anatomy of an AI System*, 7 September, https://anatomyof.ai [accessed 10 February 2022].

Crawford N. (2013), *Accountability for Killing: Moral Responsibility for Collateral Damage in America's Post-9/11 Wars*, Oxford and New York: Oxford University Press.

Crenshaw, K. W. (1991), 'Mapping the margins: Intersectionality, identity Politics, and violence against women of color,' *Stanford Law Review*, 6: 1241–1299.

Crutzen, P. (2006), 'Albedo enhancement by stratospheric sulfur injections: A contribution to resolve a policy dilemma?', *Climatic Change*, 77(3–4): 211–219.

Cuboniks, L. (2018), *The Xenofeminist Manifesto: A Politics for Alienation*, London: Verso.

Daggett C. (2015), 'Drone disorientations: How "unmanned" weapons queer the experience of killing in war,' *International Feminist Journal of Politics*, 17(3): 361–379.

Darwin, C. ([1859] 2009), *The Origin of Species by Means of Natural Selection: Or, the Preservation of Favored Races in the Struggle for Life*, New York: A L Burt.

Da Silva, F. D. (2018), 'On Heat', *Canadian Art*, 29 October, https://canadianart.ca/features/on-heat/ [accessed 28 May 2021].

Davidson, T. K., O. Part and R. Shields, (2011), 'Introduction' in T. K. Davidson, O. Part and R, Shields (eds), *Ecologies of Affect: Placing Nostalgia, Desire and Hope*, 1–15, Waterloo: Wilfrid Laurier University Press.

Davies, Margaret 2022 EcoLaw: Legality, Life, and the Normativity of Nature (Routledge, Abingdon).

Davis, A. (2016), 'Feminism and Abolition: Theories and Practices for the Twenty-First Century,' in F. Barat (ed.), *Freedom Is a Constant Struggle: Ferguson, Palestine, and the Foundations of a Movement*, 91–110, Chicago: Haymarket Books.

Davis, H. (2018), 'Art in the Anthropocene', in R. Braidotti and M. Hlavajova (eds.), *Posthuman Glossary*, 63–65, London: Bloomsbury Publishing.

Davis, M. (2017), *Asking the Law Question*, 4th edition, Sydney: Thomson Reuters.

de Leeuw, M. and S. Van Wichelen (2020), *Personhood in the Age of Biolegality: Brave New Law*, New York: Palgrave Macmillan.

De-Shalit, A. (1997), 'Down to Earth Environmentalism: Sustainability and Future persons,' in N. Foition and J. C. Heller (eds), *Contingent Future Persons*, 123–136, Dordrecht: Springer.

De Sousa Santos, B. (2015), 'Foreword to the critique influence change edition,' in W.F. Fisher and T. Ponniah (eds.), *Another World Is Possible: World Social Forum Proposals for an Alternative Globalization*, xvii–xx, London: Zed Books.

Deleuze, G. (1990). *The Logic of Sense*. London: The Athlone Press.

Deleuze, G. and F. Guattari (1987), *A Thousand Plateaus: Capitalism and Schizophrenia*, London: Bloomsbury.

Deleuze, G. (2001), *Pure Immanence: Essays on a Life*, New York: Zone Books.

Deleuze, G. (1988), *Spinoza: Practical Philosophy*, San Francisco: City Lights Books.

Deleuze, G. (1992), 'Postscript on the Societies of Control', *October*, 59: 3–7.

Deleuze, G. (2004), *Difference and Repetition*, London: Continuum.

Deleuze, G. (2004), 'How do we recognise structuralism?' in D. Lapoujade (ed.), *Desert Islands and Other Texts 1953–1974*, 170–193, New York: Semiotext(e).

Deleuze, G. and F. Guattari (1983), 'What is a minor literature?', *Mississippi Review*, 11(3): 13–33.

Deleuze, G. and F. Guattari (1988), *A Thousand Plateaus: Capitalism and Schizophrenia*, New York: Continuum.

DeLoughrey, E. (2013), 'The myth of isolates: ecosystem ecologies in the nuclear Pacific', *Cultural Geographies*, 20(2): 167–184.

Denetdale, J. (2020), '"To be a good relative means being a good relative to everyone": Indigenous feminisms is for everyone', in A. Moreton-Robinson, L. Tuhiwai-Smith, C. Andersen and S. Larkin (eds), *Routledge Handbook of Critical Indigenous Studies*, 229–240, London: Routledge.

Derrida, J. (2010), *Spectres of Marx: The State of Debt, the Work of Mourning and the New International*, London: Routledge.

Di Chiro, G. (2010), 'Polluted Politics? Confronting Toxic Discourse, Sex Panic, and Eco-Normativity', in C. Mortimer-Sandilands and B. Erickson, *Queer Ecologies: Sex, Nature, Politics, Desire*, 199–230, Bloomington: Indiana University Press.

D'Ignazio, C. and L.F. Klein (2020), *Data feminism*, Cambridge: MIT Press.

DiSalvo, C. and j. Lukens (2011), 'Nonathropocentrism and the Nonhuman in Design: Possibilities for Designing New Forms of Engagement with and through Technology', in M. Foth, L. Forlano, M. Gibbs and C. Satchell (eds), *From Social Butterfly to Engaged Citizen: Urban Informatics, Social Media, Ubiquitous Computing, and Mobile Technology to Support Citizen Engagement*, 421–436, Cambridge: MIT Press.

Dixon-Roman, E. (2016), 'Algo-ritmo: More-than-human performative acts and the racializing assemblages of algorithmic architectures', *Cultural Studies ↔ Critical Methodologies*, 16(5): 482–490.

Doherty, M. (2014), 'Oil and Dust: Theorising Reza Negarestani's Cyclonopedia', in R. Barrett and D. Worden (eds), *Oil Culture*, 366–383, Minneapolis: University of Minnesota Press.

Dolby, N. (2019), 'Nonhuman Animals and the Future of Environmental Education: Empathy and new possibilities', *The Journal of Environmental Education*, 50(4–6): 403–415.

Donovan, J. and C. Adams (eds) (2007), *The Feminist Care Tradition in Animal Ethics*, New York: Columbia University Press.

Donoghue, F. (2008), *The Last Professors: The Corporate University and the Fate of the Humanities*, New York: Fordham University Press.

Dourish, P. (2017), *The Stuff of Bits: An Essay on the Materialities of Information*, Cambridge: MIT Press.

Dow, K. and J. Lamoureux (2020), 'Situated Kinmaking and the Population "Problem"', *Environmental Humanities*, 12(2): 475–491.

Draude, C. (2017), *Computing Bodies: Gender Codes and Anthropomorphic Design at the Human-Computer Interface*, Wiesbaden: Springer Fachmedien Wiesbaden.

Draxler, H. (2019), 'Die Kunst der Diskriminierung', *Texte zur Kunst*, 113: 117–128.

Dung Kai-Cheung. *Atlas, the Archeology of an Imaginary City*, New York City: Columbia University Press.

Eales, L, and D. Peers (2020), 'Care Haunts, Hurts, Heals: The Promiscuous Poetics of Queer Crip Mad Care', *Journal of Lesbian Studies*, 24(1): 1–19.

Edney-Browne, A. (2017), 'Embodiment and affect in a digital age: Understanding mental illness among military drone personnel,' *Krisis*, 1: 18–33

Ehrlich, E. (1962), *Fundamental Principles of the Sociology of Law*, New York: Russell and Russell.

Ehrlich, P., and A. Ehrlich (1981), *Extinction: The Causes and Consequences of the Disappearance of Species*, New York: Random House.

Eisenstadt, T. A., and K. Jones West (2019), *Who Speaks for Nature? Indigenous Movements, Public Opinion and the Petro-State in Ecuador*, Oxford: Oxford University Press.

Ellis, R. (2019), 'Does the World need a new Buzzword – Syndemic – To Describe 3 Big Crises?' *National Public Radio*, 28 January, https://www.npr.org/sections/goatsandsoda/2019/01/28/689292566/does-the-world-need-a-new-buzzword-syndemic-to-describe-3-big-crises [accessed 22 February 2022].

Enemark, C. (2020), 'On the responsible use of armed drones: The prospective moral responsibilities of states,' *The International Journal of Human Rights*, 24(6): 868–888

Eng, D., and J. Puar (2020), 'Left of Queer. Introduction,' *Social Text*, 38 (4): 1–23.

Ensayos (2020), 'Hydrofeminist METitations,' New York: New Museum. https://www.newmuseum.org/pages/view/ensayos-1 [accessed 13 March 13 2021].

Ensayos (2021), *Ensayos*, https://ensayostierradelfuego.net/ [accessed 13 March 2021].

Ernstson, H. and S. Sörlin (2019), *Grounding Urban Natures: Histories and Futures of Urban Ecologies*, Cambridge: MIT Press.

Escobar, A. (2018), *Designs for the Pluriverse: Radical Interdependence, Autonomy, and the Making of Worlds*, Durham: Duke University Press.

Eshun, K. (1998), *More Brilliant Than the Sun. Adventures in Sonic Fiction*, London: Quartet Books.

Espinoza M. (2018), 'State terrorism: orientalism and the drone programme,' *Critical Studies on Terrorism* 11(2): 376–393.

Eubanks, V. (2018), *Automating Inequality: How High-tech Tools Profile, Police, and Punish the Poor*, New York: Picador.

Ewald, F. (1991), 'Insurance and Risk,' in G. Burchell, C. Gordon and P. Miller (eds), *The Foucault Effect: Studies in Governmentality*, 197–210, London: Harvester and Wheatsheaf.

Ewick, P. and S. Silbey (1998), *The Common Place of Law*, Chicago: University of Chicago Press.

Fanon, F. (1963), *The Wretched of the Earth*, New York: Grove Press.

Fanon, F. (1967), *Black Skin, White Masks*, New York: Grove Press.

FAO (1996), 'World Food Summit, Food for All', *United Nations Food and Agriculture Organization*, 13 to 17 November 1996, http://www.fao.org/3/x0262e/x0262e00.htm [accessed 12 March 2021].

Farahany, N. A., H. T. Greely, S. Hyman, C. Koch, C. Grady, S. P. Paşca, N. Sestan, P. Arlotta, J. L. Bernat, J. Ting, J. E. Lunshof, E. P. R. Iyer, I. Hyun, B. H. Capestany, G. M. Church, H. Huang, and H. Song (2018), 'The Ethics of Experimenting with Human Brain Tissue,' *Nature*, 556(7702): 429–32.

Featherstone, M. (1995), *Cyberspace/Cyberbodies/Cyberpunk: Cultures of Technological Embodiment*, London: SAGE Publications.

Federici, S. (2010) 'Feminism and the Politics of the Commons', in C. Hughes, S. Peace and K. van Meter (eds), *Uses of a WorldWind, Movement, Movements, and Contemporary Radical Currents in the United States*, 283–284, Oakland: AK Press

Fernandez, M., F. Wilding and M. M. Wright (eds) (2003), *Domain Errors! Cyberfeminist Practices*, New York: Autonomedia.

Ferrando, F. (2019), *Philosophical Posthumanism*, London: Bloomsbury.

Fisher, Anna Watkins (2020), *The Play in the System: The Art of Parasitical Resistance*, Durham: Duke University Press.

Fisher, M. (2009), *Capitalist Realism: Is There No Alternative?*, Winchester: Zero Books.

Fisher, M. (2016), *The Weird and the Eerie*, London: Repeater.

Fitsch, H. and K. Friedrich (2018), 'Digital Matters: Processes of Normalization in Medical Imaging', *Catalyst: Feminism, Theory, Technoscience*, 4(2): 1–31.

Fleming, N. (2014), 'Plants Talk to Each Other Using an Internet of Fungus', *BBC Earth*, 11 November, http://www.bbc.com/earth/story/20141111-plants-have-a-hidden-internet [accessed 21 March 2021].

Forlano, L. (2016), 'Decentering the Human in the Design of Collaborative Cities', *Design Issues*, 32(3): 42–54.

Forlano, L. (2017a), 'Data Rituals in Intimate Infrastructures: Crip Time and the Disabled Cyborg Body as an Epistemic Site of Feminist Science', *Catalyst: Feminism, Theory, Technoscience*, 3(2): 1–28.

Forlano, L. (2017b), 'Posthumanism and Design', *She Ji: The Journal of Design, Economics, and Innovation*, 3(1): 16–29.

Forlano, L. (2018), 'Posthuman Futures: Connecting/Disconnecting the Networked (Medical) Self', in Z. Papacharissi (ed.), *A Networked Self: Human Augmentics, Artificial Intelligence, Sentience*, 39–50, New York: Routledge.

Forlano, L. (2020), *The Danger of Intimate Algorithms*, Public Books: New York.

Forrest, B. (2020), 'Crip Feelings/Feeling Crip', *Journal of Literary & Cultural Disability Studies*, 14(1): 75–90.

Foucault, M. (1977a), *Discipline and Punish: The Birth of the Prison*, New York: Pantheon.

Foucault, M. (1977b), 'Nietzsche, Genealogy, History', in D. F. Bouchard (ed.), *Language, Counter-Memory, Practice*, Ithaca: Cornell University Press.

Foucault, M. ([1979] 2008), *The Birth of Biopolitics: Lectures at the Collège de France, 1978–79*, ed. M. Senellart, Basingstoke: Palgrave Macmillan.

Foucault, M. (1980), 'Truth and Power' (Interview with Alessandro Fontana and Pasquale Pasquino, 1977), in C. Gordon (ed), *Power/Knowledge: Selected Interviews and Other Writings 1972–1977*. New York: Pantheon, 109–133.

Foucault, M. (1982), 'The Subject and Power', *Critical Inquiry* 8(4): 777–795.

Foucault, M. (1991), 'Governmentality', in G. Burchell, C. Gordon and P. Miller (eds), *The Foucault Effect: Studies in Governmentality*, 87–104, Chicago: University of Chicago Press.

Foucault, M. (2003), *'Society Must Be Defended': Lectures at the College de France 1975–1976*, New York: Picador.

Fournier, E., L. Etienne-Mesmin, C. Grootaert, L. Jelsbak, K. Syberg, S. Blanquet-Diot, M. Mercier-Bonin (2021), 'Microplastics in the human digestive environment: A focus on the potential and challenges facing in vitro gut model development', *Journal of Hazardous Materials*, 415(125632): 1–15.

Fox, H. D. (2013), *Phantasmal Media: An Approach to Imagination, Computation, and Expression*, Cambridge: MIT Press.

Franklin, S. (2003), 'Ethical Biocapital,' in Sarah Franklin and Margaret Lock (eds), *Remaking Life and Death: Toward an Anthropology of the Biosciences*, 97–128, Santa Fe: School of American Research Press.

Franklin, S. (2013), *Biological Relatives: IVF, Stem Cells, and the Future of Kinship*, Durham: Duke University Press.

Franklin, S. and C. Roberts (2005), *Born and Made: An Ethnography of Preimplantation Genetic Diagnosis*, Princeton: Princeton University Press.

Frauenberger, C. (2019), 'Entanglement HCI The Next Wave?', *ACM Transactions on Computer-Human Interaction.*, 27(1): 1–27.

Fredengren, C. (2018), 'Re-wilding the Environmental Humanities: A Deep Time Comment,' *Current Swedish Archaeology*, 26: 50–60.

Fredengren, C. and C. Åsberg (2020), 'Checking in with Deep Time,' in R. Harrison and C. Sterling (eds), *Deterritorializing the Future: Heritage in, of and after the Anthropocene*, London: Open Humanities Press.

Freitas, E. de (2016), 'Calculating Matter and Recombinant Subjects', *Cultural Studies ↔ Critical Methodologies*, 16(5): 462–470.

Fritsch, K. (2016), 'Cripping Neoliberal Futurity: Marking the Elsewhere and Elsewhen of Desiring Otherwise', *Feral Feminisms*, 5: 11–26.

Fritsch, K and A. McGuire (2018), 'The Biosocial Politics of Queer/Crip Contagions', *Feminist Formations*, 30(1): vii–xiv.

Fritsch, K and A. McGuire (2019), 'Risk and the Spectral Politics of Disability', *Body & Society*, 25(4): 29–54.

Frost, S. (2016), *Biocultural Creatures: Toward a New Theory of the Human*, Durham: Duke University Press.

Fuller, M. (2007), *Media Ecologies: Materialist energies in art and technoculture*, Cambridge and London: MIT Press.

Fuller, M. (2008), *Software Studies: A Lexicon*. Cambridge: MIT Press.

Gaard, G. (1993), *Ecofeminism: Women, Animals, Nature*, Philadelphia: Temple University Press.

Gabrys, J. (2011), *Digital Rubbish: A Natural History of Electronics*, Ann Arbor: University of Michigan Press.

Gabrys, J. (2016), *Program Earth: Environmental Sensing Technology and the Making of a Computational Planet*, Minneapolis: University of Minnesota Press.

Gajjala, R. (2003), 'South Asian digital diasporas and cyberfeminist webs: negotiating globalization, nation, gender and information technology design', *Contemporary South Asia*, 12(1): 41–56.

Galle, N. J., S. A. Nitoslawski and F. Pilla (2019), 'The Internet of Nature: How Taking Nature Online Can Shape Urban Ecosystems', *The Anthropocene Review* 6(3): 279–287.

Gallese, V. (2007), 'Embodied simulation: From mirror neuron systems to interpersonal relations,' in *Empathy and Fairness: Novartis Foundation Symposium*, 278: 3–12.

Galloway, A. (2004), *Protocol: How Control Exists After Decentralization*, Cambridge: MIT Press.

Galloway, A. and C. Caudwell (2018), 'Speculative Design as Research Method: From answers to questions and "staying with the trouble"', in G. Coombs, A. McNamara and G. Sade (eds), *Undesign: Critical Practices at the Intersection of Art and Design*, 85–96, London: Routledge.

Geerts, Evelien and Groen, Amarantha. "Philosophical post-anthropology for the Chthulucene: Levinasian and feminist new materialist perspectives in more-thanhuman crisis times" Internationales Jahrbuch für philosophische Anthropologie 10, no. 1 (2020): 195-214. https://doi-org.e. bibl.liu.se/10.1515/jbpa-2020-0011.

Sodikoff, G. (2020), 'Zoonosis,' in C. Howe and A. Pandian (eds.), *Anthropocene Unseen—A Lexicon*, 529–532, Santa Barbara: Punctum Books.

Ghosh, A. (1992), 'Petrofiction: The Oil Encounter and the Novel,' *The New Republic*, 2 March, 29–34.

Giaccardi, E. and J. Redström (2020), 'Technology and More-Than-Human Design', *Design Issues*, 36(4): 33–44.

Gilbert, S., J. Sapp, and A. Tauber (2012), 'A Symbiotic View of Life: We Have Never Been Individuals' *Quarterly Review of Biology* 87(4): 325–341.

Gilligan, C. (1982), *In a Different Voice: Psychological Theory and Women's Development*, Cambridge: Harvard University Press.

Giovanardi, G. (2017), 'Buying time or arresting development? The dilemma of administering hormone blockers in trans children and adolescents,' *Porto Biomedical Journal* 2(5): 153–156.

Giraud, E. H. (2019), *What Comes After Entanglement? Activism, Anthropocentrism, and an Ethics of Exclusion*, Durham: Duke University Press.

Glissant, É. (1997), *Poetics of Relation*, Ann Arbor: University of Michigan Press.

Goodyear-Ka'opua, N. (2017), 'Protectors of the Future, Not Protestors of the Past: Indigenous Pacific Activsiom and Mauna a Wēkea' *The South Atlantic Quarterly*, 116(1): 184–194.

Gosseries, A. (2008), 'Theories of intergenerational justice: a synopsis,' S.A.P.I.EN.S, 1(1): 61–81.

Grear, A. (2013), 'Law's entities: Complexity, plasticity and justice,' *Jurisprudence*, 4(1): 76–101.

Grear, A. (2015), 'Deconstructing Anthropos: A Critical Legal Reflection on "Anthropocentric" Law and Anthropocene "Humanity"', *Law and Critique*, 26: 225–249.

Grear, A. (2020), 'Legal Imaginaries and the Anthropocene: "Of" and "For"', *Law and Critique*, 31: 351–366.

Grear, A. (2017), '"Anthropocene, Capitalocene, Chthulucene": Re-encountering environmental law and its "subject" with Haraway and New Materialism,' in L. J. Kotzé (ed.), *Environmental Law and Governance for the Anthropocene*, Surrey: Hart Publishing.

Greenaway, T. (2019), 'Food as Medicine on the Navajo Nation, *Civil Eat*s, January, https://civileats.com/2020/06/04/food-as-medicine-on-the-navajo-nation/amp/ [accessed 22 February 2022].

Gregory D. (2012), 'From a view to kill: Drones and late modern war,' *Theory, Culture & Society*, 28(7–8): 188–215.

Greve, J. and F. Zappe (eds) (2019), *Spaces and Fictions of the Weird and the Fantastic: Ecologies, Geographies, Oddities*, Cham: Springer.

Greve, J. and F. Zappe (eds) (2020), *The American Weird: Concept and Medium*, London: Bloomsbury.

Gruen, L. (2015), *Entangled Empathy: An Alternative Ethic for our Relationships with Animals*, New York: Lantern Books.

Guattari, F. ([1989] 2000), *The Three Ecologies*, London and New York: Athlone Press.

Gumbs, A. P. (2020), *Dub: Finding Ceremony*, Durham: Duke University Press.

Gumbs, A. P. (2021), *Undrowned: Black Feminist Lessons from Marine Mammals*, Chico: AK Press.

Hacking, I. (1999), 'Making Up People,' in M. Biagioli (ed.), *Science Studies Reader*, 161–171, New York: Routledge.

Halberstam, J. (2008),'Animating revolt/revolting animation: Penguin love, doll sex and the spectacle of the queer non-human,' in N. Giffney and M. Hird (eds) *Queering the Non/human*, 265–81, Hampshire: Ashgate Publishing.

Hameed, A. (2014), 'Black Atlantis,' in Forensic Architecture (ed.), *Forensis: The Architecture of Public Truth*, 712–719, Berlin: Sternberg Press.

Hamilton, J.M. (2019), 'The Future of Housework: The Similarities and Differences Between Making Kin and Making Babies,' *Australian Feminist Studies*, 34(102): 468–489.

Hamilton, J.M. and A. Neimanis (2018), 'Composting Feminism and the Environmental Humanities,' *Environmental Humanities*, 10(2): 501–527.

Hamraie, A. and K. Fritsch (2019), 'Crip technoscience manifesto,' *Catalyst: Feminism, Theory, Technoscience*, 5(1): 1–33.

Han, B.-C. (2017), *In the Swarm: Digital Prospects*, Cambridge: MIT Press.

Haraway, D. (1985), 'Manifesto for cyborgs: Science, technology, and socialist feminism in the 1980s,' *Socialist Review*, 80: 65–108.

Haraway D. (1988), 'Situated knowledges: The science question in feminism and the privilege of partial perspective,' *Feminist Studies*, 14(3): 575–599.

Haraway, D. (1989), *Primate Visions: Gender, Race, and Nature in the World of Modern Science*, London: Routledge.

Haraway, D. (1991), *Simians, Cyborgs and Women: The Reinvention of Nature*, New York: Routledge.

Haraway, D. (1997), *Modest_Witness@ Second_Millennium. FemaleMan©_ Meets_ Oncomouse*, London and New York: Routledge.

Haraway, D. (2003), *The Companion Species Manifesto: Dogs, People, and Significant Otherness*, Chicago: University of Chicago Press.

Haraway, D. J. (2008), *When Species Meet*, Minneapolis and London: University of Minnesota Press.

Haraway, D. (2011), 'Speculative fabulations for technoculture's generations: Taking care of unexpected country,' *Australian Humanities Review*, Issue 50.

Haraway, D. (2013), 'Sowing Worlds: A Seed Bag for Terraforming with Earth Others' in M. Grebowicz and H. Merrick (eds), *Beyond the Cyborg: Adventures with Donna Haraway*, 137–146, New York: Columbia University Press.

Haraway, D. (2016), *Staying with the Trouble: Making Kin in the Chthulucene*. Minneapolis: University of Minnesota Press.

Haraway, D., N. Ishikawa, S.F. Gilbert, K. Olwig, A.L. Tsing, and N. Bubandt (2016), 'Anthropologists Are Talking – About the Anthropocene,' *Ethnos*, 81(3): 535–564.

Harman, G. (2012), *Weird Realism: Lovecraft and Philosophy*, London: Zero Books.

Harney, S., and F. Moten (2013), *The Undercommons: Fugitive Planning & Black Study*, New York City: Minor Compositions.

Harper, D. (n.d.), 'Trophic,' *Online Etymology Dictionary*, https://www.etymonline.com/word/trophic#etymonline_v_39458 [accessed 1 May 2020].

Hartman, S. (1997), *Scenes of Subjection: Terror, Slavery and Self-making in Nineteenth Century America*, New York and Oxford: Oxford University Press.

Hartman, S., J. Adamson, G. Gaard, and S. Oppermann (2020), 'Through the Portal of COVID-19: Visioning the Environmental Humanities as a Community of Purpose,' *Bifrost*, 8 June, https://bifrostonline.org/steven-hartman-joni-adamson-greta-gaard-serpil-oppermann/ [accessed 22 February 2022].

Hartman, S. V. (2007), *Lose Your Mother: A Journey Along the Atlantic Slave Route*, New York: Farrar, Straus and Giroux.

Harvey, D. (2006), *Spaces of Global Capitalism*, London: Verso.

Hayles, K. (1992), 'The Materiality of Informatics,' *Issues in Integrative Studies*, 10: 121–144.

Hayles, K. (1999), *How We Became Posthuman Virtual Bodies in Cybernetics, Literature, and Informatics*, Chicago: University of Chicago Press.

Hayles, N. K. (2008), *How We Became Posthuman: Virtual Bodies in Cybernetics, Literature, and Informatics* (1st edn). University of Chicago Press.

Haynes, M. (2017), 'Animal,' in I. Szeman, J. Wenzel and P. Yaeger (eds), *Fueling Culture: 101 Words for Energy and Environment*, 35–38, New York: Fordham Press.

Heathcote G. (2018), 'War's perpetuity: Disabled bodies of war and the exoskeleton of equality,' *Australian Feminist Law Journal* 44(1): 71–91.

Hegel, G. W. F. ([1807] 2018), *The Phenomenology of Spirit*, Oxford: Oxford University Press.

Hegglund, J. (2020), 'Unnatural Narratology and Weird Realism in Jeff VanderMeer's *Annihilation*,' in E. James and E. Morel (eds), *Environment and Narrative: New Directions in Econarratology*, 27–44, Columbus: Ohio University Press.

Heitlinger, S., M. Foth, R. Clarke, C. DiSalvo, A. Light, and L. Forlano (2018), 'Avoiding ecocidal smart cities: participatory design for more-than-human futures,' *Proceedings of the 15th Participatory Design Conference: Short Papers, Situated Actions, Workshops and Tutorial-Volume 2*, 1–3, New York: ACM.

Heinze, C., T. Blenckner, H. Martins, D. Rusiecka, R. Döscher, M. Gehlen, N. Gruber, E. Holland, Ø. Hov, F. Joos, J. Brian R. Matthews, R. Rødven and S. Wilson (2021), 'The quiet crossing of ocean tipping points,' *Proceedings of the National Academy of Sciences*, 118(9): 1–9.

Hekman, S. (2014), *The Feminine Subject*. Cambridge: Polity Press.

Helmreich, S. (2017), 'The Genders of Waves,' *Women's Studies Quarterly*, 45 (1/2): 29–51.

Hemming, S., D. Rigney, S. Bignall, S. Berg and G. Rigney (2019), 'Indigenous nation building for environmental futures: Murrundi flows through Ngarrindjeri country,' *Australasian Journal of Environmental Management*, 26(3): 216–235.

Hijazee A., C. J. Ferguson, F. R. Ferraro, H. Hall, M. Hovee and S. Wilcox (2019), 'Psychological dimensions of drone warfare,' *Current Psychology* 38(5): 1285–1296.

Hildebrandt, M. (2015), *Smart Technologies and the End(s) of Law*, Cheltenham: Edward Elgar Publishing.

Hills, J. (2010), *The Struggle for Control of Global Communication: The Formative Century*, Champaign: University of Illinois Press.

Hird, M. J. (2007), 'The Corporeal Generosity of Maternity,' *Body & Society*, 13(1): 1–20.

Hird, M. J. (2013), 'Waste, Landfills, and an Environmental Ethic of Vulnerability,' *Ethics and the Environment*, 18(1): 105–124.

Hodson, L. C. (2019), 'Mermaids and Utopias: The High Seas as Feminist Space?', In I. Papanicolopulu (ed), *Gender and the Law of the Sea*, 122–143, Leiden: Brill.

Hoffman, M. L. (2014), 'Empathy, Justice, And Social Change,' in H. L. Maibom (ed), *Empathy and Morality*, 1–40, New York: Oxford University Press.

Holmqvist, C. (2013), 'Undoing war: War ontologies and the materiality of drone warfare,' *Millenium: A Journal of International Studies*, 41(3): 535–552.

Holmstedt, J. (2020), 'Humus Economicus: Soil Blindness and the Value of "Dirt" in Urbanized Landscapes,' *Formas projekt-databas*, http://proj.formas.se/detail. asp?arendeid=10874&x=250&y=20&spra k=2&redovisning=0 [accessed 12 March 2021].

hooks, b. (1984). *Feminist theory: from margin to center*, Boston MA: South End Press.

Hughes, B., L. McKie, D. Hopkins and N. Watson (2005), 'Love's Labours Lost? Feminism, the Disabled People's Movement and an Ethic of Care,' *Sociology*, 39(2): 259–275.

Intergovernmental Panel on Climate Change (2018), *Global Warming of 1.5°C*, Geneva: IPCC.

Irani, L. J. Vertesi, P. Dourish, K. Philip and R. E. Grinter (2010), 'Postcolonial Computing: A Lens on Design and Development,' *CHI '10: Proceedings of the SIGCHI Conference on Human Factors in Computing Systems*: 1311–1320.

Iovino, Serenella, and Serpil Oppermann (eds) (2014), *Material Ecocriticism*, Bloomington, IA: Indiana University Press.

Jackson, Z. I. (2013), 'Animal: New Directions in the Theorization of Race and Posthumanism,' *Feminist Studies*, 39(3): 669–685.

Jackson, Z. I. (2015), 'Outer Worlds: The Persistence of Race in Movement "Beyond the Human,"' *GLQ: A Journal of Lesbian and Gay Studies*, 21(2): 215–218.

Jackson, Z. I. (2020), *Becoming Human: Matter and Meaning in an Antiblack World*, New York: New York University Press.

Jacobsen, S.R.H. (2018), *Havbrevene*, Copenhagen: Lindhardt & Ringhof.

Jaffee, L. J. and K. John (2018), 'Disabling Bodies of/and Land: Reframing Disability Justice in Conversation with Indigenous Theory and Activism', *Disability and the Global South*, 5(2): 1407–29.

jagodzinski, j. (2018), 'From the Artist to the Cosmic Artisan: the Educational Task in Anthropocentric Times', in C. Naughton, G. Biesta, and D. Cole (eds), *Art, Artists and Pedagogy: Philosophy and the Arts in Education*, 83–95, London: Routledge.

jagodzinski, j. (2019), 'An Avant-Garde "Without Authority": The Posthuman Cosmic Artist in the Anthropocene', in P. de Assis and P. Giudici (eds), *Aberrant Nuptials: Deleuze and Artistic Research*, 233–254, Leuven: Leuven University Press.

James, E. and E. Morel (eds) (2020), *Environment and Narrative: New Directions in Econarratology*, Columbus: Ohio University Press.

Johns, F. (2013), *Non-Legality in International Law: Unruly Law*, Cambridge: Cambridge University Press.

Johnson, G. T., and A. Lubin (eds) (2017), *Futures of Black Radicalism*, London: Verso.

Johnson, M. L. and R. McRuer (2014), 'Cripistemologies', *Journal of Literary and Cultural Disability Studies*, 8(2): 127–147.

Jones, E. (2018a), 'A Posthuman Feminist Approach to Mars', *International Law Grrls*, 17 October, https://ilg2. org/2018/10/17/a-posthuman-feminist-approach-to-mars/ [accessed 22 June 2021].

Jones, E. (2018b), 'A Posthuman-Xenofeminist Analysis of the Discourse on Autonomous Weapons Systems and Other Killing Machines', *Australian Feminist Law Journal*, 44(1): 93–118.

Jones, E. (2021), 'Posthuman International Law and the Rights of Nature', *Journal of Human Rights and the Environment*, 12: 76–101.

Jones, E. (2022), 'Posthuman Feminism and Global Constitutionalism: Environmental Reflections', *Global Constitutionalism*: 1–15.

Jongsma, K. R., and A.L. Bredenoord (2020), 'Ethics Parallel Research: An Approach for (Early) Ethical Guidance of Biomedical Innovation', *BMC Medical Ethics* 21(81): 1–9.

Jue, M. (2020), *Wild Blue Media: Thinking Through Seawater*, Durham: Duke University Press.

Joshi, S. T. (1990), *The Weird Tale*, Austin: University of Texas Press.

Kafer, A. (2013), *Feminist, Queer, Crip*, Bloomington: Indiana University Press.

Kafer, A. (2019), 'Crip Kin, Manifesting', *Catalyst: Feminism, Theory, Technoscience*, 5(1): 1–37.

Kagan, J. (2009), *The Three Cultures: The Natural sciences, Social Sciences and the Humanities in the Twenty-first Century*, Cambridge: Cambridge University Press.

Luciano, D. and M.Y. Chen (2015), 'Has the Queer Ever Been Human?', *GLQ: A Journal of Lesbian and Gay Studies*, 21(2–3): 183–207.

Käll, J. (2017a), *Converging Digital and Material Bodies: Posthumanism, Property, Law*, Gothenburg: Juridiska institutionens skriftserie.

Käll, J. (2017b), 'A Posthuman Data Subject? The Right to Be Forgotten and Beyond', *German Law Journal*, 18(5): 1145–1162.

Karatani, K. (2014), *The Structure of World History: From Modes of Production to Modes of Exchange*, Durham: Duke University Press.

Karatani, K. (2020), *Marx: Towards the Centre of Possibility*, London: Verso.

Katz, S. E. (2016), *Wild Fermentation. The Flavor, Nutrition, and Craft of Live-Culture Foods*, Vermont: White River Junction.

Katz, S. E. (2020), *Fermentation as Metaphor*, Vermont: White River Junction.

Kauffman, C. M. and L. Sheehan (2019), 'The Rights of Nature: Guiding our

Responsibilities through Standards,' in J. R. May, D. Shelton, S. J. Turner, J. Razzaque, O. McIntyre (eds), *Environmental Rights: The Development of Standards*, 342–366, Cambridge: Cambridge University Press.

Kazan, H. (2018), 'The Architecture of Slow, Structural, and Spectacular Violence and the Poetic Testimony of War,' *The Australian Feminist Law Journal*, 44(1): 119–136.

Kazan, H. (2020), 'Decolonizing Archives and Law's Frame of Accountability,' *World Records*, 4: 203–214.

Keenan, S. (2019), 'From Historical Chains to Derivative Futures: Title Registries as Time Machines,' *Social & Cultural Geography*, 20(3): 283–303.

Keller, C. (2004), *Apocalypse Now and Then: A Feminist Guide to the End of the World*, Minneapolis: Augsburg Fortress Publishers.

Kennedy, D. (1986), 'Freedom and Constraint in Adjudication: A Critical Phenomenology,' *Journal of Legal Education*, 36(4): 518–562.

Khalili, L. (2020), *Sinews of War and Trade: Shipping and Capitalism in the Arabian Peninsula*, London and New York: Verso.

Khoury, C. K., A. D. Bjorkman, H. Dempewolf, J. Ramirez-Villegas, L. Guarino, A. Jarvis, L. H. Rieseberg, P. C. Struik (2014), 'Increasing homogeneity in global food supplies,' *Proceedings of the National Academy of Sciences*, 111(11): 4001–4006.

Kim, C. J. (2015), *Dangerous Crossings*, Cambridge: Cambridge University Press.

Kimmerer, R. (2013), *Braiding Sweetgrass: Indigenous Wisdom, Scientific Knowledge and the Teachings Of Plants*, Minneapolis: Milkweed Editions.

Kimmerer, R. (2017), Speaking of Nature,' *Orion Magazine*, 12 June, https://orionmagazine.org/article/speaking-of-nature/ [accessed 15 February 2022].

King, Y. (1987). 'What Is Ecofeminism?', *The Nation*, 702: 730–731.

Kirksey, E. (2015), *Emergent Ecologies*, Durham: Duke University Press.

Kirksey, E. (2018), 'Multispecies,' in R. Braidotti and M. Hlavajova (eds), *Posthuman Glossary*, 265–266, London: Bloomsbury Academic.

Kitchin, R. (2017), 'Thinking critically about and researching algorithms,' *Information, Communication & Society*, 20(1): 14–29.

Kittler, F. (1992), 'There is No Software,' *Stanford Literature Review*, 9(1): 81–90.

Klumbytè, G., C. Draude and L. Britton (2020), 'Re-Imagining HCI: New Materialist Philosophy and Figurations as Tool for Design,' *ArXiv*, 4 March, https://arxiv.org/abs/2003.02312 [last accessed 15 February 2022].

Klumbytè, G., C. Draude (2022), 'Prospects for a New Materialist Informatics: Introduction to a Special Issue,' Special Issue 'Prospects for a New Materialist Informatics,' *Matter: Journal of New Materialist Research*, 3(1): I–XIV.

Kneale, J. (2019), '"Indifference Would Be Such a Relief": Race and Weird Geographies in Victor LaValle and Matt Ruff's Dialogues with H. P. Lovecraft,' in J. Greve and F. Zappe (eds), *Spaces and Fictions of the Weird and the Fantastic: Ecologies, Geographies, Oddities*, 93–109, Cham: Palgrave MacMillan.

Koehn, D. (1998), *Rethinking Feminist Ethics: Care, Trust and Empathy*, London and New York, Routledge.

Konings, M. (2018), *Capital and Time: For a New Critique of Neoliberal Reason*, Redwood City: Stanford University Press.

Kortekallio, K. (2020), 'Reading Mutant Narratives : The Bodily Experientiality of Contemporary Ecological Science Fiction,' unpublished PhD thesis, University of Helsinki, https://helda.helsinki.fi/handle/10138/309144 [accessed 31 January 2022]

Kosek, J. (2010), 'Ecologies of Empire: On the New Uses of the Honeybee,' *Cultural Anthropology* 25(4): 650–78.

Kristensen, B. (2020), 'Welcome to the Viralocene: Transcorporeality and Peripheral Justice in an Age of Pandemics,' *Medium*, May 19, https://medium.com/@bjornkristensen/viralocene-66a954260487 [accessed 22 February 2022].

Kristeva, J. (1982), *Powers of Horror: An Essay on Abjection*, New York: Columbia University Press.

Kröger, T. (2009), 'Care research and disability studies: Nothing in common?', *Critical Social Policy*, 29(3): 398–420.

Kroker A. (2014), *Exits to the Posthuman Future*, Cambridge: Polity Press.

Krzywoszynska, A. and G. Marchesi (2020), 'Toward a Relational Materiality of Soils: Introduction,' *Environmental Humanities*, 12(1): 190–204.

Kull, K., and P. Torop (2003), 'Biotranslation: Translation Between Umwelten,' in S. Petrilli (ed.), *Translation*, 313–328. Amsterdam: Rodolpi.

Kumar, N. and N. Karusala (2019), 'Intersectional Computing', *Interactions*, 26(2): 50–54.

Kuntsman, A. and R. Stein (2015), *Digital Militarism: Israel's Occupation in the Social Media Age*, Redwood City: Stanford University Press.

Kuokkanen, R. (2019), *Restructuring Relations: Indigenous Self-determination, Governance and Gender*, New York: Oxford University Press.

Kurgan, L., D. Brawley, B. House, J. Zhang, and W. H. K. Chun (2019), 'Homophily: The Urban History of an Algorithm,' *e-flux*, October, https://www.e-flux.com/architecture/are-friends-electric/289193/homophily-the-urban-history-of-an-algorithm [accessed 15 February 2022].

Laiti, O. (2016), 'The Ethnoprogramming Model', in J. Sheard and C. S. Montero (eds), *Proceedings of the 16th Koli Calling International Conference on Computing Education Research*, 150–4, New York: ACM.

Laiti, O. (2021), *Old Ways of Knowing, New Ways of Playing: The Potential of Collaborative Game Design to Empower Indigenous Sámi*, unpublished PhD thesis, University of Lapland. https://lauda.ulapland.fi/bitstream/handle/10024/64547/Laiti.Outi.pdf?sequence=1&isAllowed=y [accessed 1 February 2022].

Lakhani, N. (2020), 'Navajo Nation reels under Weight of Coronavirus – and History of Broken Promises,' *The Guardian* 8 May, https://www.theguardian.com/world/2020/may/08/navajo-nation-coronavirus#_=_ [accessed 22 February 2022].

Langer, S. (1955), *Feeling and Form: A Theory of Art*, New York: Charles Scribner's Sons.

Latour, B. (1994), *We Have Never Been Modern*, Cambridge: Harvard University Press.

Latour, B. (2018), *Facing Gaia: Eight Lectures on the New Climactic Regime*, Cambridge: Polity Press.

Le Guin, U. (1989), *Dancing at the Edge of the World: Thoughts on Words, Women, Places*, New York: Grove Press.

Lehman, G. (1997), 'Life's Quiet Companion', in G. Carey and R. Sorenson (eds), *The Penguin Book of Death*, 223–232, Ringwood: Penguin Australia.

LeMenager, S. (2014), *Living Oil: Petroleum Culture in the American Century*, New York: Oxford University Press.

Lemm, V. (2020), *Homo Natura: Nietzsche, Philosophical Anthropology and Biopolitics*, Edinburgh: Edinburgh University Press.

Lenton, T. M., H. Held, E. Kriegler, J. W. Hall, W. Lucht, S. Rahmstorf, and H. J. Schellnhuber (2008), Tipping elements in the Earths climate system, *Proceedings of the National Academy of Sciences of the United States of America,* 105(6): 1786–1793.

Lessig, L. (1999), *Code and Other Laws of Cyberspace*, New York: Basic Books

Letzter, R. (2020), 'Are We Really Running Out of Time to Stop Climate Change?'

livescience, 26 September, https://www.livescience.com/12-years-to-stop-climate-change.html [accessed 28 May 2021].

Lévi-Straus, C. ([1958] 1963), *Structural Anthropology*, New York: Basic Books.

Levy, J. (2012), *Freaks of Fortune*, Cambridge: Harvard University Press.

Lewis, S. (2017), 'Defending Intimacy against What? Limits of Antisurrogacy Feminisms,' *Signs*, 43(1): 97–125.

Lewis, S. (2019), *Full Surrogacy Now: Feminism Against Family*, London: Verso.

Leys, R. (2012), '"Both of Us Disgusted in My *Insula*": Mirror Neuron Theory and Emotional Empathy,' *Non-Site.Org*, 5, https://nonsite.org/both-of-us-disgusted-in-my-insula-mirror-neuron-theory-and-emotional-empathy/ [accessed 1 February 2022].

Lloyd, G. (1984), *The Man of Reason: Male and Female in Western Philosophy*. London: Methuen.

Loo, S. and U. Sellbach (2015), 'Insect Affects,' *Angelaki*, 20(3): 79–88.

Lopez, G. P. (2009), 'Changing systems, changing ourselves', *Harvard Latino Law Review*, 12(1): 15–40.

Lorde, A. (2017), *The Master's Tools Will Never Dismantle the Master's House*, London: Penguin Random House.

Lorenz-Meyer, D., P. Treusch, X. Liu (2019), *Feminist Technoecologies: Reimagining Matters of Care and Sustainability*, New York: Routledge.

Lorimer, Jamie (2007), 'Nonhuman Charisma: Which Species Trigger Our Emotions and Why?', *Environment and Planning D: Society and Space*, 25(5): 911–935.

Lovecraft, H. P. ([1927] 2011), 'Supernatural Horror in Literature,' in *H. P. Lovecraft: The Complete Fiction*, 1041–1098, New York: Barnes and Noble.

Luckhurst, R. (2017), 'The Weird: A Dis/Orientation,' *Weird Fiction, Textual Practice*, 31(6): 1041–1061.

Lundblad, M. (2013), *The Birth of a Jungle: Animality in Progressive-Era US Literature*

and Culture, Oxford: Oxford University Press.

Lykke, N. (2018) 'Passionately Posthuman: From Feminist Disidentifications to Postdisciplinary Posthumanities,' in C Åsberg and R Braidotti (eds), *A Feminist Companion to the Posthumanities*. Cham: Springer International.

Lykke, N. (2019), 'Making Live and Letting Die: Cancerous Bodies between Anthropocene Necropolitics and Chthulucene Kinship,' *Environmental Humanities*, 11(1): 108–136.

Lykke, N. (2022), *Vibrant Death. A Posthuman Phenomenology of Mourning*. London: Bloomsbury Academic.

Lykke, N. and R. Braidotti (1996), *Between Monsters, Goddesses and Cyborgs*, London: Zed Books.

MacCormack, P. (ed.) (2014), *The Animal Catalyst: Towards Ahuman Theory*, London : Bloomsbury.

MacCormack, P. (2016), "Lovecraft's Cosmic Ethics," in C. H. Sederholm and J. A. Weinstock (eds), *Age of Lovecraft*, 199–214, Minneapolis: University of Minnesota Press.

MacCormack, P. (2019), 'Queering the Weird: Unnatural Participations and the Mucosal in H. P. Lovecraft and Occulture,' in J. Greve and F. Zappe (eds), *Spaces and Fictions of the Weird and the Fantastic: Ecologies, Geographies, Oddities*, 57–72, Cham: Palgrave MacMillan.

MacCormack, P. (2020a), *The Ahuman Manifesto: Activism for the End of the Anthropocene*, London. Bloomsbury.

MacCormack, P. (2020b), 'Embracing Death: Opening the World', *Australian Feminist Studies*, 35(104): 101–115.

Macdonald, G. (2012), 'Oil and World Literature,' *American Book Review*, 33(3): 7–31.

Mackay, D. and A. Fraser (2000), 'Bioaccumulation of persistent organic chemicals: mechanisms and models,' *Environmental Pollution*, 110(3): 375–391.

MacKenzie, A. and A. Munster (2019), 'Platform Seeing: Image Ensembles and Their Invisualities', *Theory, Culture & Society*, 36(5): 3–22.

MacLeod, J. (2013), 'Water and the Material Imagination: Reading the Sea of Memory against the Flows of Capital', in C. Chen, J. MacLeod and A. Neimanis (eds), *Thinking with Water*, 40–60, Montreal and Kingston: McGill-Queen's University Press.

Malabou, C. (2009), *Plasticity at the Dusk of Writing: Dialectic, Destruction, Deconstruction*, New York: Columbia University Press.

Manjikian, M. (2014), 'Becoming unmanned', *International Feminist Journal of Politics*, 16(1): 48–65.

Marchetti, C. (1977), 'On Geoengineering and the CO_2 Problem', *Climatic Change*, 1: 58–69.

Marder, M. (2012), 'The Life of Plants and the Limits of Empathy', *Dialogue*, 51: 259–273.

Margulies, J. and B. Bersaglio (2018), 'Furthering post-human political ecologies', *Geoforum*, 94: 103–106.

Margulis, L. and D. Sagan (1995), *What is Life?*, London: the Orion Publishing Group.

Margulis, L. and D. Sagan (2002), *Acquiring Genomes: A Theory of the Origin of Species*. New York: Basic Books.

Marshall, K. (2016), 'The Old Weird', *Modernism/modernity*, 23(3): 631–649.

Marshall, V. (2020), 'Removing the Veil from the "Rights of Nature": The Dichotomy between First Nations Customary Rights and Environmental Legal Personhood' (2020) *Australian Feminist Law Journal*, 45(2): 233–248.

Martin, A., N. Myers, and A. Viseu (2015), 'The politics of care in technoscience', *Social Studies of Science*, 45(5): 625–641.

Martino, A. S. (2017), 'Cripping Sexualities: An Analytic Review of Theoretical and Empirical Writing on the Intersection of Disabilities and Sexualities', *Sociology Compass*, 11: 1–15.

Marx, K. and F. Engels (2010), *Collected Works Volume 5: Marx and Engels 1845–47*, Digital Edition: Lawrence and Wishart.

Mascaro, J., J. A. Harris, L. Lach, A. Thompson, M. P. Perring, D. M. Richardson, and E. C. Ellis (2013), 'Origins of the Novel Ecosystems Concept', in R. J. Hobbs, E. Higgs, and C. M. Hall (eds), *Novel Ecosystems : Intervening in the New Ecological World Order*, 45–57, Chichester and Hoboken: John Wiley and Sons.

Massart, F., J. Harrell, G. Federico and G. Saggese (2005), 'Human Breast Milk and Xenoestrogen Exposure: A Possible Impact on Human Health', *Journal of Perinatology*, 25: 282–288.

Massey, D. B. (2005), *For Space*, London: SAGE.

Massumi, B. (1992), *A User's Guide to Capitalism and Schizophrenia: Deviations from Deleuze and Guattari*, Cambridge: MIT Press.

Massumi, B. (2015), *The Politics of Affect*, Cambridge: Polity Press.

Mbembe, A. (2003), 'Necropolitics', *Public Culture*, 15(1): 11–40.

Mbembe, A. (2019), *Necropolitics*, Durham: Duke University Press.

McCormack, B. and T. McCance (2010), *Person-Centred Nursing: Theory and Practice*, Hoboken: Wiley-Blackwell.

McGrath, M. (2019), 'Climate change: 12 years to save the planet? Make that 18 months', *BBC News*, 23 July, https://www.bbc.com/news/science-environment-48964736 [accessed 25 January 2021].

McIntyre, O. (2020), 'The Irish Supreme Court Judgment in Climate Case Ireland: "One Step Forward and Two Steps Back," *IUCN*, 28 August, https://www.iucn.org/news/world-commission-environmental-law/202008/irish-supreme-court-judgment-climate-case-ireland-one-step-forward-and-two-steps-back [accessed 3 March 2022].

McKittrick, K. (2015), *Sylvia Wynter: On Being Human as Praxis*, Durham: Duke University Press.

McNeily, K. (2018), 'What Feminist can teach us about Law on Mars,' *International Law Grrls*, 29 November, https://ilg2.org/2018/11/29/what-feminism-can-teach-us-about-alterity-and-law-on-mars/ [accessed 22 June 2021].

McRuer, R. (2006), *Crip Theory: Cultural Signs of Queerness and Disability*, New York: New York University Press.

McRuer, R. (2012), 'Cripping Queer Politics, or the Dangers of Neoliberalism.' *S&F Online,* 10(1–2), http://sfonline.barnard.edu/a-new-queer-agenda/cripping-queer-politics-or-the-dangers-of-neoliberalism/ [accessed 15 February 2022].

McRuer, R. (2016), 'Crip', in K. Fritsch, C. O'Connor, and A.K. Thompson (eds), *Keywords for Radicals: The Contested Vocabulary of Late-Capitalist Struggle,* 119–126, Oakland: AK Press.

Meadows-Fernandez, A. R. (2020), 'The Unbearable Grief of Black Mothers,' *Vox,* 28 May, https://www.vox.com/first-person/2020/5/28/21272380/black-mothers-grief-sadness-covid-19?fbclid=IwAR284rGo QHVBp_jRkHK9i1Th4XRduOGd0s QYput8WcLmJCMLmbXzsXnGvDM [accessed 22 February 2022].

MELT (Ren Loren Britton and Isabel Paehr) (2019–), *Meltionary,* meltionary.com [accessed 25 January 2021].

Mende, D. (2019), 'Editorial: "Navigation Beyond Vision,"' *e-flux*, June, https://www.e-flux.com/journal/101/274019/editorial-navigation-beyond-vision/ [accessed 15 February 2022].

Méndez Cota, G. (ed.) (2011), *Another technoscience is possible: Agricultural lessons for the posthumanities*, London: Open Humanities Press.

Mensch, J. (2011), 'Empathy and Rationality,' in B. Weber, E. Marsal and T. Dobashi (eds), *The Politics of Empathy: New Interdisciplinary Perspectives on an Ancient Phenomenon*, 17–24, Münster: Lit Publisher.

Miéville, C. (2009), 'The Weird,' in M. Bould, A. Butler, A. Roberts and S. Vint (eds), *The Routledge Companion to Science Fiction*, 510–15, London: Routledge.

Mills, M. and P. Chakravartty (2018), 'Virtual Roundtable on "Decolonial Computing",' *Catalyst: Feminism, Theory, Technoscience*, 4(2): 1–4.

Mingus, M. (2010), 'Wherever You Are is Where I Want to Be: Crip Solidarity', *Leaving Evidence,* May 3. https://leavingevidence.wordpress.com/2010/05/03/where-ever-you-are-is-where-i-want-to-be-crip-solidarity/ [accessed 1 February 2022].

Minh-ha, T. T. (1989), *Woman, Native, Other: Writing Postcoloniality and Feminism,* Bloomington and Indianapolis: Indiana University Press.

Mishra, A., K. J. Singh and P. P. Mishra (2021), 'Microplastics in polar regions: An early warning to the world's pristine ecosystem', *Science of The Total Environment*, 784(147149): 1–9.

Mol, A. (1998), 'Lived Realities and the Multiplicity of Norms: A Critical Tribute to George Canguilhem,' *Economy and Society,* 27(2/3): 274–284.

Mollison, B. (1993), *The Permaculture Book of Ferment and Human Nutrition*, Sister's Creek: Tagari Publications.

Mollison, B., and D. Holmgren (1978), *Permaculture One: A Perennial Agriculture System for Human Settlements,* London: Corgi Publishing.

Monirul I. M. (2016), 'Posthumanism: Through the Postcolonial Lens,' in D. Banerji and M. R. Paranjape (eds), *Critical Posthumanism and Planetary Futures*, 115–129, New Delhi: India Springer.

Morrison, T. 1987, *Beloved*, New York: Plume Contemporary Fiction.

Morton, T. (2016), *Dark Ecology: For a Logic of Future Coexistence*, New York: Columbia University Press.

Moten, F. (2003), *In the Break: The Aesthetics of the Black Radical Tradition,*

Minneapolis: University of Minnesota Press.

Munif, A. ([1984] 1989), *Cities of Salt*, London: Vintage Books.

Munster, Anna, A. (1999), 'Is there Postlife after Postfeminism? Tropes of Technics and Life in Cyberfeminism', *Australian Feminist Studies*, 14(29), 119–129. https://doi.org/10.1080/08164649993371

Murphy, M. (2017), 'Alterlife and decolonial chemical relations', *Cultural Anthropology*, 32(4): 494–503.

Murray, S. (2020), *Disability and the Posthuman: Bodies, Technology, and Cultural Futures,* Liverpool: Liverpool University Press.

Naffine, N. (1997), 'The Body Bag', in Naffine and Owens (eds.), *Sexing the Subject of Law*, LBC, 79–94.

Nair, S. (2017), 'Postcolonialism: Interrogating National Security and Drone Warfare', in M. Cavelty and T. Balzacq (eds), *Routledge Handbook of Security Studies*, Abingdon: Routledge.

Nakamura, L. (2008), *Digitizing Race Visual Cultures of the Internet*, Minneapolis and London: University of Minnesota Press.

Nakamura, L. and D. Haraway (2003), 'Prospects for a Materialist Informatics: An Interview with Donna Haraway'. *Electronic Book Review,* August 30, https://electronicbookreview.com/essay/prospects-for-a-materialist-informatics-an-interview-with-donna-haraway/ [accessed 4 May 2019].

Nake, F. (1994), 'Human-computer interaction: signs and signals interfacing', *Languages of Design,* 2: 193–205.

Narayan, U. (1995), 'Colonialism and Its Others: Considerations On Rights and Care Discourses', *Hypatia,* 10(2): 133–140.

National Research Council (2015), *Climate Intervention: Reflecting Sunlight to Cool Earth*, Washington DC: National Academies Press.

Nature Geoscience (2017), 'For people and planet', *Nature Geoscience*, 10(463),

https://doi.org/10.1038/ngeo2987 [last accessed 10 February 2022].

Neimanis, A. (2012), 'Hydrofeminism: Or, on becoming a body of water', in H. Gunkel, C. Nigianni and F. Soderback (eds), *Undutiful Daughters*, New York: Palgrave MacMillan.

Neimanis, A. (2013), 'Feminist subjectivity, watered', *Feminist Review* 103: 23–41.

Neimanis, A. (2017) *Bodies of Water: Posthuman Feminist Phenomenology,* London: Bloomsbury Academic

Neimanis, A. (2019) 'The Weather Underwater: Blackness, White Feminism, and the Breathless Sea', *Australian Feminist Studies*, 34(102): 490–508.

Neimanis, A., C. Åsberg and J. Hedrén (2015), 'Four Problems, Four Directions for Environmental Humanities', *Ethics and the Environment,* 20(1): 67–97.

Neimanis, A. and R. L. Walker (2014), 'Climate Change and the "Thick Time" of Transcorporeality', *Hypatia*, 29(3): 558–575.

Nicenboim, I., E. Giaccardi, M. L. J. Søndergaard, A. V. Reddy, Y. Strengers, J. Pierce and J. Redström (2020), 'More-Than-Human Design and AI', in R. Wakkary, K. Andersen, W. Odom, A. Desjardins and M. G. Petersen (eds), *Companion Publication of the 2020 ACM Designing Interactive Systems Conference*, 397–400, New York: ACM.

Nixon, R. (2011), *Slow Violence and the Environmentalism of the Poor.* Cambridge: Harvard University Press.

Noble, S. U. (2018), *Algorithms of Oppression: How Search Engines Reinforce Racism*, New York: New York University Press.

Noll, G. (2014), 'Weaponising Neurotechnology: International Humanitarian Law and the Loss of Language', *London Review of International Law*, 2(2): 201–231.

Noys, B. and T. S. Murphy (2016), 'Introduction: Old and New Weird', *Genre,* 49(2): 117–134.

Nussbaum, M. (2006), *Frontiers of Justice. Disability, Nationality, Species Membership*, Cambridge: Harvard University Press.

Nussbaum, M. (2011), *Creating Capabilities: The Human Development Approach*, Cambridge: Harvard University Press.

Nuttall, S. (2019), 'Afterword; the shock of the new old', *Social Dynamics: A Journal of African Studies*, 45(2): 280–285.

Nuttall, S. (2020), 'The Redistributed University'. *The WISER Podcast*, 11 October, https://witswiser.podbean.com/e/sarah-nuttall-the-redistributed-university/ [accessed 4 February 2022].

O'Donnell, E., A. Poelina, A. Pelizzon, and C. Clark (2020), 'Stop Burying the Lede: The Essential Role of Indigenous Law(s) in Creating Rights of Nature', *Transnational Environmental Law*, 9(3): 403–427.

O'Donoghue, A. and R. Houghton (2019a), '"Ourworld": A feminist approach to global constitutionalism', *Global Constitutionalism*, 9(1): 38–75.

O'Donoghue, A. and R. Houghton (2019b), 'Can global constitutionalism be feminist?' in S. H. Rimmer and K. Ogg (eds), *Research Handbook on Feminist Engagement with International Law*, 81–102, Cheltenham: Edward Elgar Publishing.

O'Neil, C. (2016), *Weapons of Math Destruction: How Big Data Increases Inequality and Threatens Democracy*, London: Penguin.

Orford, A. (2012), 'In Praise of Description', *Leiden Journal of International Law*, 25(3): 609–625.

Otto, D. and E. Jones (2020), 'Thinking through anthropocentrism in international law: queer theory, posthuman feminism and the postcolonial', *LSE Centre for Women, Peace and Security blog*, June 17, https://www.lse.ac.uk/women-peace-security/assets/documents/2020/Final-Jones-and-Otto-Anthropocentrism-Posthuman-Feminism-Postcol-and-IL-LSE-WPS-Blog-2019-002.pdf [accessed 30 March 2021].

Oxford University Press (2020), 'weird, adj.', OED Online, December, www.oed.com/view/Entry/226916 [accessed 25 January 2021].

Oxley, J. C. (2011), *The Moral Dimensions of Empathy: Limits and Applications in Ethical Theory and Practice*, New York: Palgrave Macmillan.

Paglen, T. (2014), 'Operational Images', *e-flux*, November, https://www.e-flux.com/journal/59/61130/operational-images/ [accessed 15 February 2022].

Palmer, H. (2020), *Queer Defamiliarisation: Writing, Mattering, Making Strange*, Edinburgh: Edinburgh University Press.

Papadopoulos, D. (2018), 'Insurgent Posthumanism', in R. Braidotti and M. Hlavajova (eds), *Posthuman Glossary*, London: Bloomsbury Academic.

Papenburg, B., L. Hausken and S. Schmitz (2018), 'Introduction: The Processes of Imaging/The Imaging of Process', *Catalyst: Feminism, Theory, Technoscience*, 4(2): 1–26.

Parfit, D. (1984), *Reasons and Persons*, Oxford: Oxford University Press.

Parikka, J. (2011), *Medianatures: Materiality of Information Technology and Electronic Waste*, London: Open Humanities Press.

Parikka, J. (2015), *A Geology of Media*, Minneapolis: University of Minnesota Press.

Parikka, J. (2018), 'Cartographies of Environmental Arts', in R. Braidotti and S. Bignall (eds), *Posthuman Ecologies: Complexity and Process After Deleuze*, 41–60, London: Rowman and Littlefield Publishers.

Parikka, J. and P. Feigelfeld (2015), 'Friedrich Kittler: E-Special Introduction', *Theory, Culture & Society*, 32(7–8): 349–358.

Parisi, L. (2004), *Abstract Sex, Philosophy, Bio-Technology and the Mutations of Desire*, London: Continuum.

Parks, L. and C. Kaplan (2017), *Life in the Age of Drone Warfare*, Durham: Duke University Press.

Parr, A. (2022), *Earthlings*, New York: Columbia University press.

Pascoe, B. (2014), *Dark Emu, Black Seeds: Agriculture or Accident?*, Broome: Magabala Books.

Paulsen, F. J., M. B. Nielsen, Y. Shashoua, K. Syberg and S. F. Hansen (2021), 'Early warning signs applied to plastic', *nature reviews materials*, https://doi.org/10.1038/s41578-021-00317-9 [accessed 1 February 2022].

Peele, J. (director) (2019), *Us*, USA: Universal Pictures.

Pellow, D. N. and L. S. H. Park (2002), *The Silicon Valley of Dreams: Environmental Justice, Immigrant Workers and the High-Tech Global Economy*, New York and London: New York University Press.

Penniman, L. (2018), *Farming While Black: Soul Fire Farm's Practical Guide to Liberation on the Land*, White River Junction: Chelsea Green Publishing.

Pentecost, C. (2008), 'Outfitting the Laboratory of the Symbolic: Toward a Critical Inventory of Bioart,' in B. da Costa and K. Philip (eds), *Tactical Biopolitics. Art, Activism, and Technoscience*, 107–25, Cambridge and London: MIT Press.

Perera, S. (2013), 'Oceanic Corpo-Graphies, Refugee Bodies and the Making and Unmaking of Waters', *Feminist Review*, 103(1): 58–79.

Petrocultures Research Group (2016), *After Oil*, Alberta: Petrocultures Research Group.

Philip, K., L. Irani and P. Dourish (2012), 'Postcolonial Computing: A Tactical Survey,' *Science, Technology, & Human Values,* 37(1): 3–29.

Philippopoulos-Mihalopoulos, A. (2017), 'Critical Environmental Law as Method in the Anthropocene', in A. Philippopoulos-Mihalopoulos and V. Brooks (eds), *Research Methods in Environmental Law*, Cheltenham: Edward Elgar Publishing.

Phillips, P. C. (1989), 'Temporality and Public Art', *Art journal,* 48(4): 331–335.

Pick, A. (2011), *Creaturely Poetics: Animality and Vulnerability in Literature and Film*, New York: Columbia University Press.

Piepzna-Samarasinha, L. L. (2018), *Care Work: Dreaming Disability Justice*, Vancouver: Arsenal Pulp Press.

Plant, S. (1997), *Zeroes and Ones: Digital Women and the New Technoculture,* 1st edn, New York: Doubleday.

Plumwood, V. (1993), *Feminism and the Mastery of Nature*, London and New York: Routledge.

Plumwood, V. (2002), *Environmental Culture: The Ecological Crisis of Reason*, London and New York: Routledge.

Popkin, B. (2009), *The World is Fat: the Fads, Trends, Policies and Products that are Fattening the Human Race*, New York: Avery Publishing Group.

Popkin, B. M, L. S. Adair and S. W. Ng (2012), 'Global nutrition transition and the pandemic of obesity in developing countries,' *Nutrition Reviews*, 70(1): 3–21.

Povinelli, E. A. (2016), *Geontologies: A Requiem to Late Liberalism*, Durham: Duke University Press.

Price, M. (2017), 'What Is a Service Animal? A Careful Rethinking', *Review of Disability Studies: An International Journal*, 13(4): 1–18.

Prigogine, I. and I. Stengers ([1984] 2017), *Order Out of Chaos: Man's New Dialogue with Nature*, London: Verso.

Prinz, J. J. (2011), 'Is Empathy Necessary for Morality?' in A. Coplan and P. Goldie (eds), *Empathy: Philosophical and Psychological Perspectives*, 211–229, Oxford: Oxford University Press.

Pritchard, H., J. Rocha and F. Snelting (2020), 'Figurations of Timely Extraction' *Media Theory*, 4(2): 159–188.

Probyn, E. (2016), *Eating the Ocean*, Durham: Duke University Press.

Puar, J. (2007), *Terrorist Assemblages: Homonationalism in Queer Times*, Durham: Duke University Press.

Puar, J. (2012), 'I Would Rather Be a Cyborg Than a Goddess: Becoming-Intersectional in Assemblage Theory', *philoSOPHIA*, 2(1): 49–66.

Radomska, M. (2017), 'Non/living Matter, Bioscientific Imaginaries and Feminist Technoecologies of Bioart', *Australian Feminist Studies*, 32(94): 377–394.

Radomska, M. (2020), 'Deterritorialising Death: Queerfeminist Biophilosophy and Ecologies of the Non/Living in Contemporary Art', *Australian Feminist Studies* 35(104): 116–137.

Radomska M, Åsberg C. 'Fathoming postnatural oceans: Towards a low trophic theory in the practices of feminist posthumanities.' *Environment and Planning E: Nature and Space*. June 2021. doi:10.1177/25148486211028542.

Radomska, M., T. Mehrabi, and N. Lykke (2020), 'Queer Death Studies: Death, Dying and Mourning From a Queerfeminist Perspective', *Australian Feminist Studies*, 35(104): 81–100.

Raghuram, P. (2019), 'Race and feminist care ethics: intersectionality as method', *Gender, Place and Culture: A Journal of Feminist Geography*, 26(5): 613–637.

Ramesh, S., H. Ramprasad, and J. Han (2020), 'Listen to Your Key: Towards Acoustics-based Physical Key Inference,' in *Proceedings of the 21st International Workshop on Mobile Computing Systems and Applications (HotMobile '20)*, 3–8, New York: ACM.

Rawls, J. (1971), *A Theory of Justice*, Massachusetts: Harvard University Press.

Reardon, J., and K. TallBear. (2012), '"Your DNA is our history": genomics, anthropology, and the construction of whiteness as property', *Current Anthropology*, 53(S5): S233–S245.

Redecker, S. von and C. Herzig (2020), 'The Peasant Way of a More than Radical Democracy: The Case of La Via Campesina', *Journal of Business Ethics*, 164(4): 657–670.

Regan, T. (1983), *The Case for Animal Rights*, Berkeley and Los Angeles: University of California Press.

Renic, N. C. (2018), 'Justified killing in an age of radically asymmetric warfare', *European Journal of International Relations*, 25(2): 408–430.

Rich, A. (1986), *Blood, Bread and Poetry*, New York: Norton.

Rieder, B. (2020), *Engines of Order: A Mechanology of Algorithmic Techniques*, Amsterdam: Amsterdam University Press.

Ripple, W. J., C. Wolf, T. M. Newsome, J. W. Gregg, T. M. Lenton, I. Palomo, J. A. J. Eikelboom, B. E. Law, S. Huq, P. B. Duffy, and J. Rockström (2021), 'World Scientists' Warning of a Climate Emergency 2021', *BioScience*, 71(9): 894–898.

Roberts, C. (2019), 'Puberty as Biopsychosocial Enfolding: Mothers' Accounts of their Early-Developing Daughters', in Sharon Lamb and Jen Gilbert (eds), *The Cambridge Handbook of Sexual Development*, 485–504, Cambridge University Press: Cambridge.

Robertson, B. J. (2018), *None of this is Normal: The Fiction of Jeff VanderMeer*, Minneapolis: University of Minnesota Press.

Robinson, C. J. (2020), *Black Marxism, Revised and Updated Third Edition: The Making of the Black Radical Tradition*. UNC Press Books.

Robinson, S. (2016), 'The Vital Network: An Algorithmic Milieu of Communication and Control', *communication +1*, 1(5): http://scholarworks.umass.edu/cpo/vol5/iss1/5 [accessed 23 March 2018].

Roeser, S., V. Alfano, and C. Nevejan (2018), 'The Role of Art in Emotional-Moral Reflection on Risky and Controversial Technologies: The Case of BNCI', *Ethical Theory and Moral Practice*, 21: 275–89.

Roff, H. M. (2016), 'Gendering a warbot', *International Feminist Journal of Politics*, 18(1):1–18.

Rose, D. B. (2004), *Reports From a Wild Country*, Sydney: University of New South Wales Press.

Rose, D. B. (2011). *Wild Dog Dreaming: Love and Extinction*, Charlottesville: University of Virginia Press.

Rose, D. B. (2012), 'Multispecies knots of ethical time', *Environmental Philosophy*, 9(1): 127–140.

Rose, D. B. (2017), 'Shimmer: When all you love is being trashed' in A. Tsing, H. Swanson, E. Gan, N. Bubandt (ed.), *Arts of Living on a Damaged Planet*, 51–61, Minneapolis: University of Minnesota Press.

Rosenthal, C. (2018), *Accounting for Slavery: Masters and Management*, Cambridge: Harvard University Press.

Rosner, D. K. (2018), *Critical Fabulations: Reworking the Methods and Margins of Design*, Cambridge: MIT Press.

Rotman, B. (2008), *Becoming Beside Ourselves: The Alphabet, Ghosts, and Distributed Human Being*, Durham: Duke University Press.

Rouvroy, A. (2013), 'The end(s) of critique: data-behaviourism vs. due-process', in M. Hildebrandt and K. de Vries (eds), *Privacy, Due Process and the Computational Turn: The Philosophy of Law Meets the Philosophy of Technology*, 143–167, New York: Routledge.

Rouvroy, A. (2020), 'Algorithmic Governmentality and the Death of Politics', *Green European Journal*, 27 March, https://www.greeneuropeanjournal.eu/algorithmic-governmentality-and-the-death-of-politics/ [accessed 9 June 2020].

Rouvroy, A. and T. Berns (2013), 'Gouvernementalité algorithmique et perspectives d'émancipation', *Réseaux*, 177(1): 163.

Rouvroy, A. and B. Stiegler (2016), 'The Digital Regime of Truth: From the Algorithmic Governmentality to a New Rule of Law', *La Deleuziana: Online Journal of Philosophy*, 3: 6–29.

Sheldon, R. (2015). 'Form / Matter / Chora: Objected-Orientated Ontology and Feminist New Materialism,' in Richard Grusin (ed.), *The Nonhuman Turn*, Minneapolis: University of Minnesota Press.

Rupprecht, A. (2016), 'Inherent Vice: Marine insurance, Slave Ship Rebellion and the Law', *Race & Class*, 57(3): 31–44.

Ruru, J. (2018), 'First laws: Tikanga maori in/and the law', *Victoria University of Wellington Law Review*, 49(2): 211–228.

Sadek, W. (2016), *The Ruin to Come: Essays from a Protracted War*, Geneva: Motto Books.

Sagan, D. and L. Margulis (2013), '"Wind at Life's Back" – Toward a Naturalistic, Whiteheadian Teleology: Symbiogenesis and the Second Law', in B.G. Henning and A. Scarfe (eds), *Beyond Mechanism: Putting Life Back into Biology*, 205–232, Lanham: Lexington Books.

Saha, P. (2019), 'Unwatched/Unmanned: Drone Strikes and the Aesthetics of the Unseen,' in N. Baer, M. Hennefeld, L. Horak, and G. Iversen (eds), *Unwatchable*, 63–70, New Brunswick: Rutgers University Press.

Samuels, E. (2014), *Fantasies of Identification: Disability, Gender, Race*, New York: New York University Press.

Samuels, E. (2017), 'Six ways of looking at crip time', *Disability Studies Quarterly*, 37(3), https://dsq-sds.org/article/view/5824/4684 [accessed 4 February 2022].

Sandahl, C. (2003), 'Queering the Crip or Cripping the Queer? Intersections of Queer and Crip Identities in Solo Autobiographical Performance', *GLQ: A Journal of Gay and Lesbian Studies*, 9(1–2): 25–56.

Sands, D. (2019a), 'Thinking Unthinkable Futures: Artificial Intelligence and Posthumanism', in C. Wood, S. Livingston, and M. Uchida (eds), *AI: More than Human*, 181–183, London: Barbican.

Sands, D. (2019b), *Animal Writing: Storytelling, Selfhood and the Limits of Empathy*, Edinburgh: Edinburgh University Press.

Sassen, S. (2001), *The Global City*, Princeton: Princeton University Press.

Sauer, F. and N. Schörnig (2012), 'Killer drones: The "silver bullet" of democratic warfare?,' *Security Dialogue*, 43(4): 363–380.

Schaeffer, F. A. (2018), 'Spirit Matters: Gloria Anzaldua's Cosmic Becoming across Human/Nonhuman Borderlands', *Signs: Journal of Women in Culture and Society*, 43(4): 1005–1029.

Schlesinger, A., W. K. Edwards and R. E. Grinter (2017), 'Intersectional HCI', in G. Mark, S. Fussell, C. Lampe, M. schraefel, J. P. Hourcade, C. Appert and D. Wigdor (eds), *Proceedings of the 2017 CHI Conference on Human Factors in Computing Systems – CHI '17*, 5412–5427, New York: ACM Press.

Schmitz, S. (2021), 'TechnoBrainBodies-in-Cultures: An Intersectional Case', *Frontiers in sociology*, 6: 1–16.

Schuppli, S. (2020), *Material Witness: Media, Forensics, Evidence*, Cambridge: MIT Press.

Sederholm, C. H. and J. A. Weinstock (eds) (2016), *The Age of Lovecraft*, Minneapolis: University of Minnesota Press.

Sendra, P. and R. Sennett, (2020), *Designing Disorder: Experiments and Disruptions in the City*, London: Verso.

Serner, W. (2020), *Last Loosening: A Handbook for the Con Artist & Those Aspiring to Become One*, Prague: Twisted Spoon Press.

Serres, M. ([1980] 2007), *The Parasite*, Minneapolis: University of Minnesota Press.

Servigne, P. and R. Stevens ([2015] 2020), *How Everything Can Collapse: A Manual for our Times*, Cambridge: Polity Press.

Servigne, P., R. Stevens, and G. Chapelle ([2018] 2021), *Another End of the World Is Possible*, Cambridge: Polity Press.

Seshadri, K. (2012), *HumAnimal: Race, Law, Language*, Minneapolis: University of Minnesota Press.

Shapiro, S. (2021), 'The Lure of Fascism - Algorithmic Neoliberalism and the World-System of Large-Scale Customization', *Sawyer Lecture, Arizona State University*, 9 February 2021,

https://www.youtube.com/watch?v=eTWDcRREbuw [accessed 20 February 2022].

Sharpe, S. (2016), *In the Wake: on Blackness and Being*, Durham: Duke University Press.

Shaw I. G. R. (2013), 'Predator empire: the geopolitics of US drone warfare', *Geopolitics*, 18(3): 536–559.

Shaw I. G. R. and M. Akhter (2011), 'The unbearable humanness of drone warfare in FATA, Pakistan', *Antipode: a Radical Journal of Geography*, 44(4): 1490–1509.

Sheets P., C. Rowling, and T. Jones (2015), 'The view from above (and below): A comparison of American, British, and Arab news coverage of US drones', *Media, War & Conflict*, 8(3): 289–311.

Shiels, M. S., A. T. Haque, E. A. Haozous, P. S. Albert, J. S. Almeida, M. García-Closas, A. M. Nápoles, E. J. Pérez-Stable, N. D. Freedman, A. Berrington de González (2021), 'Racial and Ethnic Disparities in Excess Deaths During the COVID-19 Pandemic', *Annals of Internal Medicine*, 174(12):1693.

Shildrick, M. (2015), 'Chimerism and *Immunitas*: The Emergence of a Posthumanist Biophilosophy', in S. Wilmer and A. Žukauskaite (eds), *Resisting Biopolitics: Philosophical, Political and Performative Strategies*, 95–109, London: Routledge.

Shildrick, M. (2020), 'Queering the Social Imaginaries of the Dead', *Australian Feminist Studies*, 35(104): 170–185.

Shklovsky, V. (2017), *Viktor Shklovsky: A Reader*. trans. and ed. A. Berlina. London and New York: Bloomsbury.

Sholtz, J. (2015), *The Invention of a People: Heidegger and Deleuze on Art and the Political*, Edinburgh: Edinburgh University Press.

Simard, S. (2021), *Finding the Mother Tree: Uncovering the Wisdom and Intelligence of the Forest*, New York: Alfred A. Knopf.

Simpkins, R. (2016), 'Trans*feminist Intersections,' *TSQ: Transgender Studies Quarterly*, 3(1–2): 228–234.

Simpson, L. B. (2017), *As We Have Always Done: Indigenous Freedom Through Radical Resistance*, Minneapolis: University of Minnesota Press.

Sinclair, U. (1926), *Oil!,* London: Penguin Random House.

Singer, H., T. Laird, A. Dunn, S. Lavau and B. Verlie (2019), *Hacking the Anthropocene IV*, https://hackingtheanthropoceneiv. wordpress.com/ [accessed 3 March 2021].

Singer, P. (1976), *Animal Liberation: A New Ethics for Our Treatment of Animals*, London: Cape.

Sins Invalid (2016), *Skin, Tooth, and Bone: The Basis of Movement is Our People*, 1st ed., San Francisco: Dancer's Group.

Smith, N., S. Bardzell, and J. Bardzell (2017), 'Designing for Cohabitation: Naturecultures, Hybrids, and Decentering the Human in Design,' in G. Mark (ed.), *Proceedings of the 2017 CHI Conference on Human Factors in Computing Systems*, 1714–1725, New York: ACM Press.

Smith, J. B. And E. Willis (2020), 'Interpreting Posthumanism with Nurse Work,' *Journal of Posthuman Studies,* 4(1): 59–75.

Snow, C. P. ([1959] 1998), *The Two Cultures*, Cambridge: Cambridge University Press.

Sollfrank, C. (ed.) (2018), *Die Schönen Kriegerinnen: Technofeministische Praxis im 21. Jahrhundert*, Vienna and Linz: Transversal Texts.

Sollfrank, C. (ed.) (2019), *The Beautiful Warriors. Technofeminist Praxis in the 21st. century,* New York: Minor Compositions.

Sperling, A. (2017), 'Weird Modernisms,' unpublished PhD thesis, University of Wisconsin-Milwaukee, https://dc.uwm. edu/etd/1542/ [accessed 4 February 2022].

Spillers, H. (1984), 'Interstices: A Small Drama of Words,' in C. S. Vance (ed.), *Pleasure and Danger: Exploring Female Sexuality*, 73–100, Boston: Routledge.

Spillers, H. (1987), 'Mama's Baby, Papa's Maybe: An American Grammar Book,' *Culture and Countermemory: The "American" Connection*, 17(2): 64–81.

Spillers, H. (2003), *Black White and in Color: Essays on American Literature and Culture*, Chicago: University of Chicago Press.

Spinoza, B. de ([1677] 1996), *Ethics*, London: Penguin.

Sprague, R. K. (1991), 'Plants as Aristotelian Substances,' *Illinois Classical Studies*, 16(1/2): 221–229.

Srnicek, N. (2017), *Platform capitalism*, Cambridge and Malden: Polity Press.

Standish, R. J., A. Thompson, E. Higgs, and S. D. Murphy (2013), 'Concerns About Novel Ecosystems'. In Novel Ecosystems : Intervening in R. J. Hobbs, E. Higgs, and C. M. Hall (eds), *Novel Ecosystems : Intervening in the New Ecological World Order*, 296–309, Chichester and Hoboken: John Wiley and Sons.

Stauffer, R. C. (1957), 'Haeckel, Darwin, and Ecology,' *The Quarterly Review of Biology*, 32(2): 138–144.

Sternlicht, A. (2020), 'Navajo Nation Has Most Coronavirus Infections Per Capita In U.S., Beating New York, New Jersey,' *Forbes*, 19 May, https://www.forbes.com/ sites/alexandrasternlicht/2020/05/19/ navajo-nation-has-most-coronavirus-infections-per-capita-in-us-beating-new-york-new-jersey/?sh=22b58f3f8b10 [accessed 22 February 2022].

Steyerl, H. (2019), 'A Sea of Data: Pattern Recognition and Corporate Animism (Forked Version)', in C. Apprich, W. H. K. Chun, F. Cramer, and H. Steyerl (eds), *Pattern Discrimination*, 1–22, Minneapolis: University of Minnesota Press.

Steyn, M. and W. Mpofu (2021), *Decolonising the Human*, Johannesburg: Wits University Press.

Stimpson, C. R. (2016), 'The nomadic humanities,' *Los Angeles Review of Books*, 12 July.

Stone, A. R. (1991), 'Will the real body please stand up?', in M. Benedikt (ed), *Cyberspace: First Steps*: 81–118, Cambridge: MIT Press.

Stone, C. (1972), 'Should trees have standing? Toward legal rights for natural objects', *Southern California Law Review*, 45: 450–501.

Stone, S. (1992), 'The *Empire* Strikes Back: A Posttransexual Manifesto,' *Camera Obscura*, 10(2): 150–176.

Storr, C. (2021), '"Space is the Only Way to Go": The Evolution of the Extractivist Imaginary of International Law,' in S. Chalmers and S. Pahuja (eds), *Routledge Handbook of International Law and the Humanities*, 290–301, Abingdon and New York: Routledge.

Strathern, M., J. S. Sasser, A. Clarke, R. Benjamin, K. Tallbear, M. Murphy, D. Haraway, Y. -L. Huang and C. -L. Wu (2019), 'Forum on Making Kin Not Population: Reconceiving Generations,' *Feminist Studies*, 45(1): 159–172.

Stronach, M., D. Adair, and H. Maxwell (2019), '"Djabooly-djabooly: why don't they swim?": the ebb and flow of water in the lives of Australian Aboriginal women', *Annals of Leisure Research*, 22(3): 286–304.

Suchman, L. (2006), *Human–Machine Reconfigurations*, Cambridge: Cambridge University Press.

Sullivan, H. I. (2019), 'Petro-texts, plants, and people in the Anthropocene: the dark green,' *Green Letters*, 23(2): 152–167.

Sundberg, J. (2014), 'Decolonizing humanist geographies,' *Cultural Geographies,* 21(1): 33–47.

Sutela, J. (2019) 'nimiia ïzinibimi,' *Vimeo*, 14 February, https://vimeo.com/317271977?f bclid=IwAR0rn99VZbN_7xWhjffA0P7k zKPi9iY-Ak5h0i4_ HjdQ0YKNiD8Rij8RHMw [accessed 29 April 2021].

Sweeney, L. (2013), 'Discrimination in Online Ad Delivery: Google ads, black names and white names, racial discrimination, and click advertising,' *Queue*, 11(3): 10–29.

Swinburn, B., V. Kraak, S. Allendar, Steven, et al. (2019), 'The Global Syndemic of Obesity, Undernutrition, and Climate Change: *The Lancet* Commission report,' *The Lancet Commissions*, 393(10173): 791–846.

Szeman, I. Sheena Wilson, and Adam Carlson, (2017) *Petrocultures. Oil, Politics, and Culture*, Chicago: McGill-Queen's University Press.

Taffel, S. (2019), *Digital Media Ecologies: Entanglements of Content, Code and Hardware*, New York: Bloomsbury Academic.

TallBear K. and Angela Willey, "Critical Relationality: Queer, Indigenous, and Multispecies Belonging Beyond Settler Sex & Nature," *Imaginations*, vol. 10, no.1, 2019.

Tamm, E. and E. Wägner (1940), *Fred med Jorden*, Stockholm: Bonnier.

Tansley, A. G. (1935), 'The Use and Abuse of Vegetational Concepts and Terms,' *Ecology*, 16: 284–307.

Taylor, S. (2017), *Beasts of Burden: Animal and Disability Liberation,* New York: The New Press.

Terranova, F. (director) (2017), *Donna Haraway: Story Telling for Earthly Survival,* USA: Icarus Films.

Terry, J. (1999), *An American Obsession Science, Medicine, and Homosexuality in Modern Society,* Chicago: University of Chicago Press.

Teubner, G. (2006), 'Rights of Non-humans? Electronic Agents and Animals as New Actors in Politics and Law', *Journal of Law & Society*, 33(4): 497–521.

Thacker, E. (2004), *Biomedia.* Minneapolis: University of Minnesota Press.

Thacker, E. (2011), *In the Dust of This Planet*, London: Zero Books.

The Care Collective (2020), *The Care Manifesto*, London: Verso Books.

Thiel, G. J. M. W. van, and J. J. M. van Delden (2010), 'Reflective Equilibrium as a Normative Empirical Model,' *Ethical Perspectives,* 17(2): 183–202.

Throsby, K. (2013), '"If I go in like a Cranky Sea Lion, I Come out like a Smiling Dolphin": Marathon Swimming and the Unexpected Pleasures of Being a Body in Water,' *Feminist Review*, 103(1): 5–22.

Tinsley, O. N. (2008), 'Black Atlantic, Queer Atlantic: Queer Imaginings of the Middle Passage' *GLQ: a Journal of Gay and Lesbian Studies,* 14(2–3): 191–215.

Tlostanova, M. and W. Mignolo (2009), 'On Pluritopic Hermeneutics, Trans-Modern Thinking, and Decolonial Philosophy', *Encounters*, 1(1): 11–27.

Tlostanova, M. and W. Mignolo (2012), *Learning to Unlearn: Decolonial Reflections from Eurasia and the Americas*, Columbus: Ohio State University Press.

Todd, Z. (2015), 'Indigenizing the anthropocene', in H. Davis and E. Turpin (eds), *Art in the Anthropocene: Encounters among aesthetics, politics, environments and epistemologies*, 241–254, London: Open Humanities Press.

Todd, Z. (2021), 'Weaponized Fossil Kin and the Alberta economy,' *speculative fish-ctions*, 19 January 2021, https:// zoestodd.com/2021/01/19/weaponized-fossil-kin-and-the-alberta-economy/ [accessed 8 February 2022].

Treusch, P. (2017), 'Naturecultures of Immunological Principles: A discussion on the politics of the CLONALG algorithm from a feminist materialist perspective', *International Journal of Gender, Science and Technology*, 9(2): 141–58.

Treusch, P. (2020), *Robotic Knitting: Re-Crafting Human-Robot Collaboration Through Careful Coboting*, Berlin: transcript Verlag.

Tronto, J. (1995), 'Care as a basis for radical political judgment'. *Hypatia*: 10(2): 141–149.

Tronto, J. C. and B. Fisher (1990), 'Toward a feminist theory of caring', in E. K. Abel and M. K. Nelson (eds), *Circles of Care: Work and Identity in Women's Lives*, 36–54, New York: SUNY Press.

Tsing, A. (2015), *The Mushroom at the End of the World: On the Possibility of Life in Capitalist Ruins*, Princeton: Princeton University Press.

Tsing A., H. Swanson. E. Gan and N. Bubandt (eds) (2017), *Arts of Living on a Damaged Planet: Ghosts and Monsters of the Anthropocene*, Minneapolis: University of Minnesota Press.

Tsing, A., J. Deger, S. Keleman Saxena, and F. Zhou (2021), *Feral Atlas: The More-Than-Human Anthropocene*, Redwood City: Stanford University Press.

Tsosie, R. (2007), 'Indigenous people and environmental justice: the impact of climate change', *University of Colorado Law Review,* 78: 1625.

Tuin, I. van der (2018), 'Diffraction,' in R. Braidotti and M. Hlavajova (eds), *Posthuman Glossary,* 99–101, London: Bloomsbury Academic.

Tuin, I. van der (2018), 'Neo/New Materialism,' in R. Braidotti and M. Hlavajova (eds), *Posthuman Glossary*, 277–279, London: Bloomsbury Academic.

Tuin, I. van der and R. Dolphijn (2012), *New Materialism: Interviews & Cartographies*, Ann Arbor: Open Humanities Press.

Trewawas, A. (2015), *Plant Behaviour and Intelligence*, Oxford: Oxford University Press.

Tuhiwai Smith, L. (2021), *Decolonizing Methodologies*, London and New York: Bloomsbury Academic.

Ulmer, J. (2017), 'Slow Ontology,' *Qualitative Inquiry*, 23(3): 201–211.

Vandana, S. (2013), *Making Peace with the Earth*, London: Pluto Press.

VanderMeer, A. and J. VanderMeer (eds) (2011), 'Introduction,' *The Weird: A*

Compendium of Strange and Dark Stories, xv–xxiv, London: Corrus.

VanderMeer, J. (2008), 'The New Weird: "It's Alive?"' in A. VanderMeer and J. VanderMeer (eds), *The New Weird,* ix–xvii, San Francisco: Tachyon Publications.

van Dooren, T. Kirksey E. and Münster U. (2016), 'Multispecies Studies: Cultivating Arts of Attentiveness,' *Environmental humanities,* 8(1):1–23.

Vehlken, S. (2019), *Zootechnologies: A Media History of Swarm Research,* Amsterdam: Amsterdam University Press, 2019

Venn, C. (2009), 'Neoliberal Political Economy, Biopolitics and Colonialism: A Transcolonial Genealogy of Inequality,' *Theory, Culture & Society,* 26(6): 206–233.

Veprinska, A. (2020), *Empathy in Contemporary Poetry after Crisis*, London: Palgrave Macmillan

Verbeek, P.-P. (2010), 'Accompanying Technology: Philosophy of Technology after the Ethical Turn,' *Techné* 14(1): 49–54.

Vermeulen, P. (2015), *Contemporary Literature and the End of the Novel: Creature, Affect, Form*, London: Palgrave Macmillan.

Verstraete, M. (2019), 'The Stakes of Smart Contracts,' *Loyola University Chicago Law Journal,* 50: 743–795.

Viveiros de Castro, E. (2015), *The Relative Native: Essays on Indigenous Conceptual Worlds*, Chicago: HAU Press.

V NS Matrix. (1991), *Manifesto.* https:// vnsmatrix.net/essays/manifesto [accessed 4 May 2022].

Vogel, S. (1988), 'Marx and Alienation From Nature,' *Social Theory and Practice,* 14(3): 367–387.

Waal, F. de (2010), *The Age of Empathy: Nature's Lessons for a Kinder Society*, London: Souvenir Press.

Wajcman, J. (2007) 'From women and technology to gendered technoscience,' *Information, Community and Society,* 10(3): 287–298.

Wakkary, R. (2020) 'Nomadic practices: A posthuman theory for knowing design,' *International Journal of Design,* 14(3): 117–128.

Wandersee, J. H. and E. E. Schussler (2001), 'Toward a theory of plant blindness,' *Plant Science Bulletin,* 47(1): 2–9.

Wasserstrom, J. (2020), *Vigil: Hong Kong on the Brink,* New York: Columbia Global Reports.

Watkin, C. (2020), *Michel Serres: Figures of Thought*, Edinburgh: Edinburgh UP.

Watt-Cloutier, S. (2015), *The Right to Be Cold: One Woman's Fight to Protect the Arctic and Save the Planet from Climate Change*, Minneapolis: University of Minnesota Press.

Weheliye, A. G. (2014). *Habeas Viscus: Racializing Assemblages, Biopolitics, and Black Feminist Theories of the Human.* Duke University Press.

Weil, K. (2018), 'Empathy,' in R. Broglio, U. Sellbach and L. Turner (eds), *The Edinburgh Companion to Animal studies,* 126–139, Edinburgh: Edinburgh University Press.

Weinbaum, A. (2019) *The Afterlife of Reproductive Slavery: Biocapitalism and Black Feminism's Philosophy of History*, Durham: Duke University Press.

Weinstein, J. (2016), 'Vital Ethics: On Life and In/difference,' in A. Hunt and S. Youngblood (eds), *Against Life,* 87–118, Evanston: Northwestern University Press.

Weizman, E. (2008), *Hollow Land: Israel's Architecture of Occupation*, London: Verso.

Wenzel, J. (2014), 'Petro-Magic Realism Revisited: Unimagining and Reimagining the Niger Delta,' in R. Barrett and D. Worden (eds), *Oil Culture,* 211–225, Minneapolis: University of Minnesota Press.

Whitehead, A. (2017), *Medicine and Empathy in Contemporary British Fiction: An Intervention in Medical Humanities,* Edinburgh: Edinburgh University Press.

Whitehead, A. N. (1978), *Process and Reality: An Essay in Cosmology,* D. R. Griffins and

D. W. Sherburne (eds), New York: Free Press.

Whyte, K. (2017), 'Way Beyond the Lifeboat: An Indigenous Allegory of Climate Justice', in D. Munshi, K. Bhavnani, J. Foran, and P. Kurian (eds), *Climate Futures: Reimagining Global Climate Justice*, 11–20, Berkeley: University of California Press.

Whyte, K. P. and C. Cuomo (2017), 'Ethics of Caring in Environmental Ethics: Indigenous and Feminist Philosophies', in Stephen M. Gardiner, Allen Thompson (eds), *The Oxford Handbook of Environmental Ethics*, 234–247, New York: Oxford University Press.

Wilcox, L. (2015), *Bodies of Violence: Theorizing Embodied Subjects in International Relations*, Oxford: Oxford University Press.

Wilcox, L. (2017a), 'Embodying algorithmic war: Gender, race, and the posthuman in drone warfare', *Security Dialogue,* 48(1): 11–28.

Wilcox, L. (2017b), 'Drones, swarms and becoming-insect: Feminist utopias and posthuman politics', *Feminist Review,* 116(1): 25–45.

Williams, O. (2006), 'Food and Justice: The Critical Link to Healthy Communities', in D. N. Pellow and R. Brulle (eds), *Power, Justice, and the Environment: A Critical Appraisal of the Environmental Justice Movement,* 117–130, Cambridge: MIT Press.

Williams, R. (1976), *Keywords: A Vocabulary of Culture and Society,* London: Fontana.

Wilson, B. (2019), *The Way We Eat Now. Strategies for Eating in a World of Change,* London: Fourth Estate.

Wilson, S. (2014), 'Gendering Oil: Tracing Western Petrosexual Relations', in R. Barett and D. Worden (eds), *Oil Culture*, 244–263, Minneapolis: University of Minnesota Press.

Winseck, D. R., and R. M. Pike (2007), *Communication and Empire: Media, Markets, and Globalization, 1860–1930,* Durham: Duke University Press.

Wolfe, C. (2003), *Animal Rites: American Culture, the Discourse of Species, and Posthumanist Theory*, Chicago: University of Chicago Press.

Wong, A. (2020), *Disability Visibility: First-Person Stories from the Twenty-First Century,* New York: Vintage Books.

Wunderling, N., J. F. Donges, J. Kurths, and R. Winkelmann (2021), 'Interacting tipping elements increase risk of climate domino effects under global warming,' *Earth System Dynamics,* 12: 601–619.

Wynter, S. (2001), 'Towards the sociogenic principle: Fanon, Identity, the Puzzle of Conscious Experience, and What it is like to be Black', in A. Gomez-Moriana and M. Duran-Cogan (eds.), *National Identities and Sociopolitical Changes in Latin America*, 30–66, New York: Routledge.

Wynter, S. (2003), 'Unsettling the Coloniality of Being/Power/Truth/Freedom: Towards the Human, after Man, Its Overrepresentation—An Argument', *CR: The New Centennial Review*, 3(3): 257–337.

Wynter, S. and K. McKittrick (2015), 'Unparalleled Catastrophe for Our Species?'. In K. McKittrick (ed.), *Sylvia Wynter. On Being Human as Praxis*, 9–89, Durham and London: Duke University Press.

Yager, P. (2011), 'Literature in the Ages of Wood, Tallow, Coal, Whale Oil, Gasoline, Atomic Power, and Other Energy Sources', *PMLA*, 26(22): 305–326.

Yamin-Pasternak, S., A. Kliskey, L. Alessa, I. Pasternak, P. Schweitzer (2014), 'The Rotten Renaissance in the Bering Strait. Loving, Loathing and Washing the Smell of Foods with a (Re)acquired Taste', *Current Anthropology*, 55(5): 619–648.

Yoshida, K. (2018), 'A Constitution for Mars: A Call for Founding Feminists', *International Law Grrls*, 4 October 2018, https://ilg2.org/2018/10/04/a-constitution-for-mars-a-call-for-founding-feminists/ [last accessed 22 June 2021].

Young, J. (1996), 'Tempest,' *Cryptome*, http://cryptome.org/tempest-old.htm/ [accessed 15 February 2022].

Yung, L., S. Schwarze, W. Carr, F. S. Chapin, and E. Marris (2013), 'Engaging the Public in Novel Ecosystems', in R. J. Hobbs, E. Higgs, and C. M. Hall (eds), *Novel Ecosystems : Intervening in the New Ecological World Order*, 247–256, Chichester and Hoboken: John Wiley and Sons.

Yunkaporta, T. (2020), *Sand Talk: How Indigenous Thinking Can Save The World*, San Francisco: HarperOne.

Yusoff, K. (2018), *A Billion Black Anthropocenes or None*, Minneapolis: University Of Minnesota Press.

Zehfuss, M (2011), 'Targeting: Precision and the production of ethics,' *European Journal of International Relations* 17(3): 543–566.

Zegart, A. (2018), 'Cheap Fights, Credible Threats: The Future of Armed Drones and Coercion,' *Journal of Strategic Studies,* 43(1): 6–46.

Zimmer, C. (1998), *At the Water's Edge: Macroevolution and the Transformation of Life*, Toronto: The Free Press.

Zumbansen, P. (2007), 'The Law of Society: Governance Through Contract', *Indiana Journal of Global Legal Studies*, 14(2): 191–233.

Zumbansen, P. (ed.) (2020), *The Many Lives of Transnational Law: Critical Engagements with Jessup's Bold Proposal*, Cambridge: Cambridge University Press.

Zylinska, J. (2018), *The End of Man: A Feminist Counterapocalypse*, Minneapolis: University of Minnesota Press.

TREATIES AND CASES

Case Concerning Military and Paramilitary Activities In and Against Nicaragua (Nicaragua v. United States of America); Merits, International Court of Justice (ICJ), 27 June 1986.

Convention on the Rights and Duties and Duties of States (Montevideo Convention) 1933.

Bell v Tavistock [2021] EWCA Civ 1363, case CO/60/2020, *judiciary.uk,* https://www.judiciary.uk/wp-content/uploads/2021/09/Bell-v-Tavistock-judgment-170921.pdf [accessed 10 February 2022].

City of Pittsburgh, Code of Ordinances, Title 6, art 1, ch 618, 'Marcellus Shale Natural Gas Drilling Ordinance' (2010) https://library.municode.com/pa/pittsburgh/codes/code_of_ordinances?nodeId=COOR_TITSIXCO_ARTIRERIAC_CH618MASHNAGADR [accessed 23 November 2020].

EU Artificial Intelligence Act Proposal, Proposal For A Regulation Of The European Parliament And Of The Council Laying Down Harmonised Rules On Artificial Intelligence (Artificial Intelligence Act) And Amending Certain Union Legislative Acts, Brussels, 21.4.2021 Com(2021) 206 Final 2021/0106(Cod)

Judgment No. 09171-2015-0004, Ninth Court of Criminal Guarantees, Guayas Province, Republic of Ecuador (23 April 2015) 55–59.

Judgment No. 11121-2011-0010, Provincial Court of Justice, Loja Province, Republic of Ecuador (30 March 2011).

Judgment No. 166-15-SEP-CC, Case No. 0507-12-EP, Constitutional Court of Ecuador, Republic of Ecuador (20 May 2015)

Judgment No. 269-2012, Civil and Mercantile Court, Gala´pagos Province, Republic of Ecuador (28 June 2012).

NASA (2020), 'The Artemis Accords: Principles for a Safe, Peaceful, and Prosperous Future,' *NASA,* https://www.nasa.gov/specials/artemis-accords/img/Artemis-Accords_v7_print.pdf [accessed 8 April 2021].

Republic of Ecuador, Constitution of 2008, trans. Georgetown University, https://pdba.georgetown.edu/Constitutions/Ecuador/english08.html [accessed 23 November 2020].

Te Awa Tupua (Whanganui River Claims Settlement) Act. (2017) (New Zealand)

Te Urewera Act, (2014) (New Zealand).

United Nations Department of Economic and Social Affairs, Sustainable Development Goals, United Nations, https://sdgs.un.org/goals [accessed 22 February 2022].

UNDP (2018), *Disability Inclusive Development in UNDP Summary,* New York: United Nations Development Programme.

UNGA (1979), *Agreement Governing the Activities of States on the Moon and Other Celestial Bodies* (The Moon Agreement), 18 December, UNGA Resolution 34/68.

UNGA (1967), *The Treaty on Principles Governing the Activities of States in the Exploration and Use of Outer Space, including the Moon and Other Celestial Bodies* (The Outer Space Treaty), 27 January, UNGA Resolution 2222 (XXI)

US Federal Register (2020), 'Encouraging International Support for the Recovery and Use of Space Resources' Executive Order 13914 of 6 April, https://www.federalregister.gov/documents/2020/04/10/2020-07800/encouraging-international-support-for-the-recovery-and-use-of-space-resources [accessed 8 April 2021].

UN 1987. *Report of the World Commission on Environment and Development: Our Common Future.* Brundtland Report. United Nations Assembly. Session 42. eller United Nations 1987. Our Common Future – Brundtland Report. Oxford: Oxford University Press.

UN 1972. *Report of the United Nations Conference on the Human Environment.* Stockholm, 5–16 June 1972. New York: United Nations.

UNEP 2018, Future Generations vs. Ministry of Environment and Others, https://leap.unep.org/countries/co/national-case-law/future-generations-vs-ministry-environment-and-others

Printed in the USA
CPSIA information can be obtained
at www.ICGtesting.com
LVHW012106220624
783667LV00003B/332